Neutrality and Impartiality

A substantial part of the studies for this book was carried out within the framework of GRIPH, Groupe de Recherche Interculturelle et Philosophique, of Montreal.

A grant from UNESCO towards the cost of preparing this work, together with a parallel edition in French, is gratefully acknowledged.

Neutrality and Impartiality

*The University and
Political Commitment*

BY

ANDREW GRAHAM

LESZEK KOLAKOWSKI

LOUIS MARIN

ALAN MONTEFIORE

CHARLES TAYLOR

C. L. TEN

W. L. WEINSTEIN

EDITED BY

ALAN MONTEFIORE

*Fellow and Tutor in Philosophy
Balliol College, Oxford*

CAMBRIDGE UNIVERSITY PRESS

Published by the Syndics of the Cambridge University Press
Bentley House, 200 Euston Road, London NW1 2DB
American Branch: 32 East 57th Street, New York, N.Y. 10022

© Cambridge University Press 1975

ISBNS
0 521 20664 2 hard covers
0 521 09923 4 paperback

First published 1975

Photoset and printed
in Great Britain by
REDWOOD BURN LIMITED
Trowbridge & Esher

Contents

Preface

This is an open-ended and not very systematic book about a certain rather untidy family of concepts – such concepts as those of neutrality, impartiality, objectivity, open-mindedness and so on. It is also a book in which use is made of these concepts to discuss certain issues concerning the position of universities in their internal and external relations and that of university teachers and researchers in relation to their subjects, their students and their wider political commitments. And finally it is a book in which a number of people from different countries with very different backgrounds of theoretical and practical experience come together to discuss those matters. With the exception of Part III the reader would in general find no particular difficulty in moving among the various sections and contributions as if from one independent discussion to another. Nevertheless, its authors think of the book as having a certain overall unity. It may therefore be helpful to start with a word or two of explanation of the basis on which it has been compiled.

In some parts of the world many of the most politically conscious and active members of the universities have over the last few years been demanding that the university as such should take up deliberately partisan social and political positions. Most of those who take this line would reject as hypocritical or, at best, as irresponsibly naïve the traditional 'liberal' claim that the proper business of the university lies in the disinterested search for true knowledge and in the transmission of the concern for this search, just as they would reject the traditionally accompanying claim that this is an essentially academic concern and, as such, strictly non-political. In other parts of the world these positions are virtually reversed. There, many of the most politically conscious and active members of the universities have been demanding that the university as such should be recognised as politically independent, that it should be treated and should treat itself as politically neutral and that its individual members should be allowed in their individual capacities to take up any political stance they might please, including that of political indifference. Those who take this line reject any claims by the authorities established in their societies to determine the nature of professional university activities in the name of what are alleged to be the higher interests of society, insisting that the academic vocation and the freedom of the individual alike presuppose and imply the duty of the university and the right of its members to abstain from all political activities.

Whatever else may be unclear in the often heatedly unclear contexts of these conflicts and debates, it is at least evident that issues of great importance for the whole status of university research and education are here at stake (and, indeed, of much other education beside). But what issues precisely? The key terms are often used differently not only by members of different sides, but even by members of what appears to be the same side – quite often indeed by one and the same man on maybe not so different occasions. Moreover, it is not uncommon to find terms which could (and should) be used to mark important distinctions being used in practice as if they were casually interchangeable with each other. In such circumstances clear mutual understanding would rarely seem possible; and though clear understanding is no sufficient condition of closer agreement, it is certainly a necessary condition of any agreement on which the parties concerned might rely. Indeed, before questions of agreement or disagreement can even arise, it is hard to think clearly for oneself without having in the process to pin down the different key terms to more or less fixed relations to each other. An attempt to make a start on doing just this was the first point of origin of this book.

Pure conceptual analysis, however, may not only appear dry and remote – that, after all, is a risk which only propagandists and pedagogues need take really seriously; it may actually become too dry and remote for it to rank even as acceptable conceptual analysis. If a major purpose of analysis is to make possible clearer thought and debate, the debate itself will provide the only ultimately serious testing ground for the analysis. Moreover, if these debates had not had the interest and importance that they do, there would not have been the same motivation to undertake the analysis in the first place. In other words, the analysis of the relevant concepts and their use in substantive discussion are closely bound up with each other as different aspects of one complex enterprise; and it was a shared concern for the issues at stake in these discussions that provided the book with its second point of origin.

In practice, the book got itself under way in 1969 when I undertook to work out a first rather rough and incomplete set of analyses of some of the central concepts involved and to circulate them to the other contributors. Selected parts of these first background analyses constitute Part I of the present book; they have been cut down and somewhat recast, but nothing has been removed to which any of the other contributors have made explicit or implicit reference in their papers, however inadequate it may now appear; nor has anything of importance been added in this Part, however badly it may now seem to me that certain things need adding. This means that it must be read as a first, provisional approximation. Part II contains the papers of all the other contributors. Part III contains (some of) my present further thoughts on the matters raised in Part I, seen now in the light of the discussions of Part II, as well as in that of many subsequent critical discussions in and out of seminars.

But this is in a number of ways an over-bald statement of the position. For one thing, it is already obvious that, whatever the differences of emphasis, there can be no neatly separate distribution of the conceptual and substantive aspects of the discussions among the several parts of the volume. For another, it is worth mentioning that some of us were able to have quite extensive discussions with each other during the latter part of 1969 and 1970, when some of the papers of Part II were moving from earlier to subsequent drafts. In particular four of us were fortunate enough to be able to take advantage of an invitation from the Department of Philosophy at the University of Montreal to join in holding a colloquium on the topics here under consideration, in April 1970. The interest which both English and French speaking participants derived from this experience of working together, out of their very different philosophical backgrounds, in this hospitable bilingual and bi-cultural context, persuaded them that it would be worthwhile to seek to publish the eventual volume in the two languages simultaneously. The problems of translation, in both directions, have been as instructive as they have been difficult; they have also unavoidably been the cause of a rather considerable delay in final publication.

There are two other acknowledgements that should be made in the Preface. An earlier version of section 2 of Part I was included in a contribution to a conference organised in October 1969 by L'Association Internationale des Futuribles at Perugia and subsequently published (in Italian) in their journal, *Futuribili*, no. 18, and in *Proteus*, Vol. I, no. 3. I am most grateful for permission, kindly given in advance, to reproduce the substance of that contribution here. Finally, especial thanks are due to Jeremy Mynott of the Cambridge University Press for the immense care with which he has worked through the whole book. But for him it would have remained in a far more imperfect state.

Oxford, 1974   A.M.

Notes on the contributors

Andrew Graham Fellow and Tutor in Economics at Balliol College, Oxford, and a University Lecturer in Economics. He is currently (1973–4) on partial leave of absence from Oxford while acting as a Policy Adviser at 10 Downing Street. He was previously an Economic Assistant at the Department of Economic Affairs 1964–6, an Economic Assistant at the Cabinet Office 1966–7, and an Economic Adviser attached to the Prime Minister's Office 1968–9.

Leszek Kolakowski Born 1927 in Radom, Poland. Professor in Warsaw University and Chairman of the Section of History of Philosophy until 1968; expelled from the University in March 1968 for political reasons. Visiting Professor at McGill University, Montreal, and University of California, Berkeley. From 1970 Fellow of All Souls College, Oxford. Author of books dealing with history of philosophy and of religious ideas in sixteenth and seventeenth centuries and with philosophy of culture.

Louis Marin Born 1931 in France. Studied at the Ecole Normale Supérieure in Paris. Has taught at L'Ecole Pratique des Hautes Etudes and the Universities of Nanterre, Paris I, California (San Diego) and is currently at Johns Hopkins (Baltimore, U.S.A.). From 1965 to 1967 was Director of the Institut Français in London. His books include *Sémiotique de la Passion, Topiques et Figures* (1971); *Etudes Sémiologiques – Ecritures, Peintures* (1971); together with Claude Chabrol, *Sémiotique narrative: les récits bibliques* (1971); *Le Récit Evangelique* (1974). He has also published a translation, with introduction, of Radcliffe-Brown's *Structure and Function in Primitive Society*; has edited (and contributed to) a volume entitled *Utopiques – jeux d'espaces* (1973); has published editions of *La Logique de Port-Royal* (1970) and *Pensées de Pascal*; and has contributed articles to innumerable learned and cultural journals.

Alan Montefiore Read P.P.E. – Politics, Philosophy and Economics – at Balliol College, Oxford, from 1948 to 1950. From 1951 to 1961 taught philosophy, a lot of it moral and political philosophy at the then new University College of North Staffordshire, now the University of Keele. In 1961 returned to Balliol as Fellow and Tutor in Philosophy. Tutor for Admissions in Balliol 1962–7. Has written or edited books on *Moral Philosophy, British Analytical Philosophy* and *Philosophy and Personal Relations* (the latter being a joint Anglo–French–French Canadian enterprise); and published articles in a variety of professional journals.

Chin Liew Ten Born in Malaysia. Studied philosophy at the former University of Malaya in Singapore (now the University of Singapore), and then at the London School of Economics. From 1964 to 1970 taught philosophy at the University of Singapore. Left Singapore in 1970 to join the Philosophy Department, Monash University, Australia, where he is now a Senior Lecturer. Currently working on a book, *Mill on Liberty*.

Charles Taylor B.A. McGill (History) 1952, B.A. Oxford (P.P.E.) 1955, John Locke Scholar, Oxford, 1955, D.Phil Oxford 1961. At present Professor of Philosophy and Political Science at McGill; has also taught at l'Université de Montréal, Princeton, University of California at Berkeley. Sometime Fellow of All Souls. Publications: *The Explanation of Behaviour* (1964), and a number of articles on philosophy of mind, philosophy of psychology, philosophy of politics. A book on Hegel is to be published shortly. Also active in politics. Ran a number of times for Canadian Federal Parliament; member of Federal Executive, New Democratic Party of Canada.

W.L. Weinstein Fellow and Tutor in Politics, Balliol College, Oxford. Has been Tutor for Admissions there 1967–71; other university experience in America, East Africa and Australia. Political theorist; articles published on liberalism, freedom, privacy; writing book on rival conceptions of freedom.

PART I

1 Preliminaries

Those who hold to a liberal view of the university would all agree on insisting on the crucial importance of the distinction between the academic and the political; those who reject the liberal view hold on the contrary that it is a distinction without any tenably honest or serious difference. Liberals believe in detachment, disinterestedness, impartiality, open-mindedness, objectivity and political independence and neutrality. Their most serious opponents do not merely reject these values; they regard them rather as constituting a characteristically self-interested illusion.

As a first statement of the position this is, of course, highly oversimplified; but so too are the terms in which many of those involved in conflicts over the desirability or undesirability, possibility or impossibility, of a liberal university, are accustomed to fight out their theoretical and practical disagreements. Over-simplified and hence also both confused and confusing. This is why it seems important to make some explicit attempt to clarify the conditions of meaningful employment of these and related terms. In making this attempt, however, I should make it clear that I am not primarily interested in the niceties (or the lack of them) of ordinary language. As far as ordinary English is concerned at any rate, it seems in fact to be used in this area with considerable imprecision and apparently easy interchange;and the same is doubtless true for other languages.Naturally, it is preferable not to stray too far from commonly acceptable usage; but what is important is to see what distinctions can be made, and which are most worth making, without worrying beyond reasonable limits over the exact stylistic felicity of assigning any particular term to any particular concept.

Before embarking on this discussion there is one important disclaimer to be made. I have already used the word 'liberal' and it recurs often in what follows. Nevertheless, I do not propose to attempt any serious analysis either of the history or of the current uses of this term, but rather to continue to use it in what I should have under pressure to admit may be little more than a general gesticulatory way. My gestures may be understood in the light of that vague pattern of associations between the concepts of a liberal society and a liberal education and those of the values already mentioned, of a readiness to give free expression and unprejudiced consideration to every point of view, of tolerance of disagreement, of the absence of hidden bias, political or other, and so on. Most of these latter concepts will come under explicit discussion. But to my use of the term 'liberal' itself there is no deep theoretical significance to be attached; and if I place it in certain contexts in inverted

commas, it is not – of course – to indicate any attitude of contempt
for the notion, but simply as a reminder of the fact that while it may
stand for an essentially contestable concept, I make in these discussions no attempt either to define or to contest it.

In using it in this rather relaxed way, however, it is as well to be
quite explicitly aware that 'liberal' is also very much a fighting word
and, what is more, one which may be uttered either with pride or
with scorn. (One may compare, for example, the salute 'He is a man
of great learning and truly liberal cast of mind' with the dismissal
'He may know a great deal, but he remains just another "wishy
washy" liberal'.) One of the sources of pride has been the view that
there is no line of distinction to be drawn between a 'liberal' education and a rational education as such – all other forms of so-called
education being no more than so many varieties of indoctrination.
One of the grounds of scorn has been the appeal sometimes made to
'liberal' values apparently simply in order to avoid practical action
against even the worst features of an inequitable *status quo*. This is
not the stage at which to enter into arguments about whether either
of these points of view is in general justified. It is anyhow natural
that those who interpret their experience of established liberal authority in this latter way should take a preoccupation with such
alleged values as objectivity and impartiality as anything but objective and impartial. And so I must at least make it clear that I cannot
start by making or by repudiating in advance any claim for the objectivity or the impartiality of my own discussion of these concepts.
It would in any case be foolish to do so before having settled on
some reasonably firm suggestion as to how the terms should best be
understood.

2   Neutrality, indifference and detachment

First, however, we may turn to some considerations concerning the
concept of neutrality and certain of its closer conceptual relations.
Here what I take to be the central point may be made at the outset in
the form of a straight, simple assertion: to be neutral is always to be
neutral as between two or more actual or possible policies or parties. There may be some sense in taking as a limiting case neutrality
towards some one party or policy other than oneself or one's own
policy, (where the actual or possible conflict in question would
simply be one between oneself and the other party). But there can be
no sense in any suggestion of total or absolute neutrality, if that is to
be understood as meaning a neutrality with respect to every possible
policy or to each and any option that might ever be exercised by

anyone else whomsoever. Questions of neutrality arise in reference to situations of actual or possible conflict between parties or policies; one cannot be neutral if there is, so to speak, nothing to be neutral between.

This first assertion I take to be pretty well self-evident. My second suggestion is less so: to be neutral in any conflict is to do one's best to help or to hinder the various parties concerned in an equal degree.[1]

It follows from this that one can only be neutral in a given situation in so far as one is in a position to exercise some sort of influence on it and has some effective choice as to whether to exercise that influence or not. Neutrality thus interpreted is, we may say, both an intentional and a causal concept in the sense that it relates to the directed, or at any rate to the directable, causal impacts that one agent may or may not have on the policies of another. This dual status will be of great importance in subsequent analysis.

It is obvious that a whole range of further problems will arise from this first way of delineating the concept of neutrality, including many of those associated with that of intentions. But these complexities may be held aside for the moment. It is at least evident that neutrality, so defined, has to be distinct both from (what may reasonably be called) indifference and detachment. To be indifferent in any situation, or when faced with a choice of any sort, is to have no personal preferences one way or the other. Detachment may be regarded as the setting aside of whatever personal preferences one may happen to have; it is compatible with indifference, but does not presuppose it. To illustrate these distinctions by way of just one example: faced with appeals for help from two conflicting political parties I may decide to remain *neutral* between them, that is to say to do my best to provide them with help or hindrance in equal degree. This is quite compatible with my retaining a strong personal preference in favour of one side rather than the other; that is, I may be in no way *indifferent* to the outcome of the conflict. In making up my mind to remain neutral, however, I may have considered the matter in an entirely *detached* spirit, by reference, for instance, to my legal or other institutional responsibilities and abstracting wholly from my own personal preferences.

The concept of neutrality is also to be distinguished from that of disinterestedness. There are two main ways in which this concept

[1] In the limiting case mentioned above, this may be construed as doing one's best neither to help nor to hinder the other party or policy in question in any special way; that is, to act exactly as one would anyhow have acted had the party or policy never existed. Clearly, this possibility only arises as a genuine option when the party or policy in question stands in no particular relationship of opposition or support to any antecedently or independently conceived policies of one's own.

may be taken. According to the first, to be disinterested in any given situation is simply to have no interests of one's own at stake; or at any rate no interests of which one is aware. According to the second, one may use the term to refer to the attitude of a man who, although he did have interests at stake, succeeded in setting them aside from the considerations which he allowed to weigh with him in coming to his decision or in determining his attitude. If one prefers to take the term in the first way only, one might, by way of conceptual compensation, extend the meaning of 'detachment' to cover the setting aside of considerations of interest as well as the setting aside of personal preference. This suggestion in fact raises further problems of considerable importance and complexity concerning the relations between the concepts of interest and preference; we shall have to return to them in a later section (see p. 30 below). For the moment, however, we may return to a more direct consideration of the concept of neutrality itself.

My approach to a definition of 'neutrality' has been in terms of an agent's doing his best to help or to hinder to an equal degree all the parties concerned in any situation of competition or conflict. A main reason for seeking a definition of this form, rather than one in terms of avoiding giving any help or hindrance at all to any of the parties involved, is that it is a necessary condition for the concept of neutrality to have any genuine application that it should be open to the potential neutral to choose whether or not to exercise an influence on the situation of conflict. This means that there must be some sort of causal or otherwise practical relationship existing between him and at least some of the parties to the conflict in question. But if this is the case, it is hard to see on what principles one could establish a base line to serve as a starting point from which potential neutrals might choose to provide no help or hindrance to anyone involved in the conflict; since, from whatever standpoint one might assess his actions as providing neither help nor hindrance to any of those involved, there must always be some other standpoint from which it may be complained that differential help or hindrance is in effect being provided from behind the base line. For at the very least, and even if he does nothing else, the potential neutral may always be seen as helping one side to the extent of not providing the help that he *could* have been affording to the other in virtue of his definitionally necessary causal involvement in the situation.

On the other hand, the reference to equal (rather than to no) help or hindrance to all the parties concerned runs into certain *prima facie* difficulties of its own. These can best be illustrated in terms of a situation where the parties to the conflict are of evidently unequal strength. To take an example which has no political significance in itself, but which brings out the point very well: two children may each appeal to their father to intervene with his support in some dispute between them. Their father may know that if he simply 'refuses to intervene', the older one, stronger and more resourceful, is bound to come out on top. If he actively intervenes with equal help or hindrance to both of them, the result will necessarily be the same. If he wants to make sure that they both have roughly equal chances of success (that is, if he wants to render the outcome of their conflict as nearly unpredictable as possible), then he has, in practical terms, to help one of them more than the other. In other words, the decision to remain neutral, according to the terms of our present definition, would amount to a decision to allow the naturally stronger child to prevail. But this may look like a very odd form of neutrality to the weaker child.

One way of reacting to this point might be to argue that the option of neutrality is open only where there is no clear basis for distinguishing between the initial balances of strength and weakness of the various parties to the conflict. But does one then judge that the availability of a neutral option depends on the actual balances of strength and weakness of the conflicting parties? Or on the estimate that the potential neutral may make of the relevant balances? Or on the estimate that it would be reasonable for him to make given the information at his reasonable disposal?[2] In practice, it may be argued, in situations of serious academic or political conflict the initial balances of strength and weakness are probably very rarely to be seen as evidently equal. This may in part be due to the fact that there is here a disturbing unclarity in the very notion of 'an initially equal balance'. But there also seems to be something unsatisfactory in an account of neutrality which relates it directly to an initial balance, where 'initial' must seemingly turn out to refer either to the moment at which the potential neutral first considers the problem, or to that at which it might reasonably be thought that he should first have considered it, or to the moment at which he judges the conflict itself to have arisen, or to that at which he might reasonably have judged it to have arisen . . . or to some other moment of similarly complicated subjective order.

In the face of all this, might one not do better to argue to the paradoxical conclusion that not only are there situations in which no option of neutrality exists, but that the concept of neutrality actually turns out never to have any coherent application at all? But this too seems unsatisfactory. Indeed, we know very well that, provided the terms of what is to be counted as help are specified closely

---

[2] Such a reference to reasonableness would, of course, raise its own further characteristic set of problems.

enough, it is possible to lay down fairly firm conditions for various forms of legal or 'technical' neutrality; and why, it is natural to ask, should such conditions not serve as bases for wider and less technical accounts?

This suggests another way of trying to deal with the problem: namely to accept the different apparent paradox that the adoption of a neutral attitude might very well work in favour of one party to a conflict or to the detriment of another; and that the fact that such probabilities might be known to the potential neutral need not exclude the possibility of his actually taking up a neutral attitude.[3]

Whatever the solution to this problem turns out to be, further crucial distinctions must now be made; for the knowledge that whatever he does, including taking up a 'subjectively neutral' attitude, is likely to work in favour of some one or other of the parties to the conflict, *will* sometimes mean that there is no neutral option available. We shall return to this point later on. For the moment, we may simply accept as a consequence of our partial definitions the possibility that a man may adopt an attitude of neutrality, knowing very well that in so doing he is likely to favour the chances of one side against another, so long as the fact that this is likely to be so derives solely from such aspects of the positions, expectations or manoeuvres of one or both of the conflicting parties as are independent of the potential neutral's own original position or actions – he could not, obviously, take up an attitude of neutrality *in order to* favour one side rather than the other (except, perhaps, when certain technical and strictly delimited forms of neutrality are in question). This last stipulation admittedly brings elements of evaluation (of what may relevantly constitute 'independence') quite openly into the structuring of the concept of neutrality; but this is perhaps a source of realism and of strength rather than of weakness.

I turn meanwhile to another problem: how should one distinguish and understand the distinctions between the assessment of specific actions as neutral or un-neutral, the assessment in this light of general policies and the assessment of roles or positions within a complex of social relationships? An illustration of the importance of getting these distinctions straight may be given by the case of a referee in a game. Many of the particular actions and decisions of such an official are bound to give direct help or hindrance to one side or the other; moreover, the referee who blows his whistle and points to the penalty spot knows perfectly well which side he is helping. But it would seem absurd to suggest that even in games there could in principle be no such thing as a neutral referee.

---

[3] Whether or not his own interests are also involved is of itself of no direct relevance; neutrality does not have to be disinterested.

As far as formally constituted games are concerned, the problem, however tricky in detail, seems essentially to be one of careful formulation. A neutral referee will, roughly speaking, be one who works with the clear and well trained intention of helping or hindering either side in completely equal measure *with respect to his application of the rules of the game,* whatever the nature of the performance that either side may produce in the course of it. His intention has to be well trained as well as clear in the sense that, beyond a certain point of incompetence, mere subjective intention will fail to guarantee neutrality. It is a matter of complete indifference to him *qua* referee whether it is one side or the other that has incurred a penalty. It is true that in imposing a penalty he is hindering the offending side and helping its opponents, but he would have behaved in exactly the same way had their positions been reversed. There is nothing in his role which could lead him to aim at helping one side rather than the other; his relations to them are defined in terms of the complex game situation within which they are competing and within that framework he stands in precisely the same relations to each of the competing sides. Since his individual actions as a referee all spring from his role within the total game situation, their neutrality has to be assessed in the light of his overall role and of his attitude towards it rather than in that of the particular and contingent help that they bring to one side or the other in the course of the game. An un-neutral referee, on the contrary, would be one whose actions were calculated to help one side at the expense of the other (apart, perhaps, from the special and controversial case of outstanding and culpable, if yet uncalculating, incompetence); and the very nature of the example makes it clear that no such calculation could be based on mere concern for a strict application of the rules of the game. In practice it may often be difficult, if not impossible, to decide whether a given referee is acting neutrally in the required sense or not. Nevertheless, however difficult it may be to judge particular cases and particular referees, the general basis of the distinction between a neutral and an un-neutral referee would seem reasonably secure.

The example of a game may provide some helpful lessons for other more complex cases; but for the moment I shall make just two further points about it:

(a) A referee may know in advance of some particular game that one of the contestants is a much stronger competitor than the other. It might even be that unless something extraordinary happened, the result would be a foregone conclusion. But the known unequal strength of two competitors clearly does nothing to alter the role of the referee nor his relations, through the rules of the game, to those competing; and since the neutrality of his actions derives from the neutrality of his role, it raises no special problem for their neutrality either.

(b) The role of a referee is closely bound up with the way in which a game is both constituted and governed by its rules. But games and referees are not the only activities, institutions or officials to have their nature determined by rather closely defined rules. It is interesting to try to see how far the position of a judge in relation to those who appear in the courts before him can be assessed in analogous terms. It is a familiar claim of liberal political and legal theorists that in a well run society the judiciary will be neutral *vis-à-vis* all of its members, just as it is a familiar protest of many left-wing thinkers that there can be no such thing as overall judicial neutrality. Obviously it may be important to distinguish between the neutrality of the judiciary as such and the practical neutrality of judge X or Y when faced with offenders of one class or another; or between the neutrality of the judiciary acting within the framework of the law and that of the law or of the legislators (though this latter distinction may sometimes be hard to maintain). One must also distinguish between the problem of neutrality that confronts a given man, who has to decide whether to continue as a judge within what he regards as an unacceptable legal system, and that of the judge struggling actually to administer laws of which he disapproves, but which he feels that he should nevertheless try to administer in strictly neutral fashion. There will be times, too, when the judge may himself in effect be called upon to share in the making of the very law that he has to administer. How, one will have to ask, is one to understand his role as defined by law and in relation to society in general? How far is it analogous to that of the referee in relation to the game and to the rules? Here, as so often, we can expect no socially invariant answer.

Many of these problems may perhaps be expressed in their most general form by asking a version of the well known philosophical riddle 'When is a game no longer a game?' At this stage, however, I propose to turn back to the claim, bound to be made by any classical liberal, that there would be something wrong with a definition which could have the effect of refusing the status of neutral to someone *simply* because, whichever way he acted in a given situation, the foreseen or foreseeable consequences of his actions must, independently of his own motives or intentions, have an influence on the balance of power within some given conflict.

The point can be illustrated by a by no means implausible example. A doctor, whose total personal commitment is to the healing purpose of his profession, may through the force of unwanted circumstances find himself responsible for the care of patients whose fate is of great political importance. There were, for example, German doctors who found themselves in this sort of situation with key Nazi officials as their patients. The doctor may know that if he restores his patient to his full normal activity he will return to play a central role in, say, the organisation of concentration camp industries; conversely, if his patient dies or remains an invalid, this will be a serious setback to their organisation. It would be absurd, so runs the liberal objection, to accuse the doctor of being non-neutral on the side of the Nazis simply because he treated his Nazi patients as any dedicated doctor would treat any patient whatsoever. In a way the peculiar and even dramatic nature of this particular example serves to bring out the point more clearly; for if it would be absurd even in these circumstances to accuse the doctor of partisanship, how much more absurd to raise such accusations in the hundred and one more humdrum situations in which doctors have to care for people whose health may be known to be of some importance to some relatively workaday political party or cause.

I do not think that this example presents a knock-down objection; but nor do I think that there is a knock-down answer to it. Its discussion, however, cannot be straightforward for there are a number of complex factors involved. The first of these concerns the problem of how to relate the different descriptions under which one and the same action may apparently be identified – if, indeed, it is not already misleading to suggest that different action descriptions may refer to one and the same action in advance of any clear indication of how to determine criteria of identity for the one or the other. What, for example, was the doctor actually doing in our example? Was he simply treating his patient or was he restoring a Gestapo leader to full activity? Or was he doing both of these things at the same time? Do these questions pose issues of substantial importance or simply a series of tiresome philosophical riddles?

To this last question the answer is 'both'; but that the nature of their entanglement is such that though one has to start by trying to answer the riddles, to do so effectively is so far to do nothing more directly substantial than to avoid falling into distracting confusion. However, on these points we may avoid further immediate discussion by accepting the terminology and distinctions proposed by A. J. P. Kenny in his article on 'Intention and Purpose in Law', which do at any rate provide us with a clear framework for discussion:

I have in the past distinguished between *performances*, the bringing about of states of affairs in the world (e.g. killing a man, baking a cake, opening a door), and *activities* which go on for an indefinite time and have no particular terminus (e.g. running, laughing). Substantially the same distinction has been made by von Wright as a distinction between *act* which is the effecting of a change, and *activity* which keeps a process going. I adopt his terminology, and following him I shall make a distinction between the result and the consequence of an act. The result of an act is the end state of the change by which the act is defined. When the world changes in a certain way there may follow certain other changes, perhaps by natural necessity. In that case we may say that the second transformation is a consequence of the first and of the act which brought the first about. The relation between an act and its result is an intrinsic relation, and that between an act and its consequence is a causal relation. The consequence of one act may be the result of another and the activity involved in the two may be identical.[4]

Secondly, there arise questions of intention and responsibility. Take the case of an agent performing two acts, A and B, which are so related that the doing of A has as its (causal) consequence the doing of B; and consider too the factors of the agent's knowledge and desires. 'The agent knows he is doing A and wants to do A and knows he is doing B by doing A, but does not want to do B.' Kenny exemplifies this possibility by reference to a man getting out of bed knowing that he is waking the baby by doing so, although not wanting to wake the baby; so far as the structure of the case goes this is straightforwardly analogous to the position of the doctor who knows that he is helping the Gestapo by restoring his patient to full health, although not wanting to help it. The question is whether the man's waking the baby or the doctor's helping the Gestapo is to be counted as intentional.

On this point many lawyers in fact apparently still agree with Bentham in classifying such performances as intentional (Bentham's phrase was 'obliquely intentional'). This is something that Kenny himself rejects. Certainly there may be significant differences between cases in which an agent performs A knowing that it is likely to have as its consequence the doing of B, but where he does not himself want to do B, and cases where, on the other hand, he either does A expressly in order that it should lead on to the doing of B or where he at least foresees the consequential doing of B and is content to do it. There are certain important purposes for which the weight which Kenny lays on the factor of the agent's own desires may be importantly misleading. Often enough one may be faced with a choice effectively limited to two possible courses of action only, neither of which in any way corresponds to one's own actual desires. So far as English idiom is concerned at any rate, an agent who found himself in such circumstances would be perfectly justified in saying of whichever act he had chosen deliberately to per-

[4] The article is included in *Essays in Legal Philosophy*, edited by Robert S. Summers (Blackwell, 1968); see especially p. 150, from which this quotation comes, and those immediately following.

form that he did not want (i.e. desire) to do it. It is true that he might also have said that he wanted (i.e. was willing) to do it as the least of all possible evils. It remains that one may bitterly regret or resent having to do what one nevertheless chooses to do as the least undesirable of all available courses of action.

However this may be, one of the main reasons for settling on the ascription of intentions lies in its relationship to assessments of responsibility, and for this purpose it may not matter too much what one decides to say about the agent's wanting or not wanting to perform the least undesirable of the acts open to him or about the precise state of the conceptual relationships between intending and wanting. Similarly, one of the main interests in deciding on the neutrality or the non-neutrality of anyone's actions lies in the relevance of such decisions to assessments of responsibility. So the substantial questions may now be asked whether we should hold the man getting out of bed responsible for waking up the baby or the doctor for providing effective assistance to the Gestapo by his conscientious treatment of one or more of its most important members.

Here there can surely be no purely conceptual way of deciding whether such men should be held responsible for such actions or not. One might try to draw up a list of factors which have most influence on most people's ordinary assessments of responsibility: for example, the closeness of the connection between the doing of the wanted A and the doing of the unwanted B, the degree of direct involvement of the agent in whatever performance constituted the doing of B, the degree of importance of B – together with such other problem factors as the types of constraint, influence or temptation under which the agent may have been acting. But the sense of any such list is heavily conditioned by evaluative as well as by purely conceptual considerations. Just where does one look to identify one's ordinary man? What counts as important and who decides on the counting? Are assessments of moral or social responsibility judgements on which everyone has in the last resort to make up his own individual mind?

These last questions further relate to certain familiar but still highly complicated issues concerning the ways in which the very concepts of evaluation may vary from one society to another, especially the different ways in which the individual may be seen as either the ultimate author of his own values or, on the contrary, as the learner and discoverer of standards that are given to him as from without. To illustrate, very crudely, just one aspect of these matters: Two people from different cultural backgrounds might nevertheless agree that, other things being equal, the importance of B would be a crucial factor in determining the degree of responsibility to be attributed to an agent undertaking A in the knowledge that it would lead to the doing of B. But while one of them might assume that each individual had in the end to assess the importance of B on the basis of his own personally determined scale of values, the other might take it for granted that the matter had nothing to do with his own personal inclinations or preferences, but was determined by, say, the needs and standards of his community or the measured will of God.

Unfortunately for brevity, not only is the illustration excessively crude, but the precise implications of this sort of divergence are far from obvious. We may ignore for the moment the major oversimplification of supposing that these different conceptual patterns may not be found within one and the same individual. It may now seem reasonable to suppose that someone who works within a framework of evaluative concepts such that individuals have necessarily each ultimately to determine their own values is likely to lay substantial weight on the subjective or intentional factor in assessments of responsibility. But this is still compatible with the existence of major differences in the nature of such assessments. On the one hand such an 'individualist' may naturally be led very far in the direction of insisting that an agent's responsibility for the reasonably foreseeable but unwanted consequences of his acts will depend primarily on the maxims or intentions which underlie them and only secondarily on the contingently attendant circumstances of what others, taken singly or together, may do or intend. On this view no other (sane and adult) person or persons can saddle me with the responsibility for their deaths merely by informing me in advance that they will commit suicide if I publish a paper on neutrality; my responsibility is engaged only if I actually intend these consequences or to the extent that I have to regard the persons concerned as less than fully sane or autonomous and thus as constituting part of my given environment. But there is another natural line of 'individualist' thought which leads in the direction of imputing an inescapable total responsibility to each individual for *all* foreseeable consequences of his acts, even if these include the unjustifiable reactions of others, whatever they may be. The rationale of this position is very different from that which may be adopted by someone working within a framework of evaluative concepts such that individual preferences, desires, choices, decisions and so on have always to be distinguished from values which, as such, are determined by some factor or factors beyond the individual himself. Such a man will have to ground his assessments of individual responsibility on whatever he sees as given commitment to a shared humanity and as the given importance of the consequences likely to flow from the reactions of others to the acts of any one agent.

Nevertheless, different though their rationales may be, the effective outcomes of these two positions may on occasion appear very much the same.

As far as assessments of neutrality are concerned these are, of course, background questions and cannot be fully unravelled here. Moreover, though it is true that one of the main interests in deciding on the neutrality or non-neutrality of anyone's actions lies in the relevance of such decisions to assessments of responsibility, the two assessments need on no view come to the same thing. There may sometimes be sharp disagreements over whether any option of neutrality really exists; but even those who insist that it does, and that the would-be neutral does *not* have to assume responsibility for *all* the foreseeable consequences of his neutrality, would still agree that he may be held responsible for his decision to remain neutral. Thus, the referee who knows in advance which team is bound to win if he acts as a neutral referee should, does not thereby incur the responsibility for the victory of team A over team B; he is simply responsible for the way in which he conducts the game. He has, that is in effect to say, a certain area within which he may freely decide what his responsibilities are to be; if he had chosen to act in an improperly un-neutral manner, he would then have incurred some share of the responsibility for the outcome of the game.

How far can the position of the doctor be compared with that of the referee? The neutrality of this latter's position rests, I have suggested, on that of his role. The 'liberal' may well wish to argue that the neutrality of the doctor's position springs from the political neutrality of his role as a doctor. There is obviously something in this; the problem is just how much and where exactly does it lie? The position of the referee is determined by relation to the rules, some sub-section of which actually constitutes the game of which he is a referee. It may be possible to identify in certain societies bodies of rules which, for all legal purposes at any rate, actually determine the role of a doctor. However, membership of a society is not exactly like taking part in a game. For one thing, while people who are dissatisfied with the nature of a particular game may seek to reform the rules in order to provide a new variation, those who prefer the existing game need neither abandon their version of it nor take part in whatever new game may be invented. Social life rarely provides such freely open alternatives. To argue about the position and proper responsibilities of a doctor in relation to his fellow members of society, or in relation to his fellow human beings in general, cannot be over lightly assimilated, therefore, to arguing about the best way of defining the role and position of a referee.[5]

[5] It may be noted, moreover, that whereas to be a doctor is to fulfil a certain role, there is

There is one last point to be mentioned at this preliminary stage. A 'liberal' doctor working within the framework of a 'liberal' society may in general be able to distinguish clearly enough between the non-political nature of his acts and the political relevance of some of their foreseen but unwanted consequences in such a way as to leave himself free of all responsibility for the latter, and hence as to leave totally unimpaired the political neutrality of his actions *qua* doctor. But the phrase 'within the framework of a liberal society' deserves underlining. For what if the foreseen but unwanted consequences of his actions are likely to contribute towards undermining the very existence of the 'liberal' framework within which he is working? What if, as in my example, the patients under his care are determined and able to contribute towards bringing about a society in which even the role of a doctor would be politicised?

This question may seem to be a peculiar one; for how, it may be asked, could even a fundamental change of political structure bring about a change in the role of a doctor? In any society whatsoever it must surely be defined by the goal or *telos* of his activity, namely that of caring for the sick. But is it to be taken for granted that the class of possible patients is the class of humanity as a whole and not any particular sub-class of it? Doctors are no doubt accustomed to finding themselves faced with appalling dilemmas in which, through the operation of one mechanism or another, the successful treatment of one group of persons may be bound up with the exclusion of others from the same or different forms of treatment. Often the mechanisms in question turn on problems of competitive investment of scarce resources, problems which may certainly be seen as having their political aspects. Still, the doctor may argue that it is not *qua* doctor that he or anyone else decides on the differential allocation of resources to one social project or another; as doctor he is concerned only with their distribution between different medical purposes. It is far from uncontroversial that even within this relatively circumscribed context, the distinction between the medical and the political can always be kept sharp. Let this, however, pass for the moment. What if the doctor finds, as in our example, that his successful treatment of one person seems bound to lead to the suffering or actual loss of life of very many others as a result of the renewed political activity of the first, if and when restored to health? Even here he may still want to claim that his conflict is in no sense a political one, on the grounds that it arises directly out of that non-political concern for human life which lies at the heart of the doctor's activity.

---

hardly any such role as getter-out-of-bed; which suggests that it may anyhow be a mistake to put too much of the weight of the argument on the somewhat blurred concept of a role.

Against this, it is clear that other societies might set such limits on the doctor's role as would direct his concern only to certain sub-classes of the sick; this might go with a belief that other classes of human beings had no particular call on medical help; or it might be part of a view which held that each society had the obligation only to look after its own sick; or even that certain groups of people ought actually to be liquidated. What, then, would be the position of a doctor, with a universal concern for humanity, if it seemed that a likely consequence of his successful treatment of a particular group of patients would be their living to succeed not merely in causing widespread suffering, but in so modifying society that such roles as that of a doctor would be understood in much more restrictive ways?

I am not sure that it would actually be impossible for a liberal, universalist doctor to continue meaningfully to maintain the essentially non-political nature of his role and actions even in such a case. The concept of the political is, after all, essentially contestable. But there is at least a certain practical incoherence in the position of anyone who, while claiming a universal status for his role, so understands it that he regards himself as committed thereby to actions whose most probable impact would be to destroy the very conditions on which its continued existence depends. For myself, I should be inclined rather to say that when the very structures of society are called into question, the range of the political increases, maybe alarmingly, and the space for political neutrality shrinks until there may be hardly any left. When such points are reached, those who would want to be liberals may have to abandon all present pretence of political neutrality in order the more clear-sightedly to formulate and to work for a programme for the achievement of a society in which the possibility of such neutrality may in the end be restored.

3   Objectivity, impartiality and open-mindedness

Of the three terms listed here, the first has a particularly varied set of patterns of usage behind it; but the second also shows a disconcerting degree of more or less idiomatic interchangeability with other terms of the same general family; and even the third has quite commonly more than one connotation. I shall not try to plot the varieties of already existing and possibly extendable uses of these three terms; nor could I claim any other kind of systematic completeness for my discussion. Instead I start by trying simply to indicate the sense of the three concepts to which I shall refer under these headings by way of a sketchy example.

Consider, then, the position of a teacher of politics who has to explain and discuss with his class a situation of contemporary political relevance. It is virtually certain that if the situation is of any serious degree of complexity, it will not be seen and understood in the same way by all the parties involved; that is, they are likely to differ not only in their objectives, but more fundamentally in the ways in which they assess their common context of action and hence in the ways in which they think that their own and their opponents' objectives should be formulated. A teacher of politics has, among other things, to decide whether to try to set out the situation in each and all of its rival versions and not merely in his own; and whether he is to go beyond bare exposition to try to distinguish between truth and falsity, confusion, distortion and viably honest points of view in each of the versions which he expounds. A 'liberal' professor would presumably do his best to be impartial (let us say) in the sense of trying to set out every relevant view as to the nature of the situation, including those opposed to his own, and moreover to set them out fully and fairly by using their own terms of reference and trying to expound them as they would be expounded by their own partisans; he would strive for objectivity in the sense that he would do his best to check all these different versions of the situation against the background of such facts as were available to him – which could not, of course, be facts as they were 'in themselves', but only and necessarily facts such as he understood them to be in the light of the available evidence and of what he took to be the most accurate principles of interpretation rather than in that of his own personal preferences and interests; he would aim at open-mindedness in the sense of being always ready to take into fresh consideration any new facts and any new interpretation of old facts which might seem to have any relevance.

It may help to bring out the intended sense of these concepts briefly to point to some of the most obvious objections that might be made to the formulations that I have just suggested. Put at their briefest and most brutal, they will amount to the familiar charge that these famous values of objectivity, impartiality and openness of mind may perhaps be liberal, but are certainly imaginary, if not deliberately fraudulent. For one thing, no one in his senses would try (even supposing that he could succeed) to set out literally every view that may be held on issues that he has to study or to discuss with a class of students, if for no other reason than that some views will be so absurd as not to be worth his serious treatment. No geographer or astronomer, for example, would be considered as biased or narrow-minded simply because he refused to spend time on careful exposition and consideration of the views of the Flat Earth Society. Criteria of relevance are, of course, value laden. But even if one ignores this difficulty, it may still be impossible to expound every point of view that one accepts as relevant on a given issue without in effect rejecting the view that one is expounding, if not by the terms, then at least by the deliberate context of one's exposition. (How, for example, could a 'liberal' professor expound in the manner of one of its own exponents a thesis according to which it would be wrong to allow equal opportunities of expression and exposition to ideologically hostile points of view and which at the same time insists on the equal theoretical and practical importance of some version or other of the doctrine of the unity of theory and practice?)

It will be objected too that no one, not even a 'liberal' professor, has access to a realm of pure and evaluatively neutral facts, least of all a realm of pure facts relating to the nature of social and political situations; for there will be said to be no such realm. It is true, it must be conceded, that no one can simply carve out the facts to suit himself merely by choosing some favoured or convenient description; it is in this sense, as a reminder of and as a way of expressing these constraining limits, that it may occasionally be worth insisting that the facts are what they are in themselves, independently of what anyone may think about them. But this in no way limits the truth or force of the 'fact' that the concepts, the descriptions and the categories that one has to use as soon as one starts to reflect on the facts of any situation, but above all one that is social or political, must themselves derive from, rest on and reflect a certain human experience. But whatever universal element there may or may not be in human experience as such, in any particular case it necessarily takes the form of the experience of a certain culture or of a certain society; and whatever derives from and reflects the experience of a certain culture or society reflects at the same time its interests and values. Hence the idea of being able to check competing social theses against the facts of the social political situation to which they refer, as if such facts could in themselves be neutral and non-evaluative, turns out to be another illusion.

Finally, one may add to this sample list of objections, there is an unbridgeable gulf between, say, the position of a member of a despised, humiliated and persecuted minority, intent on creating at least a certain dignity for himself through (what he sees as the only possible route of) violence and revenge, and that of a member of the 'liberal' majority intent on 'taking into consideration' such a minority position. To take it into consideration is to set it among other possible points of view; but this is at once to falsify it, since for anyone who holds it seriously there *is* no other possible point of view. No one who is open-minded in the 'liberal' sense can take into genuine consideration the viewpoint of someone who feels that his status as the kind of human being that he has to be, demands a (perhaps desperate) rejection of open-mindedness.

Some liberals may be tempted to reject objections of this sort as totally wrong-headed; but this would be an insensitive reaction. A more wary liberal teacher of politics might start to sketch out a reply, somewhat along the lines of a Max Weber or a Gunnar Myrdal, by saying:

(1) That he is well aware that any piece of research, any course of study, implies both a selection of subject matter and a selection within the subject matter – a selection of theoretical method as well as a selection of relevant facts.

(2) That this selection will naturally be a function both of the interests and values of whoever is responsible for it and beyond him, to some greater or lesser extent, of the society or culture of which he is a member. One might add that a study whose subject matter was chosen entirely at random, that is, one which might be relevant to no particular interest or which was undertaken in the light of no particular value, need by the same token have no particular importance for anyone (in so far as such a mechanical randomness of choice may not itself be taken as expressive of the value-system of the society in which, or the individual by whom, such a choice might be made).

(3) That in order to eliminate any possibility of misunderstanding or of hidden persuasiveness, the teacher should start by making an explicit and unreserved declaration of his own values and interests in the subject.

(4) That although there is more than one sense in which his choice and interpretation of the facts may be said to be bound to 'express' or to 'represent' certain values, it does *not* follow that what he says about the facts will or even could entail any particular value judgement about them. For the truth of what he says must ultimately be determined by the sorts of observations that in principle any competent observer could make; and the acceptance of this truth would leave everyone free to be for, against or indifferent with respect to the states of affairs which he claims to depict – free, that is to say, to make their own value judgements about them.

Such a teacher would most probably agree that there might be situations in which perfect objectivity or impartiality should be sacrificed in the interest of even more important values; and also that there could be occasions on which the adoption or maintenance of objective and impartial attitudes might be very un-neutral in its effect on some given conflict. The first point may be illustrated by one fairly simple example. There could be situations in which the objective and impartial exposition of all the main locally competing views on interracial relations by a teacher whose pupils came from families most liable to harbour or to suffer racial prejudice, might actually serve to inflame rather than to disperse it. Such a result might be even more likely if the teacher himself belonged to the group that was the focus of the prejudices in question; or to the extent that the arguments of the racists were comparatively simple to grasp and that the evidence against them was, however powerful, nevertheless somewhat complex. It is unfortunately optimistic to suppose that the causal results of the presentation of a rational and objective argument must always be to lead the audience in the direction of greater rationality and objectivity. In such circumstances the thorough-going liberal teacher, opposed as he must be to racialism, might well conclude that it was better to try to create non-racialist attitudes among his pupils even at the expense on this occasion of a fully objective and impartial presentation of all the relevant facts and views.

Any more wary liberal teacher is thus bound to admit the possibility of internal conflict between his own values in circumstances which are themselves less than ideal. He is equally bound to admit the impossibility in principle of finding criteria which could, if satisfied, provide a guarantee that his treatment of a given problem had reached a standard of perfect objectivity and impartiality. This is to admit that perfect objectivity and impartiality cannot in any practical terms be known to exist; that is to say that one may never succeed, and that in any case one could never obtain a conclusive guarantee of having succeeded, in presenting every one of the rival viewpoints in a situation of conflict in just such ways, both as to terms and to context, as their own partisans would have chosen, together with a full recital of *all* the facts which might from the different viewpoints be held to be relevant, presented successively in all the various interpretations to which such facts might be susceptible – always supposing that under these different interpretations one would even find oneself with recognisably isomorphic sets of 'facts'.

It is at this point, however, that open-mindedness comes to the rescue and, in doing so, shows how closely it is bound up with objectivity and impartiality. To be open-minded is after all to be unremittingly sensitive to the possibility that one may not yet have succeeded in being as impartial and as objective as one may have intended and hoped; that there may still be new facts to be discovered, old facts whose relevance has yet to be reassessed, new interpretations to be considered of the total situation or of certain aspects of it. One might say that objectivity and impartiality exist as ideals of reason; or that while to aim at objectivity is necessarily to aim at truth, in actual practice the most objectively presented account may always in as yet unknown fact turn out to be false. To say that perfect objectivity and impartiality may never be known to exist in the facts of things actually said or done is not at all the same thing as to say that they exist in no meaningful way whatsoever. The crucial point, for this kind of liberal at any rate, is to articulate the concepts of impartiality and objectivity clearly and distinctly enough for them to serve as guiding values, as ends for our intentions, our attitudes and our actions. He might say, then, that a teacher's presentation of his subject was objective and impartial to whatever extent it succeeded in setting out all the facts and the rival interpretations of them in just such ways as the rival partisans would have chosen, and that his conduct or attitude as a teacher could be regarded as objective and impartial just in so far as he was genuinely striving after such a presentation.

This last formulation poses something of a problem, for it suggests that a teacher whose attitudes and intentions were fully objective and impartial might nevertheless fall so far short of the aims that he set himself as to give a thoroughly unobjective and unimpartial presentation of the situation that he was dealing with. But surely it cannot be enough to declare oneself impartial and objective in order actually to be so, even if the declaration is entirely sincere? Naïve goodwill alone can hardly be enough. A certain degree of insight and understanding is also required; and to know exactly how to take into consideration and to expound very different viewpoints from one's own may demand not only the qualities of a quick and sympathetic imagination, but also considerable training. This point has, of course, important implications for the aims and methods of a liberal education; but also, and more fundamentally, for the proper understanding of the very concepts of objectivity and impartiality and, for that matter, of neutrality as well.

What in fact might one say of people whom one believes to be subjectively sincere in their claim to be striving for objectivity and impartiality, but whose representation of a given situation is patently 'biased' in the direction of their own vested interests? One possibility, of course, is that they have an imperfect grasp of the concepts of objectivity and impartiality (or that they are simply using these terms in some quite different way from that which I have sketched out here). More interestingly they may have allowed or persuaded themselves to ignore the fact that their presentation actually fell far short of the accessible standards of objectivity and impartiality, and that the particular way in which it fell short fitted in to a remarkable degree with their own interests and ambitions. This need not mean that they were deceiving themselves in believing that they believed themselves to be striving after objectivity and impartiality; but it would mean that they were deceiving themselves in believing that they were really doing so.

It is important to notice that the problem here is one of honesty and insight rather than one concerning the interestedness or disinterestedness of a man's efforts to be impartial and objective. After all it might very well be in one's interests to be impartial and objective and one might oneself see this very clearly. One might, for example, be employed as a teacher of politics in an institution which was not prepared to renew the contract of any teacher whose presentation of his material to his students was not consistently impartial and objective. According to our present definitions at any rate, there are no logically binding relationships between the concepts of objectivity and impartiality on the one hand and those of neutrality and disinterestedness on the other hand. The crucial point is rather that while we may count a man's attitude as objective and impartial even though his performance falls short of the standards that he sets himself, provided only that his efforts are sincere and reasonably clear-sighted, we are bound to an equal insistence on this second provision of reasonable clear-sightedness; sincerity alone is simply not enough.

The reason why we are bound to measure the objectivity and impartiality of a man's attitudes in part at least by reference to the sincerity of his intentions, and not merely by reference to the actual standard of his performance, is that objectivity and impartiality are, like neutrality, partly intentional concepts. This claim may be tested by considering the sense in which a machine might be described as impartial or objective. Clearly, an effective way of securing a full and undistorted account of the proceedings of a conference at which competing views are put forward and incompatible policies propounded, would be to obtain a complete audio-visual record of what had taken place. One could, no doubt, understand a description of the recording apparatus (or the record that it produced) as impartial or neutral in as much as it did indeed produce a full account of all the rival points of view exactly as set out by their respective partisans and in as much as it certainly intended no differential support or opposition to any of the parties involved. In so far as objectivity is defined by reference to an effort to check against the facts as one understands them, the question of the objectivity of a merely recording apparatus could hardly arise. But then the question of its neutrality is already an odd one; the reason why we can say with such evidence that it has and could have had no intention of according differential support or opposition to any of the parties involved is simply that recording apparatus is not the sort of thing to which intentions can be ascribed. In fact the best way of understanding a description of such apparatus as impartial is probably as a compressed way of saying that if such a report had been produced by any rational intention-pursuing creature such as man, we should have regarded it as wholly impartial; for a main point of our use of such concepts as objectivity, impartiality and neutrality is surely to assess the attitudes and performances of potentially rationally intentional beings like ourselves. This is why it is only in a derivative sense that predicates such as objectivity, impartiality and neutrality can be ascribed to natural phenomena or to artefacts whose intentionality is derived from that of their creators. Or to put the point differently: the degree to which it may seem acceptable to describe the behaviour of a machine as neutral, impartial or objective will depend on the extent to which it may seem natural to construe its behaviour as intentional.

On the other hand, it is also clear that the conscious intentions of an agent cannot provide the only criteria for our assessment of his performances. We are unavoidably interested in the actual effects of his performances on other individuals and on society in general; and in so far as we are assessing his performances under such headings as those of impartiality or neutrality, we must necessarily suppose the agent himself to be interested in their impact on other people. Moreover, whatever view we may take about the self-evidence to the agent of his own intentions, it is very hard to suppose that he must necessarily be consciously aware of the full motivational and purposive significance of all his own acts. Thus we are also bound to refer to what may be called the objective nature of his performances even in assessing the objectivity, impartiality or neutrality of his own attitudes. For one thing it constitutes part of the logically necessary framework within which to assess the degree and direction of his own self-insight or self-deception; for another it is a necessary condition for assessing him as objective, impartial or neutral that we should be able to treat him as a potential partner in a rational discussion of the actual nature of his performances.

It would seem, then, that the sense of such concepts as objectivity, impartiality and neutrality must be governed by some indirect and variable balance of reference to both subjective and objective factors. It is, immediately, much less clear what the nature of this balance might be; there is here no more than a suggestion for one particular direction of further work. But it would be a natural *a priori* speculation that different people in different circumstances and operating from different viewpoints should be led to give very different emphasis to either the objective or the subjective factors –

even sometimes to the paradoxical point of stressing the importance of the one to the implicit near exclusion of the other. It is certainly interesting to note in passing that 'liberal' theorists have on the whole tended to emphasise subjective factors as compared to the sometimes near exclusive emphasis on objective ones by certain socialist theorists. This is not, perhaps, very surprising, given the liberal evaluation of the status of individuals as such and the socialist emphasis on the importance of extra-individual social relations; on the other hand it probably does not reflect any logically necessary balance of emphasis. However, this point too is one for further study.

Finally, how far can a 'liberal' answer the objections: (i) that when a viewpoint makes a certain kind of connection between theory and practice there can be no proper exposition of the theory that does not itself embody, or is not accompanied by, the kind of practice in question; (ii) that it is impossible to take into genuine consideration certain viewpoints of a radically non-liberal kind without adopting them as one's own; (iii) that viewpoints of certain kinds are in any case not open to understanding, let alone adoption, by anyone who has not himself had the requisite experience?

To what sorts of viewpoints and to what kinds of experience is this last objection supposed to apply? A strong case *can* be made for the view that the possession of certain interpretive concepts is a necessary condition for having certain experiences;[6] but since their possession is hardly likely to be a sufficient condition also, it would not follow that an understanding of the experience depended on having shared in it oneself. Nor is there here any point in reproducing the standard arguments against the claim that it is in principle impossible to understand the experiences of anyone else. In any case the claim is not one for which anti-liberals are particularly likely to argue; they are far more concerned with distinguishing between the understanding of radically different experiences that is impossible and the understanding that *is* possible on the basis of common experience. So for present exploratory purposes the best thing may again be to take the short cut of a particular example.

There is, then, an obvious sense in which it may fairly be said that those who are blind from birth cannot fully understand the experience of the sighted or those who are sighted the experience of those who are congenitally blind. Members of one group cannot really know what it is like to be a member of the other. Yet this does not mean that the one group can understand nothing about the radically different experiences of the other, nor that the blind can make

[6] Such a case might be made with reference to certain more or less sophisticated aesthetic concepts and experiences.

nothing of the language of sight. So much we may here take for granted. The crucial question is whether either group can understand enough to be able to take into properly impartial and objective consideration the special viewpoints of the other. For there *would* be something absurd in claiming impartiality for a sighted expositor of the views of the blind – or, indeed, for an expositor of any views whatsoever – if it was clear that he had no idea of the point of what he was saying, however complete and in a sense accurate his 'exposition'; if the performance of a recording apparatus can be assimilated to that of a man, assimilation may also take place in the opposite direction.

There is, however, no reason why this should necessarily be the case; perhaps no one would suppose that it should, if they did not somehow believe that understanding must be a matter of all or nothing. Of course, the sighted expositor cannot directly share the outlook of the congenitally blind that he is reporting. And, other things being equal, his report may for certain purposes be less persuasive than it might have been, had it been presented by someone who had himself been blind from birth. But effective persuasion and faithful, clear and impartial exposition by no means always come to the same thing. There can hardly be any mechanically determinate rules either for attaining oneself or for assessing the degree of someone else's attainment of understanding, but in general the higher the level of generality at which the position of the blind is considered, the more easily should the sighted, expositor and audience alike, be able to understand it; the wider the ranges of experience on which communication ultimately relies and the more complex the conceptual ramifications through which references to experience are mediated, the less exclusive need be the reliance on just those aspects of experience which sighted and blind cannot share. Analogy and metaphor may also do much to help. So too will depth of experience and sensitivity and a sympathetic imagination; though it should be obvious, it is strangely possible to forget that human understanding is not an exclusively intellectual operation.

All this brings us back to the point that to the extent that capacity for understanding is one of its necessary conditions, impartiality may demand a certain kind of apprenticeship or training and even a certain kind of personality. It may also demand a certain capacity for understanding on the part of the audience; or, more exactly perhaps, a reasonably justified belief on the part of the expositor that his audience is capable of an adequate degree of understanding. This necessary reference to the capacities of the audience complicates the situation in a number of ways. A sighted expositor might know very well, for example, that if he succeeded in setting out 'fully and fairly' the position and view of the blind by 'using their own terms of reference' and by 'expounding them as they would expound them themselves', his particular audience would in fact understand much less of the situation than if he had used other methods of communication, which to the blind themselves would not naturally have been available. So let us now say that impartiality demands that the expositor should use such terms of exposition as would have been used by the blind themselves had such terms been available to them and had they properly understood the nature of the relevant audience. But there is, of course, no reason why such expositors should always have to take the capacities of their audiences as given; and often there is very good reason why they should not. So to the extent that exposition is an on-going and not a once and for all process, impartiality may demand a readiness and a capacity to train one's audience to an impartial understanding.

In this way the point is also reinforced that impartiality is not to be thought of as fully attainable in every situation, as if it was always already in principle there, waiting to be discovered complete and perfect in the facts of an accomplished act. It is rather, as already suggested, a principle or guide of action, sometimes comparatively easy to know how to follow, often difficult and uncertain. Above all, the liberal may insist, the impartiality of the sighted in their approach to the demands and viewpoints of the blind is bound to their open-minded effort to achieve as close an understanding as possible. Once again, however, the criteria of impartiality include references not only to effort but also to the chances of success. When failure is too gross and should have been too easily predictable, effort, however sincere, can no longer be regarded as enough. Once again too, there can be no definitionally determinate point at which failure does become too gross; the matter is one for complex and always potentially controversial judgement.

So impartiality and the degrees of understanding on which it depends are always matters of debatable more or less. What, however, of the remaining objections that there are viewpoints (of a radically non-liberal kind) that 'it is impossible to take into genuine consideration without adopting them as one's own'; and that 'when a viewpoint makes a certain kind of connection between theory and practice, there can be no proper exposition of the theory that does not itself embody, or is not accompanied by, the kind of practice in question'?

As to the first, I am tempted to say merely that the only way to make this argument stick is to render it virtually empty – that is, through one form of definition or another. There is anyhow surely something intolerably paradoxical in the claim that one's view can be intelligible only to someone who already accepts it; from this it would follow that attempts to convince anyone else to accept it can only be construed as attempts at encouragement to jump into the unknown, indeed the unknowable, in advance. Moreover, whenever a believer lapsed from his convictions, one would have to say either that he had now forgotten what he had previously believed or, more probably, that it has turned out that he had never really understood after all. Some forms of religious belief are presented in just such a way; one is called upon to make a 'leap of faith'. But this is a manifestly unsatisfactory line to take in the exposition, advocacy or defence of a would-be rational or scientific doctrine; and even in the case of avowedly partly non-rational doctrines, which place the acceptance of the unprovable or even of paradox at the centre of faith, it is once more hard to see how to prevent the making of such acceptance into an actual criterion of full understanding from becoming an empty definitional point and thus useless in any really important or challenging marginal cases.

It is true that all this needs much detailed elaboration if proper account is to be taken of the subtly various ways in which action can and even must be so related to belief as to show that there can be no sharply distinguishing break between them. It is also most probably true that a teacher of Confucian philosophy, for example, or of Marxism, who does not himself seek to put into practice the principles that he expounds, cannot put them over in the same ways as those in which at least certain kinds of Confucian or of Marxist would themselves do so. But he *can* say what it would be to expound them in those ways; and although this is evidently not exactly the same thing, it is close enough to be able to convey a clear understanding – including a clear understanding of the bases in Confucian or Marxist theory for criticising the methods and attitudes of the non-Confucian or the non-Marxist teacher of the subject as, at the best, inadequate.

However, this case is not strictly analogous to that of the sighted and the congenitally blind. In that case, it may be argued, as likewise in cases concerning rich and poor, man and woman, black and white, no one who has not himself had the relevant experience can 'really' understand what he who *has* had it tries to explain of his position or outlook; lack of experience, it is claimed, involves some necessary lack of insight into what the terms of exposition are used to convey. In the case where it is argued, in the appropriate fashion, that practice and theory are each constructive aspects of each other, an absence of the relevant context of practical experience or resolve will be held to change the very terms of belief and exposition; one may understand what it would be to believe or to expound the theory that one does not practise, but one cannot actually believe it or expound it as those who do believe it would do.

This does indicate a very special limitation on the possibilities of attaining full impartiality, as I have tried to mark out the concept. It is not only easier for a liberal to give impartial expositions of some types of theories rather than others; there are some types of theory which, by their very nature, place limits on such impartial exposition as the liberal can coherently aim at. Moreover, there is one further characteristic twist to this story. In the case of any theory whatsoever which the expositor believes to be either logically or factually faulty, there is a certain commonplace tension between the requirements of impartiality and objectivity. To expound the theory in the manner of one of its own adherents is, presumably, to present it in terms which 'contextually imply' one's own – i.e. the speaker's – acceptance of it. But already the context of exposition must place this 'acceptance' in brackets; and the objective scrutiny of the theory which follows its exposition, must make clear the expositor's actual rejection of it. Nevertheless, in so far as one restricts one's attention to the exposition itself and ignores its wider context, it is possible to respect the terms of reference which would be accepted by the theory's own adherents. A liberal expositor would naturally believe that there must be some important logical flaw in any Confucian or Marxist type theory which insisted on such an integral interconnection between theory and practice. Hence he would tend to assimilate to the standard case such limitations as he might admit to his impartial exposition of such theories; the limitations would hardly encroach on the fairness of his actual expositions, though they would obviously (and, he would hold, properly) modify their impact. For the Confucian or the Marxist themselves, however, the case would be very different. It would not be merely that the liberal expositor had, in their eyes, made an inaccurate assessment of the merits of the theory that he was expounding; it would be that, lacking the relevant context of practice, he had failed accurately to expound it at all. Hence his lapse from an anyhow impossible impartiality would be much more serious – not, of course, as a failure to achieve the impossible, but as a necessarily dishonest (and typically self-deceived) pretence at having come near it.

This does not mean that Marxists or Confucians (of the relevant type) could not for their part give impartial expositions of non-Marxist or non-Confucian theories; or at any rate such expositions as adherents of these theories must properly acknowledge to be impartial, as long as *they* do not claim that the very meaning of the terms of belief must in principle find partial expression in the practice of the believer. It does, however, go to show in what sense impartiality may be regarded as a peculiarly liberal value; and also why it may make no sense to aim at a universally impartial explication of the concept of impartiality.

4   Disinterestedness, independence and lack of bias

This section provides an opportunity to pick up just a few of the loose ends of further associated concepts.

The point was made in brief passing on page 5 that the concept of disinterestedness is to be distinguished from that of neutrality. The remainder of the relevant paragraph ran as follows:

'There are two main ways in which this concept [of disinterestedness] may be taken. According to the first, to be disinterested in any given situation is simply to have no interests of one's own at stake; or at any rate no interests of which one is aware. According to the second, one may use the term to refer to the attitude of a man who, although he did have interests at stake, succeeded in setting them aside from the considerations which he allowed to weigh with him in coming to his decision or in determining his attitude. If one prefers to take the term in the first way only, one might, by way of conceptual compensation, extend the meaning of "detachment" to cover the setting aside of considerations of interest as well as the setting aside of personal preference. This suggestion in fact raises further problems of considerable importance and complexity concerning the relations between the concepts of interest and preference; we shall have to return to them in a later section.'

The way in which these problems arise may be seen as follows. To prefer that one side should come out on top in any situation of conflict must presumably be to expect or to be liable to derive greater satisfaction from one possible outcome of the conflict than from the other or others. It may often happen that a man has no interest in a conflict in which he is not directly involved other than the satisfaction that he would derive from the success of the one side as against that which he would derive from the success of the other. But, it may now be argued, his natural interest in his own satisfaction would make it absurd for him or anyone else to claim that he was a disinterested party. This sort of point may be made of football supporters who may have nothing at stake in the success of their chosen team beyond their (perhaps even fanatical) pleasure in its success and pain at its failure, of people who have an intense but not further motivated dislike of seeing Jewish noses in their golf clubs or black faces among their near neighbours or of those who cannot bear the thought that others may be better off or happier than themselves, even though an attack on the other's situation could bring no material improvement in their own. So quite generally, it may be alleged, to have preferences, that is not to be indifferent, is already to have an interest in the success of that party in whose favour or for the sake of whom one is less than indifferent.[7]

Even if something like this is accepted, however, a distinction has still to be made between the concepts of indifference and disinterestedness; the argument would show only that indifference was a necessary condition of disinterestedness, not that it was also a sufficient one. I may have interests of which I am presently unaware, which I may have forgotten or of which I may never even have known. It is true that I may likewise have forgotten my own normal preferences and need to resubmit myself to an experience to rediscover whether I like it or not; and this means that one may have to choose between talking of having forgotten whether one is indifferent or not and insisting that to be indifferent is simply to be without presently recognised preferences. But in any case I may at the same time be aware of my long term interests and yet be presently indifferent towards them; I may as of now be indifferent even to virtually certain prospects of future pleasure for myself. Perhaps the argument may still be pushed that if I am really indifferent to prospects of which I am aware, then the realisation of these prospects cannot be said to be in the interests of the person that I now am; or, a different sort of argument, that there are significant differences of sense between such expressions as 'interested' and 'in his interests' or 'disinterested' and 'not in his interests'. Alternatively, it may be insisted that one should make room for some rather emphatic distinctions between what is in a man's material interests, what would be in his interests according to common expectations of what a man may naturally want, what would be in his interests according to conventional standards of what is a good state for a man to be in, and what is in his 'real interests' – where the reality of his interests may, and perhaps must, be left open to be determined by the standards accepted as relevant by the speaker (which may themselves directly be determined by the standards of his own community or which may demand that the matter be settled by the clearest expression of opinion that one can get from the man whose interests are in question or . . . etc., etc.).

[7] The term 'indifference' may also be used to indicate not only an absence of preference, but an absence of any feeling whatsoever. Thus a different kind of spectator at a football match may have no preferences as to the outcome, but still find it intensely exciting as compared with his companion, whom the whole performance leaves unmoved or 'totally indifferent'. This (perfectly legitimate) use of the term is related to but evidently different from the one I am working with here.

Any exhaustive discussion of these concepts and their attendant problems would certainly have to take all these possibilities, and others too no doubt, into explicit account. No matter how one opts among the various possible distinctions, however, there will remain a need to draw some sort of line, however shifting and liable to blur, between having a preference and having an interest, such that a man cannot turn anything into being in his interest simply by preferring that it should be so. Preferences can shift with the whim of the moment; interests are relatively more stable. Or preferences may be based on ignorance and misunderstanding, while interests have to do with a man's real (i.e. objectively ascertainable) underlying position. Or again, and most importantly, while my interests are by definition my own proper business, my mere preferences may extend to what is strictly somebody else's business and not my own proper concern at all. To make a very closely related point the other way round: somebody else's interests have far more claim to my serious consideration, even if they happen to conflict with my own preferences, than do his mere preferences alone.

It is, of course, true that at least on many and perhaps on all fully coherent views of man and his morals his interests must ultimately be determined by some privileged sub-class of his actual or potential preferences. Nevertheless, it is certainly difficult, if not actually impossible, to work out a coherent account of a society in which anything that anyone might do would be held to affect the interests, and thus to become the proper business, of anyone and everyone else whenever they had any kind of preference that he should act in some other way. Some may wish to argue, perhaps, that in the case of certain kinds of feelings their combined strength and nature may give a man a proper interest in whatever behaviour they may range over. But however this may be, unless we are prepared to let everybody decide at his own discretion just what part or aspect of other people's behaviour is part of his own proper business and in deciding make it so, we must be prepared to draw a line somewhere (though not necessarily always in the same place in each succeeding context) and thereby to accept as a continuing possibility that a man may have preferences in some situations of conflict, where his interests on the contrary are in no way involved.

The second term, independence, may also be understood in either of two main ways. It may be taken to refer to the absence of any constraining or partly constraining factor, or of any factor that might exercise an effectively causal or manipulative influence, either by managing to pass unrecognised or through gaining the kind of acceptance that may be given it out of weakness rather than from constraint. Alternatively, the term may be taken to refer not to the absence of such factors, but to their failure to secure any effective results. There will be cases, always difficult to assess, where one might want to claim that independence had been maintained even though a given influence had been present and the outcome had in fact been precisely that which the influencing factor might have been expected to produce, but where, so it is claimed, this outcome would in any case have been the same even if the factor had not been present. The distinction between these two concepts, or these two ways of taking the term 'independence', can sometimes be most important; one might wish to mark it, for instance, by retaining the term 'independence' for the first case, but using that of 'autonomy' for the second.

If one uses the terms on this basis, one might relate them through the consideration that independence could be considered a sufficient, but not a necessary, condition for autonomy.

To consider the third concept, a biased report or position of any kind is quite simply one that fails of impartiality, objectivity or open-mindedness. It follows straightforwardly from what has been said earlier on that neither interestedness nor partisanship (that is to say, lack of neutrality) are in themselves sufficient to render a report, position or attitude biased. There are many possible reasons for which one might decide to limit the impartiality, objectivity or open-mindedness of one's report or of the position that one takes up. One, but only one, of these possible reasons would be the desire covertly to influence the preference or attitudes of others in the direction of one's own. The term 'tendentiousness' may be reserved for the framing of a report or the taking up of a position with this end in view. It is clear that on these definitions not all biased reports need necessarily be tendentious. It is slightly less clear, however, whether tendentious reports are to be treated simply as a sub-class of those which are biased. This question turns on whether one might make a fully impartial, objective or open-minded presentation of a case in order covertly to influence somebody else's preferences or attitudes. I am inclined to think that this possibility is in fact ruled out by the definitions I have suggested. This depends, of course, on stressing the word 'covertly'; we have already seen that objectivity, impartiality and open-mindedness need not necessarily be neutral. However, the point is one that it is perhaps more important to be aware of than to decide.

5   The concept of the political

For many ordinary people, in contemporary Western countries at any rate, politics is quite simply the general, if ill-defined, area of debates and disputes between the political parties. If one asks them what they mean by 'political' in the phrase 'political parties', it becomes clear often enough from their answers that for them its meaning is almost entirely extensional – that is to say that it is simply used to refer to the parties that actually exist and for any that might arise to compete with them on the same sort of terrain and under the same sort of rules as those that govern their present activities. This sort of use and understanding of the term 'political' is not, of course, going to stand up to much pressure. Nevertheless it, or the tacit assumptions that underlie its use, may have a good deal to do with the position of many of those who think that education, morals and politics can be, and maybe even should be, held rigorously apart. They may believe without obvious difficulty, for instance, that it is possible to limit oneself to the teaching of facts about the history and nature of party politics in a wholly neutral and impartial way – and that this is the only way in which education and (party) politics should ever come into contact. There is nothing surprising about such a use of the term nor about the existence of such beliefs within the framework of a pluralist and multi-political party 'liberal' society.

This is one extreme. At another stand those sociologists who insist that the scene for political activity is set as soon as any two or more people have to settle on a course of action involving a choice between two or more partially or wholly exclusive policies. As one of my own politics tutors (Professor S. E. Finer) used to say, 'If I want red curtains to hang in our living room, while my wife wants blue, then we already find ourselves in a (domestic) political situation.' There are thus family politics, school politics, office politics, university politics, local politics, national politics – politics everywhere, in fact, where conflicts of policy may arise between one person or body of persons and another. To take part in such politics is to act in such a way as to influence the final policy outcome; to act as a politician is to direct one's actions to the deliberate shaping of such policy in one way rather than in another. Politics in this most general sense is the resolution of choice, wherever two or more people are somehow implicated in the outcome, and where, in principle at least, they may or may not disagree.

No doubt, to mark out certain continuities and to play down certain discontinuities in this way does encourage certain sorts of insight; there are undeniably important analogies between the methods and attitudes of even family, let alone academic politics and those of politics as practised on the widest national scale.

Nevertheless, to approach politics from the starting point of conflicting individuals *is* to go to one kind of extreme. Moreover, it is not the only approach that may allow the term to refer to some such wide and fluctuating range. The area of the political is probably better first conceived of as lying somewhere between the two extremes to which I have just referred as setting outside limits; it may be thought of as the area of *public* policy. This, of course, displaces the burden of immediate analysis onto the term 'public'.

The problem is, then, whether it may be possible to mark out in any meaningful way an area of *public politics,* which would be wider than that of conventional party politics as defined by reference to an existing framework of institutions, but narrower all the same than the area of policy conflict between *any* two or more persons in *any* situation in which the policy of one might be incompatible with the policy of another. One clear starting point is provided by the general definition of 'public' which was offered by Sir George Cornewall Lewis in 1832, and endorsed by Brian Barry in his book *Political Argument* (Routledge and Kegan Paul, 1965), and on which, he says, it is impossible to improve:

Public, as opposed to *private,* is that which has no immediate relation to any specified person or persons, but may directly concern any member or members of the community, without distinction. Thus the acts of a magistrate, or a member of a legislative assembly, done by the same persons towards their family or friends, or in their dealings with strangers for their own peculiar purposes, are called private . . . In the language of our law, public appear to be distinguished from private acts of parliament, on the ground that the one class directly affects the whole community, the other some definite person or persons.

Barry also cites Bentham (*The Theory of Legislation*) and again it is worth repeating the quotation:

1st. *Private offences.* Those which are injurious to such or such assignable individuals. The assignable individual is such or such an individual in particular, to the exclusion of every other; as Peter, Paul or William other than the delinquent himself. 2nd. *Reflective offences, or offences against one's self.* 3rd. *Semi-public offences.* Those which affect a portion of the community, a district, a particular corporation, a religious sect, a commercial company, or any association of individuals united by some common interest, but forming a circle inferior in extent to that of the community . . . 4th. *Public offences.* Those which produce some common danger to all the members of the state, or to an indefinite number of non-assignable individuals although it does not appear that any one in particular is more likely to suffer than any other.

There are two main themes running throughout these passages.

First and most prominently, there is the insistence on the non-assignable individual, the no specific person in particular, the 'n'importe qui'; public policies are policies which might have an impact on any member of the community – not necessarily on any role-holder (i.e. the holder of any role, no matter which), but on any individual in so far as the role or roles concerned may in one way or another be open to him. This is a very shorthand and not altogether satisfactory way of putting it. For example, a policy affecting all adult males may well be a matter of public politics, even though it is obvious that many members of the public must of necessity fall outside its direct scope. This might reflect a common attitude that those who are not adult males are in some important sense not full members of the community nor, therefore, of the relevant public (certain political struggles turn precisely about this question of who shall be counted as belonging to the public body politic – women, people between the age of 18 and 21 etc.). Or it might be that all other members of the public may be affected, if strictly indirectly still directly enough, by the policy in question; if it is that of adult male conscription, boys will grow up, wives may have to part from husbands and anyhow everybody's defence is at stake. Again, it may be that there are in effect two or more mutually entangled bodies politic, where the members of the one are for some, but not all, purposes members of the other and where there may in many cases be some important impact on the members of the other, of policies directly affecting members of the one – cf. (so-called) apartheid societies.

Secondly, there is the recurring reference to the notion of 'the community' as the natural – or, as one might say, definitional – habitat of the non-assignable individual. For Bentham, public offences are 'those which produce some common danger to all the members of the state' or at any rate 'to an indefinite number of non-assignable individuals'; here the notion of the state is used in place of that of 'the community', but it seems clear enough that in this context at any rate he is using the two more or less interchangeably.[8]

In most universities of the English-speaking world, students of politics will be familiar with the game of collecting and comparing different definitions of the term 'state', different ways of distinguishing it from (or identifying it with) such other terms as 'society' (or 'civil society') or 'nation', different ways of connecting it up with such further concepts as those of 'law' or 'government'. One can well understand how someone starting off with the modest ambition of making at any rate *one* reasonably precise claim about some aspect of the subject may be driven on and on through this interconnected web into trying to set up a whole new conceptual

[8] Semi-public offences are said to be 'those which affect a portion of the community'.

framework of his own. At this stage, however, it must be enough simply to be aware of these complexities. Let us pretend for the moment that we can at least agree on a relatively clear under- standing of the sense of the term 'community' – by 'clear' I do not, incidentally, wish necessarily to imply 'distinct' in the sense of being precisely marked off at the edges from all surrounding concepts, but clear at least in its central focus. Let us now consider the proposal that politics be understood as the area of public policies; that public policies be taken to be those which might have an impact on any non-assignable member of the community; and to make a positive virtue out of the fact that what may count as constituting the com- munity may vary widely from one context to another.

What is the nature of this variability and why should it be regarded as virtuous? By way of illustration, consider at a purely colloquial level the number of different communities to which any typical individual may claim or be claimed to belong. I myself, for example, may be counted as being a member of at least the follow- ing: the academic community, the British community, the Anglo- Jewish community, the community of those living in the city of Oxford, the Balliol community (and just what this may be is at least as contentious as is the precise nature of any other community), the community of mankind; and no doubt many more besides. Some of these community groups are so related that to belong to one is *ipso facto* to belong to another; others are not. Some communities exist in highly institutionalised structures; others exist rather as the causal implications of the modern world economy or simply in the aspirations of certain outward looking individuals or groups. Some are so constituted that there need in principle be no doubt as to who is a member and who is not; others have looser or less determinate criteria of membership, so that there may exist at their fringes an indefinite number of people who may fairly be counted either as members or non-members depending on one's own particular assessment of the relevant criteria. Clearly, one might say that these are not all communities in the same sense as each other. What, then, is the point of using the same term throughout?

The main point, for immediate purposes, is to refer in each case to certain bonds of social organisation – though 'organisation' may be too strong a term or carry too heavy a suggestion of systematically institutionalised behaviour – through which certain non-assignable individuals may be linked to others. Once again there is no point in indulging in verbal legislation. The word 'community' can also quite properly be used to refer to the intimate sharing of a way of life by a group of determinate and wholly assignable individuals. One must remember, however, that even in a small community, such as a monastery for example, where everybody is perfectly well known to everyone else, policies which are designed to apply to the members identified simply through the roles that they may hold, are policies designed to apply to non-assignable individuals. Peter may be Abbot at the moment, but he may be replaced tomorrow; old Brothers may die and new ones may be admitted. Even in a totally closed 'community', a society that I might, for example, have founded with members of my class at school, to which no new members are to be admitted and which will diminish eventually to disappear with our deaths – even in such a 'community' certain of the policies that affect my relations with the others may do so in virtue of the non-assigned and reallocable roles that we happen to hold within the society rather than in virtue of our personally assignable identities. Similarly, certain aspects of family structures may present these non-assignable characteristics; here one has roughly to distinguish those cases in which one places people on the family map in terms of their relationships to that eminently assignable individual, oneself, from those in which one is considering the non-assignable individuals who may in general stand in certain relationships to each other – for example, the class of all those cousins who may at one stage or another of their lives fall in love with each other.

Be all this as it may, it may very reasonably be complained that to talk simply of 'certain bonds of social organisation' is to talk excessively vaguely. Even in preliminary sketch-work, something further is needed. Here the following four factors are worth mentioning:

(I) There is a factor of relative richness or complexity or seriousness in the bonds or relationships in question. A society whose members are held together only by interests of merely casual concern may provide the framework for characteristically political activity; but to the extent that none of the outcomes really matter to those involved, they will be only 'playing at politics'. This is not to say that societies formed even with the explicit aim of providing a framework for such play may not come to assume a far from playful importance in the lives of their members; at this point the playing at politics merges into the real thing.

(II) There is a closely related factor of relative self-sufficiency within the area of interests for which the society or community caters. That is, for a community to be a community in the relevant sense it must not only cater for some relatively important need or interest of at least some significant proportion of its members; it must do so successfully, at least to the extent that they are not in practice left always to seek any possible satisfaction of these needs in some totally different and disconnected set of social relationships. The needs or interests in question may be either material, affective, aesthetic, recreational or whatever (nor need they necessarily be those whose pursuit is the explicit aim of the community, if indeed it has one). One can talk of the banking community as easily as of the community of Quakers in general or of the local Quaker community in particular.

(III) There is a factor of relative mutual concern. A community has already ceased to exist when there is no longer any significant proportion of its members who really care about the maintenance or the well-being of the community itself or about that of any of its members (at least in their capacities as members of the community). It goes without saying that this concern need have little or nothing to do with personal or indeed any other kind of affection; it may go along with a great deal of hostility and conflict. But if there is nothing else but plain hostility or indifference, if there is not even the commitment of recognised mutual material dependence or association through acceptance of a common tradition, then there is not, in the relevant sense, community.

(IV) There is this important factor of non-assignability, that the bonds of social organisation through which the community is characterised, should serve to link together certain personally non-assignable individuals.

It is clear that the first three of these are all in their different ways messy, imprecise, something more or a little bit less factors. How far this is true even of this fourth factor remains a more obscure and controversial question. In principle individuals can hardly be more or less in their particularity; but the terms through which the relevant links between them may or must be expressed may leave much more of a margin of uncertain variability.

Such factors allow accordingly for different assessments of situations depending on the nature of one's understanding and of one's point of view. That is, they allow for and make more naturally intelligible the natural fact that different people may quite properly disagree over what, either in general or in particular, is to count as an institutionalised community and over what sorts of relations, struggles and policies are to count as political – and why. A crucial importance of such disagreements lies in the fact that to count issues as political is not just to label or to classify them; it is to classify them as being the proper business of all full members of the relevant community. It is important to note, moreover, that where one type of community is, as it were, contained in another, issues which may be matters of public policy within the narrower community may be of essentially private concern in reference to the wider. Thus, the internal politics of, say, the Oxford Wrestling Society, of which I am

not a member, are none of my personal or public business, unless
and until the ways in which this society conducts its affairs start to
have some unprovoked impact on me, or on the ways in which some
society to which I belong (which could be simply the wider community) tries to conduct *its* affairs.

The suggestion may seem to be implicit in what has been said so
far that all politics take place within communities of some degree of
mutual concern; if so, it should be explicitly removed. Politics may
obviously lie in the relationships between such communities; there
may for some purposes be point in insisting that all particular communities must be regarded as belonging to the overall community of
mankind, but, as things are, the point is (perhaps unhappily) a restricted one. Politics is involved wherever the policies of one community of non-assignable individuals conflict with those of another
– or even, *à la limite*, with those of some assignable individual
foreigner.

The starting point for this analysis that was provided by Bentham
and Sir George Cornewall Lewis belongs to a way of conceiving
societies or communities as being formed out of the associations of
independently existing individuals, whose essential and prior
assignability is not taken into consideration so far as the terms of
these associations are concerned. An apparently very different
starting point might have been found from within the tradition
which tends rather to see individuals as the residual, emergent par-
ticularisations of what, to start with, is wholly and essentially social.
From the first point of view, it is natural to think of individuals' involvements in politics as beginning only where they are prepared to
abstract from their constitutive particularity. From the second, it is
more natural to think of individuals' involvements in politics as
ceasing only when the (for the time being) limits of their social commitments are reached. From the first point of view, areas of public
community politics are created by individuals for their own common or overlapping purposes; from the second, it is the area of private, individual action that has to be carved out of the social. I
should myself be inclined to argue that there is a level of formal,
abstract analysis at which these two approaches can be seen as
coming in the end to the same thing; and that while the fact that I
have here taken one starting point rather than the other may give a
certain *de facto* bias to my presentation of the argument, no such
bias is logically written into the argument itself. Nevertheless, it
may well be that this is one of the points at which the neutral clarity
of the distinction between the '*de facto*' and the 'logical' should not
be taken over lightly for granted.

All this may help to illustrate what I meant in referring to the variability of the concept of 'community'; it is now time to say why this variability may be regarded as a virtue. Here, after all these complications, the main point is once again a simple one. It is that in practice the relevant distinction between the private and the public *is* relative, shifting and controversial; that what may be seen by one man as private may appear to another, under another aspect or from another perspective, as a properly public matter; and that there should be nothing unintelligible about this.

In a way, no doubt, Bentham himself already recognised this variability or relativity. One may feel uneasy, however, with the form that his recognition took and with the nature of his distinction between *Public* and *Semi-public offences*. For Bentham the semi-public stops short of the fully public clearly enough, because he sees clearly before him the one genuine public, the full public of the community or state. It may be that for many important purposes the state (in some sense, into whose precise definition we need not venture here) is nowadays the most important community unit of all. But this certainly need not be, nor has it always been, nor is it everywhere, the case where people have been or may one day be engaged in what is recognisable as public political activity. Even in present-day society of the nearly all-powerful nation state, there is from the standpoint of the individual nothing private about, say, local politics, commercial politics or the politics of the various churches. Of course, if one takes it for granted that the national community constitutes the only true public, then one may want to make Bentham's sort of distinctions. I do not want to say that – in their context – they are wholly mistaken; but it *would* be a mistake to take them as more absolute than they are.

In fact, however, one's uneasiness with Bentham may go somewhat further than this. Politics is concerned with the choice and effective adoption and pursual of public policies; but at times the most important politics of all may be that concerned with the choice and effective adoption, pursual or rejection of policies whose carrying out would have some impact on the very structure of that community or society which determines the domain of the kind of 'public' that is in question. This can happen, of course, in communities of all types and at all levels; the proposals may range from suggestions for moderate constitutional reform through plans for mergers with other societies to projects for total enforced dissolution. Often communities or societies may be so related that modifications in the structure of one will result in modification in the structure of another or others. Moreover, what may count as a community or society in its own right from one point of view may from another point of view appear as a significant or even crucial aspect of the structure of some more widely articulated body. Or vice versa; there are points of view from which the wider body may have an interest or importance only as providing the framework within which the more specific or more narrowly defined body may persist. Thus, there is to be taken into account not only the obvious fact that consensus may break down (if it ever really existed) on the most general structure of society or the state as it exists at any one time; but also the related fact that to call this structure into question may be *ipso facto* to bring into question the structural nature of all those many other collateral or sub-societies, which may be partly or wholly conditioned by the nature of the state at the same time as they condition it.

To sum up, then, this rather impressionistic section on the concept of 'politics'. Politics, in the sense which seems most helpfully relevant, is the area of public policy; and public policies are those which may affect any (though not necessarily every) non-assignable member of the relevant community. The notion of a community is an essentially variable, relative and contestable one, which means that the notions of 'public' and 'politics' are in their turn essentially variable, relative and contestable. But this is an advantage rather than a disadvantage, since it serves to bring out something of the interconnection of the different areas and levels of politics; of how and why it is that what may seem to be political at one level or from one perspective may seem not to be so from another; and maybe even to suggest a natural explanation of the phenomenon that quarrels over what is public or private, what is political or non-political, over what is or what ought to be the structure of society itself, may sometimes turn out to be among the most important political quarrels of all.

I do *not* present these remarks as a complete definition of the concept of 'politics'. All the same there is one further quasi-definitional point that should be noted. 'Politics' is very often presented as having something to do not only with public (or community) policies, but more specifically with government. My passing over of this standard conceptual connection may be mistaken, but it is at any rate not a mere oversight. It is doubtful whether one could easily speak of all groupings that one might wish to recognise as communities as having 'governmental' institutions; but there could very well be in such communities a great deal of community politics – that is to say, manoeuvrings by which different parties sought to guide or to impel the community in one direction or another in contexts where the interests of its members would be non-assignably affected.[9]

---

[9] Of course, if anyone does want to extend the use of the term 'government' to whatever es-

6   The concept of the academic

If one's main substantial concern is with such questions as the possibility or impossibility, desirability or undesirability of the political neutrality of the university, it would appear only systematic to enquire also into such concepts as that of the academic. Most of the points that I should want to make and that do not begin to emerge from what I have tried to say in other less direct contexts are, however, already largely familiar. For the moment, therefore, I merely mention a very few brief and essentially recapitulatory considerations.

First, and very obviously, nobody could ever have supposed that either the university as such or that members of universities acting in their capacities as such, could or should be expected to remain neutral in the face of any and every conflict that may confront them, no matter what the issues might be. On the contrary, people of whatever social or political views will agree that there will be certain conflicts in which a university or its members will be committed, by the very nature of their responsibilities, to taking sides. Disagreement there will certainly be as to how far these responsibilities stretch and over the nature of the conflicts in which the university will be thereby committed to take up one position or another; but it would be senseless to argue that no such conflict could ever arise.

Equally there is no reason to expect that universities or their members should always act in a disinterested way, in either of the two senses of disinterestedness that were distinguished earlier on. Even the most 'liberal' member of a university must see himself as having his own characteristic interests *qua* member of the university, interests which he will regard it as his duty to defend. He would no doubt insist that it would be wrong for him, when considering university matters, to take into consideration his own personal interests or those of any extra university group to which he might also belong; but conversely he would recognise an obligation to watch over the interests of his university or college. This is not to say that 'liberals' would think there is any particular obligation on members of universities to be *personally* indifferent with regard to university matters in the sense of having no preferences of their own; but they would presumably think that they should generally be detached, in

---

tablished patterns of community decision taking there may be, and these could depend on roles which called for no stable membership but which were simply available on appropriate occasions, no one need have any last-ditch objections.

as much as they should set aside such purely personal preferences or inclinations when acting in their capacities as members of the university. They may allow, however, a number of perfectly acceptable exceptions to this general rule; there are, for example, quite proper reasons why personal preferences should be allowed to play a role in deciding the subjects on which one is to lecture or the area in which one is to conduct research.

On the other hand liberals, as of course many others to whom this term might not apply, *would* insist that universities and their members, when acting as such, should aim in all their judgements and actions at as complete an objectivity, impartiality and open-mindedness as possible. They should avoid bias and tendentiousness. Ideally, on the 'liberal' view, they should be given complete independence in the sense that they should be free of any constraining or partly constraining factors, both those that might be open for all to see and those that might pass unrecognised by taking advantage of, for example, internal university weakness. They should have an absolute right to remain indifferent towards any matter which does not directly concern them in their university capacities, though obviously not towards matters which do so concern them; 'liberals' may naturally disagree over just where the line is to be drawn, but they will agree readily enough on the principle. If university teachers cannot remain disinterested and should not remain neutral in conflicts which do concern them in their professional capacities, they have a duty to remain professionally disinterested and neutral in conflicts which do not touch on their university functions.

These are all and obviously among the sorts of points that one might expect to be made by almost any university 'liberal'. It is obvious too that their detailed interpretation may lead to what may be acknowledged to be perfectly acceptable controversy by those who in general are of equally liberal mind; and also that it is in the nature of the case that serious conflicts may arise between different characteristically 'liberal' values. Finally, it is obvious that all these points presuppose some generally understood and accepted framework of social and political concepts and values within which the relevance of one consideration to another may be assessed and within which permissible controversy may take place. Nobody need suppose that the distinctions just mentioned are simple or clear-cut, but they do provide points towards which a would-be 'liberal' may direct his conduct. He must recognise that political and academic considerations may have direct practical bearing on each other within a general framework or social structure; but the structure that he recognises is at the same time one in which the possibility of their essential distinction is taken for granted.

I recall these points not in order to make the further and equally obvious one that the 'liberal' is by no means the only possible view of the proper functions of universities and their relations to society as a whole, nor yet to mount any immediate argument in favour of or against any of the possible rival views. The question is rather whether, or under what limiting conditions, this liberal conception of a university is honestly conceivable. If, as I should myself wish to argue, it turns out to be conceivable under some but not all conditions, the further question arises as to the ways in which the realisation of these values at different levels of university life may in differing circumstances be linked with the maintenance or sacrifice of other competing moral, personal or social values. The answers that may seem possible or appropriate to both of these questions will depend on the now openly interlocking issues of how all the key concepts with which we have to deal are to be understood; and this understanding will in turn both depend on and further influence the network of underlying values or norms that are presupposed in whatever distinction between the academic and the political is to be made or reformed.

PART II

Impartiality and bias in economics[1]

ANDREW GRAHAM

One of the joys of being an academic economist is that one can pursue all sorts of mad ideas. But should one also be able to teach mad ideas? Isn't that irresponsible? Moreover, are mad ideas and extremity of view different things or only different descriptions of the same thing? Of course, one rarely asks such questions, at least of oneself, because madness is a disease caught only by one's colleagues – like when one goes to the Uffizi Gallery and thinks how objectionable all the tourists are. The only difficulty in the analogy is that we probably agree on what the characteristics of a tourist are, but no such agreement exists about the characteristics of mad ideas.

However, when one moves out of the academic sphere these questions are immediately of more than academic interest and, as a result, they take a sharper form. It is, for example, impossible to get a job as a Civil Servant if one is known to be a supporter of the Communist Party. Why is this? Is it just because such people are distrusted, or is there some other reason why extremity of political view rules one out from a job, and why one job rather than another? Is there some necessary connection between strong political views and an inability to give an unbiased account, or is it just that others expect one not to try to be unbiased?

Until recently I worked as an economic adviser attached to the British Civil Service and it was questioning by the security personnel in connection with this job, together with a growing awareness of the influence of economists on policy formation, that first prompted these thoughts. Yet it is only since then, while I have been teaching, that I have realised how similar are the questions which can be asked of academics.

However, let us begin with advice both because of my familiarity with it and because the questions have an extra clarity in this context. There would, for example, be general agreement that an adviser should be objective in the sense of basing his advice as far as he can on the facts and that he should not intentionally select the facts to support his own views. Indeed, many would go further than this and say that in addition there must be a clear line drawn between giving advice of a factual nature and making policy recom-

[1] Part of this chapter was given as a paper to the Oxford economics sub-faculty seminar in November 1970. The remainder was completed in May 1971.

49

mendations. They would argue not only that this distinction *can* be made, but moreover that social scientists *ought* to recognise it and then limit themselves to the first stage because to go beyond that is to bring in one's own views with no moral principle to support doing so. Politicians are elected whereas advisers are not.

Those who hold this view might liken the job of the economist to working for the magazine *Which*. This magazine, published by the Consumers' Association, looks at groups of consumer products, considers the features which consumers might want and then reports on how adequately each of these products meets these features. Thus, if they were preparing a report on cars they would consider the features which people are likely to be interested in, such as speed, acceleration, fuel consumption etc. They would then do a series of identical tests on each car so as to measure these performance characteristics and report these results together with the costs of the cars (including running costs, options available etc.). In the light of this the consumer can then make his choice – he considers which of the characteristics he wants (and how much) and works out the necessary trade-offs, e.g. whether a little more performance is worth the cost of rather higher fuel consumption.

In addition, however, the reports usually also include certain qualitative tests where the employees of the company (or a random sample of people) give ordinal rankings to features such as comfort on which there are no agreed standards of measurement; and they usually end their reports with a recommended 'best buy'. Thus, except perhaps for the last two features, they can claim that they are quite impartial since each car gets measured in exactly the same way, and they can claim they are objective as the results of the tests merely report the observed facts which in no way depend on the chance mood or deeply held political views of the observer. Finally, the organisation is reported to take great care to protect its impartiality (and that of its employees as well) by keeping itself quite independent of any financial or institutional connections with the manufacturers of the goods it is testing, and to ensure its objectivity by reporting very fully the methods which have been used in measuring the performance characteristics.

How adequately does this account correspond to the work of the economist? Let us suppose for the moment that the politician has fairly clearly defined aims so that the economist knows when looking at any policy measure that he has to report its effects on, say, inflation and employment. But then how does he go about this? First, he will need to look at the economy to see what the currently existing situation is. This will require decisions both about what facts are relevant and what interpretation should be placed on these. Secondly, he will need to consider how the economy is likely to develop in the absence of any change in policy. Thirdly, he must assess how the forecast situation would be altered by the policy under examination; and finally, he has to think about any complementary measure that might be appropriate taking account of the existing legal, institutional, and financial framework.

So, let us follow this through and begin at the beginning with the data which the economist uses. Suppose that the politician asks 'what is the present level of unemployment in this country?' then one might think a straight factual answer could be given to this. But a moment or two of reflection show that there are some 100 quite sensible answers to this question! Does the politician want it to be (1) U.K. or G.B.? (2) seasonally adjusted or not? (3) if so, by what method? (4) including or excluding school leavers? (5) just those registered at labour exchanges or including an estimate for those not registering? (6) males, females or both? (7) just 'wholly unemployed' or including the 'temporarily stopped' – both of these being terms of art and dependent on the conventions fixed earlier by the statisticians?

At very least, therefore, I need to know why the politician wants these figures. Is it an adequate answer to be told he just wants to know how many people are actually out of work? This *seems* simple. I give him the figures of those registered at the labour exchanges, I include both males and females, school leavers and temporarily stopped, and I do not seasonally adjust. However, I must be careful. On the one hand many of the temporarily stopped *have jobs* but were just not working on the day that the unemployment count was taken, while on the other hand I can infer from past movements in the figures that there are people willing to work, such as housewives and the elderly, but who are not bothering to register;[2] so that the figures are biased upwards for the first reason and downwards for the second.

In order to deal with this I write a *brief* report giving the figures including and excluding the temporarily stopped and giving a 'guesstimate'[3] at the number of unregistered, and I describe as clearly as I can how I got them and how they should be interpreted. Now, the first two figures are objective in the sense that any economist knowing the data would have used the same ones and even though the third figure includes some element of personal judgement in it that is no reason to suppose that it is biased. But how have I *described* these figures? The unemployed can be thought of in two

---

[2] One has observed that *de*creases in the registered unemployment figures have been accompanied by considerably more than proportional *in*creases in the employment figures.

[3] A horrible but useful word in the present state of economics.

rather different ways. The politician can be concerned for them in purely social terms – here are x many people for whom he wants to do something. Or alternatively, in more directly economic terms, the unemployed represent a waste – many of them want to work and are capable of producing goods but either cannot find a job at all or cannot find one at a wage in line with their expectations. Which terms have I used? If looking at them from an economic point of view, I might have included such sentences as 'not all these people should be regarded as "out of work" in the sense that they are (or would be) employable. Some of them are unlikely ever to work either because they do not wish to or because of mental or physical handicaps.' I might add, seemingly scientifically, 'it has been estimated that some x thousand of them are hard-core unemployed'. Now, few would judge this as politically biased advice but what do we mean by hard core? Many of them *could* be employed at a cost. The question is 'how much?' and though the economist can give information on this it is not his job to decide whether it is worth it.

Thus, even at this extremely elementary level where we are dealing directly with the data, we find that it is the outcome of previous interactions between producers and consumers; that is between the institutional arrangements by which it could be collected, and the decisions of economists and statisticians about the information useful to collect and the categories in which it should be arranged. Moreover, we may note that the description which we give to this data begins the process of influencing the politician's way of looking at the world and the further questions that he is then prompted to ask; while if we are not very careful, we may, however unconsciously, be making implicit assumptions in our choice of data or in the descriptions which we attach to this data with which he does not agree. We have not yet identified any *necessary* reason to suppose that we are biasing his judgement by our choice of information, and even if we are this is not our intention; but we are clearer on how many choices have to be made and how easy it is for that choice to be biased *un*intentionally.

But let us now move to a second problem at a rather higher level of abstraction. Suppose the politician asks what is causing inflation (and this ought to be a simpler question than asking for a policy recommendation to cure it) then most writers are at least agreed in describing it as the process of rising prices accompanied by money wages rising faster than output. But on a closer analysis their descriptions begin to vary and blur into a diagnosis of its causes. There are several competing theories of inflation, but I shall restrict myself here to very simplified accounts of two of them. One says that the economy at the aggregate level acts just like a single market (or is perhaps just the total of many single markets). Now simple market theory predicts that in the short run an increase in demand will be met partly by an increase in price and partly by increase in output, but that in the long run as output has more time to respond, prices are unlikely to rise and might even fall. So on this theory continuous increases in prices would be evidence that demand exceeded the output available and that this output could not increase because one had reached full employment. The other theory agrees that this will happen at full employment but suggests that increases in price can also occur below full employment and need not be caused by demand exceeding supply. Indeed it claims this to be so on the grounds that there is a crucial difference between looking at the parts (the single markets) and looking at the whole (the economy). It says that once one considers the whole economy then money which is paid out in wages creates its *own* demand. Thus the rate of increase in *money* wages and prices need not be determined *just* by demand exogenously given (i.e. from outside the system as it is in the case of a single firm) but can also be determined by the level of the money bargains struck between unions and employers (i.e. on this view money demand can be endogenously determined, that is within the system where the system is the whole economy).[4]

What is more these two different diagnoses lead naturally to different policy prescriptions. On Theory 1 (the demand pull) lowering exogenous demand (e.g. by cutting government expenditure) lowers the demand for real goods and this both directly reduces the price of goods and indirectly the demand for labour and thus also its price (i.e. wages). On Theory 2 (the cost push) lowering exogenous demand as before will again lower the demand for real goods, but may well *not* alter significantly the bargaining power of the unions *vis-à-vis* management so that the rate of growth of *money* demand (prices and wages) could go on largely as before, but with the level of real demand for goods lower and unemployment higher.

Now what would be required in the light of this if our economist were to attempt to be unbiased in his report to the politician? First, he would need to give an account of both these theories (and of the several variants of each) in terms sympathetic to each theory.[5] Secondly, he would need to collect and summarise the evidence for and against all these theories both from the past and from other countries. And thirdly, he would need to consider the present evidence about the situation in this country. But the evidence is by no

[4] I am intentionally assuming that the money supply is not acting as a constraint. This could be either because velocity increases, or because the monetary authorities are acting passively, or because the money supply is itself endogenous.

[5] This is more difficult than it sounds. Even on the basis of the very short accounts which I have given the reader will probably find it easy to see to which of the two theories I subscribe.

means unequivocal. Indeed it is common for economists to use the same facts but described differently in support of conflicting theories – and in this case there is the added complication that the very thing to be explained, that is rising prices, would be taken as strong evidence of excess demand by one school of thought yet considered irrelevant as evidence by the others (though not irrelevant to their causal explanation, since, on their argument, past rises in price will strengthen the demands of the unions).

A further example is that at one point in this debate it was thought that the fact that earnings increased faster than wage rates was strong evidence in favour of Theory I. Professor Paish wrote in 1957 'this is again much more in conformity with a picture of wages pulled up by competition between employers for scarce labour than of wages pushed up by Trade Union pressure against the opposition of reluctant employers'. But, a year later, Thomas Balogh referring to the *same* evidence was writing, 'it is . . . perhaps even more likely that it is brought about by the bargaining strength of the unions (due to full employment) being used to cut hours rather than force up wage rates and thus to obtain increases in over-time earnings (and push up the latter relative to wage rates)'.

What then is our adviser to make of all of this? What is the relation between theory in economics and the facts? Should he just leave these rival accounts to speak for themselves (and remember that the politician values brevity greatly), or should he perhaps in his attempts to save the politician's time be extremely selective in his remarks and concentrate on his own opinion? And, if so, how does *he* choose between competing theories?

Ideally, before he would accept a theory he would require:

   (i) that the assumptions used should seem broadly justified;
  (ii) that the theoretical deductions from these assumptions should be valid;
 (iii) that the account of the causal mechanism should be theoretically or intuitively convincing;
 (iv) that the statistical evidence collected should be consistent with the theoretical predictions;
  (v) that the figures used in these tests correspond adequately to the structure of the theory;
 (vi) that the theory is supported by historical evidence, both as regards the timing of events and the causal links involved;
 (vii) that predictions (as opposed to explanations of the past) based on this theory have fallen within acceptably small statistical margins of error;
(viii) and, finally, that there should be no competing theory which meets all these requirements in a more satisfactory manner.

Yet does all this, even supposing it were the case, amount to much more than saying that one needs to *feel* that the economy *could* work in a certain way, that it did *appear* to work in that way in the past, and that therefore one's best guess is that it will do so in the future?

However, the chance of all this occurring is not high. Most economic theories are usually not precise about what is to count as evidence and, even if they are, the data may be inaccurate or unclear – we have already seen how many alternative measures of unemployment are possible. Moreover, economists can usually only observe what might count as an effect and have to infer back to its cause. For example, in the recorded figures *actual* supply and demand are always equal, so we can never directly observe disequilibrium but only the symptoms of it – we observe inflation but we infer cost push or demand pull. If therefore the facts are said to be in conflict with the theory, it is always open to those holding the theory to disagree with the facts as observed or reported, or to argue that the particular set of facts produced is irrelevant to the theory, or that the facts are incomplete, or as a final but most powerful last-ditch defence, to 'reinterpret' the facts. Only if the facts are very persuasive will the theory be amended and then probably only marginally to add a 'special case' to the theory.[6] Conclusive theory (let alone revolution in theory) is a rare event and as much due to the strength, persistence and persuasiveness of the protagonists as to the force of the facts.

Nor is this all. We need also to recognise that facts can enter our discussions in two different ways. Theories start from assumptions and work through to predictions. But in the application of economics, which are the facts meant to correspond to – the assumptions or the predictions? *If* the theory is logically sound the assumptions contain the predictions within themselves so that to argue that a theory should be rejected because its predictions do not correspond to the facts may just be another way of disagreeing about the assumptions. I shall have more to say about this below but it is sufficient here to note that in all situations in the real world facing the adviser there will be certain facts – often a large number of them – which the practitioners agree to be relevant but which are outside the usual theoretical structure; and, of course, the practitioners themselves may disagree on what this range of facts is and on what weight should be given to what evidence. For example, this writer would have wanted to argue that anyone trying to forecast the economic situation in America during the period of late 1969 and 1970

[6] This was the status to which Keynes had been reduced until he was recently resurrected and 'reinterpreted' by Leijonhufvud.

should have included among his facts not just what the New York Federal Reserve Bank was doing as seen in economic terms, e.g. expanding or contracting the money supply by so many percent, but also what they thought they were doing and what their public announcements said they were doing – the two were often different. But others, even if agreeing with this view, would have disagreed about both the interpretation and the weight to be given to this sort of evidence. (Interestingly enough a famous American economist wrote to a colleague of mine claiming that his intuition told him certain things about the likely development of the International Monetary System and that this was positive economics!)

In the light of this what can we now say of our adviser and of his prospects of being impartial in his choice of theories? Does this choice and the weight which he gives to which facts depend merely on chance? This seems unlikely (though on present evidence one can put it no higher than that). We have so far implicitly been assuming that the economist himself has no preferences on the weight to be attached to various aims; but any man has preferences. What concerns us at this stage is how these preferences might be correlated with the way in which the economist would diagnose the situation, and, if they were positively correlated, whether this necessarily means that his choice of theory and therefore his advice is biased, or whether alternatively he might still be able to be detached and lay these preferences on one side.

Surely the reasonable supposition would be that such a positive correlation does exist since on the one hand theories imply policies and it would seem to be intellectual cowardice to believe a certain theory, or more likely a *group* of theories, and then not to favour the policies suggested by those theories, while on the other hand if one just has pure political prejudice it would at least be rational to believe those theories which supported one's prejudices. Moreover, though it is no more than circumstantial evidence, one does speak of 'schools' of economists and these schools are identified both with groups of theories and with the groups of policies that those theories imply. Those who believe in that group of theories consistent with an efficiently operating free market system tend also to like the outcomes which these theories predict and to be most in favour of the policies which these theories imply, such as free trade, controlling inflation via demand and with the minimal amount of government intervention; while those economists who believe that, even if the market operates, then it operates slowly, are also those who attach great cost to this slowness, and who thus wish to see tax and subsidy policies designed to complement or supplement the market system, or direct government control to supplant the market system.[7]

Furthermore the policies which each group advocates would often tend to make more likely the very assumptions from which they work in the first place. For example, on the one hand policies to cut tariffs would allow the market to work more freely and policies to restrict the development of monopolies are designed to restore (or protect) the working of the market; while on the other hand, price control policies restrict the working of the market and central allocation of resources removes it altogether.

Now assuming for the moment that there is this correlation between theory and political views, what more can we say about it? If it is the case that I believe Theory X *because* of my political views then it is logically impossible for me also to be impartial in my choice of theory and my diagnosis of the situation must be biased. On the other hand if I hold a political view because I think Theory X the most applicable, then it is still possible at least *in principle* for me to be open minded. Unfortunately we do not know whether it is political views which create theories or theories which create political views, though we may suspect that it is neither wholly one nor the other.

Perhaps the most convincing account would be one in which economics and politics, and theory and practice, continually interacted one on the other, particularly since it is difficult to conceive of situations when this interaction does not occur. Economists can only begin to speculate sensibly on how a particular economy operates when they have some data. But data implies classification and thus a reason or theory for so classifying. Moreover, the mere collection of data can react back on the initial situation. Getting data not only imposes costs on people (firms and individuals have to fill in forms), but may also make them aware of new issues or cause them to act differently in relation to existing ones. For example, an enquiry to a firm asking how many graduates they employ could cause it to count the graduates for the first time and to make the firm wonder whether it should have more of them. Similarly, if one collects figures on wage claims in order to devise policies to stop inflation this could actually increase the inflation by giving each trade union leader the information he needs to make sure that his union gets at least as much as the next.

The more influential that economists are and the more that political decisions are taken on the basis of economic theory, the more likely it is that this interaction occurs. It can be argued quite plausi-

[7] Perhaps at a more fundamental level they dislike the income distribution the market system produces. In principle, *any* income distribution *could* be combined with a free market, but in practice it tends to produce an unequal one and then be left that way.

bly that because governments in the U.K. in the 1950s and early 1960s chose to try to correct the balance of payments by restricting demand, so businessmen gradually learnt to expect this, became increasingly pessimistic and less inclined to expand. One possible interpretation of the results of this policy is that it worked initially but that later it was defeated by the expectations it had itself created.

However, we must tread carefully. This interaction shows that what we are studying changes (not always in the direction we want!) and that part of the reason for the change is just *because* we study it. This makes life more difficult (and even suggests that it may never be possible to have a large body of agreed theory in economics), but lack of knowledge and imprecision in the subject does *not* mean that bias necessarily follows. Of course, the scope for bias is increased by such imprecision but it only becomes impossible in principle to exclude it if it can be shown that the theories which I think applicable at a particular point in time are chosen because of my own biases from whatever cause. Yet whether they are is an unanswerable question because to explain why I think what I think is itself to think something, and this then calls for *further* explanation.

In the face of this, all the adviser can do is to search as much as possible into his own beliefs and prejudices and to try to discount them when giving advice, while accepting that he can never know for sure whether he has succeeded. Moreover, whether he *would* succeed and whether you would believe that he had really tried would still depend on the form and strength of his preferences as well as on the particular problem under discussion.

Despite these difficulties we would still agree that there are facts we can know about the world irrespective of political views. Also, it is clear that in some cases it will not matter which particular set of facts we take or how we look at them because the world will still look roughly the same. Whereas in other cases there will either be violent disagreement on which facts ought to be taken or on how they ought to be interpreted.

Now the interesting thing is that the dividing line between these two is neither stable nor clear. It will shift over time as new evidence and new interpretations appear (and by no means always in the direction of adding to agreed knowledge, since views previously held to be authoritative are often at a later date called into question).

It can, however, also shift at any moment in time as the level of debate or focus of interest changes. In the case of the Balogh/Paish dispute it made little difference *whose* earnings had risen since whichever series of figures they took would have shown them rising faster than wage rates. However, if they *had* agreed that the crucial feature was the bargaining strength of the unions, then the 'facts' they took and the descriptions they gave to them would probably have changed. For example, some of those who think that inflation is caused by too much demand do accept that wages are determined in a bargaining process, but then go on to claim that it is the strength of demand which largely determines the outcome of the bargain. Those who argue in this way might choose to look at disaggregated evidence to show that demand in particular industries was correlated with the discrepancy between wage rates and earnings in *those* industries. While the response of cost push theorists to this would then probably be to argue that it is misleading to look at an industry on its own since the reason earnings went up may be in an attempt to re-establish differentials with *other* industries.

As well as disagreeing about which facts are relevant we may also disagree about what the facts represent and what we can infer from them. Consider, for example, the models used for forecasting activity in the economy. It is commonplace for these short-term forecasting models to take exports as largely exogenous (being primarily determined by the level of world demand which is outside the control of any one country) and to assume that imports are endogenous (being primarily determined by the level of demand within the country). This has some intuitive appeal and is supported by empirical work. But one must look more carefully at the assumptions underlying these models. Their development can be traced back to how people understood the Keynesian theory of income determination and the development of National Accounts. This theory was largely concerned with the under-utilisation of existing capacity rather than with the growth in this capacity – not surprisingly since it was the former problem that was of over-riding importance in the 1930s. However, the result is that models based on this assume either that supply (capacity) is fixed, or that it just grows at a steady rate independent of demand. No interaction is allowed in which the level of demand could affect the rate of growth capacity or vice versa. These models are therefore only appropriate as long as these assumptions hold and whether one agrees that they do depends on the use to which they are put. In the U.K. they have typically been the background information to budgetary policy and the major effects of this on demand probably take one or two years to work through. Yet in terms of policy the model is heavily biased in favour of deflation as a means of reducing a deficit in the balance of visible trade. According to the model a reduction in demand (deflation) lowers imports, but leaves exports unaffected for ever, whereas, as mentioned above, there are reasons for thinking that lowering demand now can cause manufacturers to become more pessimistic about the future and thus to reduce investment which may lower the *supply* of exports in the future.

Now one may say that all this latter example shows is that the model was used wrongly and that surely all economists would agree that in the short run imports are endogenous and exports exogenous, whereas in the long run we are not so sure; but to argue in that way is to miss the point. All we know is that these assumptions appear to fit experience in the U.K. in the 1950s and 1960s, while what matters for policy is whether these assumptions will apply in the future. But, this is *not* necessarily independent either of the policies which might be pursued or of what else is assumed to be happening to the economy. It may be that the only reason that exports appeared exogenous in the past was because the particular measures used to reduce demand had little effect upon unit costs, or because other countries did not react to the fall in our imports (their exports) by competitive deflations – and one can think of plenty of reasons why their reactions in the future might be different. Indeed, we are now close to the nub of the problem. All the *real* debates in economics are about which assumptions apply, and when they apply, and by how much they apply; and it was the controversial *use* of the model in this case which caused the appropriateness of its assumptions to be questioned. Moreover, the most pervasive, insidious, and least understood assumption in all economics is that the future will be like the past. We may like to think that we have understood the relationship between two economic variables, but what happened in the past, and thus the economic relationships which we observed, was the outcome not only of a set of policies on the part of the government and a pattern of desires on the part of individuals, but also occurred within a given institutional, political, legal and social framework. To assume, therefore, as a guide to policy, that past relationships *will* hold is, by omission, to advocate that they *should* hold.

This important claim may become clearer if we now look more closely at the sort of assumptions which economists make. But before doing that I should admit that I am in the process of dropping an assumption myself. At the beginning of this paper it was implicitly assumed that we could define the limits of an 'economic' problem on which economists would be more or less competent to advise. But this is not so and we must now face this difficulty. In practice, there is only political economy. Economics only exists within a social context. Thus the economist in approaching any problem must decide what he is to take as 'given'. In doing this he would typically distinguish between, on the one hand, those things which are largely outside his (or his government's) control, and, on the other hand, those which might be changed by policy. In the first group would fall such things as the policies of other countries, or the growth in world trade (since it is unlikely that any one country could affect it drastically), or relationships which he has observed in the past and which he has no obvious reason to think will change sharply. In the latter group would fall things such as tax rates, or government expenditure, or nationalised industries' prices. But what criteria does he use when selecting *within* this latter group? Everything cannot be changed all the time and certainly not immediately. Direct tax rates are normally only changed at the time of the Budget, and most government expenditure is authorised at least a year in advance. But even this requires judgement since in the U.K. most things *can* be changed by legislation as long as the government retains the support of its backbenchers. Moreover, economics does not fall into neat and tidy boxes. Any one policy affects many things. To increase tax rates (in order, for example, to improve the balance of payments by deflating demand) will also lower employment, change the distribution of income, perhaps decrease the rate of growth of prices, and affect some industries and some regions more than others. Thus, which policies *should* be changed, whether they *can* be changed, and, if so, how *fast* they can be changed will all be controversial questions. Nor will the answers be independent of each other – if tax rates *can* be increased quickly then one may not *need* to cut public expenditure.

Further, there will be an interrelation between our decisions about the assumptions in this group and those in the data group. The more widely we draw the policy group and the more we assume that policies *are* changed, the less will be the area of data which we can take as given. It is reasonable to predict that there will be some point at which other countries' policies *will* be changed as the result of measures taken by us (though to say *when* this will be so requires considerable political judgement in addition to such economic analysis as may be possible).[8]

However, can we even maintain our original distinction between what is data and what is policy? For example, whether or not we should take a certain economic relationship as given will itself be an exceedingly controversial question. Some would argue from looking at the past that any change was likely to be small, while others would respond that this merely reflected that attempts to change it were badly executed or were themselves small. But once we mention

[8] For example, economists can say something about the likely economic effects on other countries of a devaluation by the U.K., but to forecast whether they will follow us or not requires both an understanding of their economic and political situation and an insight into their reaction. Yet our judgement of the likely efficacy of a devaluation is heavily influenced by the answers to such questions.

the execution of policy then the debate goes wider than economics and includes the institutions through which policy is operated and through which the economic relationships express themselves. Indeed, one of the most divisive issues in politics is whether society can be changed and, if so, by what means and how quickly.[9]

Now the joint effect of many inter-relationships (one policy affects several aims), *and* of relationships which can themselves be altered by policy, plays havoc with the traditional distinction between ends and means. I cannot tell the politician what is the least cost method of improving the balance of payments because full employment and the distribution of income which are affected by the policy are ends in themselves – so my answer depends on the valuation which I attach to these. Nor is this all; most economists recognise *this* problem and then get out of it by arguing that we should present our calculations to the politicians and allow *them* to attach values and to decide how much of one thing is to be traded for how much of another. But this will not do either. The calculations which we present depend upon relationships which may themselves be changed by policy. We can only say that $y\%$ more growth costs us $x\%$ more inflation when many things, usually unspecified, are taken as given.[10] It is in this sense that the real debates in economics are about assumptions.

Moreover, we have now come full circle. At the very outset we began by looking at data and we have ended with the economist trying to decide what it is, and with much of the onus for decision about this resting on him. Looking back at our 'hard-core' unemployed it is worth re-emphasising that how many should be included in that category will depend very largely on the policies we assume to be pursued. Many of the unskilled can be trained, the physically handicapped might be cured or their ability to perform jobs improved through artificial limbs, the mentally sick can be helped through psychiatric care, and many who at present choose not to work would want to do so at some level of incentive. What I said about how many of them were unemployable would *only* have been justified on the implicit assumption that such policies were not possible and whether that was so or not depends entirely on the context

[9] In the jargon of economics we conventionally distinguish between parameters and variables, but which is which, and when, is what is at issue.

[10] There are two other features which do not affect the drift of the argument, but which add greatly to its complexity in practice. First, people differ on whether a policy is an end or a means. For example, economists typically look at free trade in terms of its effect on full employment and on standards of living, but some may regard it as good in its own right (people *ought* to be allowed to trade if they want to) or else attach importance to it for non-economic reasons (e.g. it adds to the colour of life). Secondly, the calculation of trade-offs is problematic even when one has made the necessary assumptions, since they are neither linear, nor necessarily reversible.

in which I was asked the question.

We must now drop our final assumption. The economist in practice is not just the passive answerer of questions. He also advises on the general lines of policy, on both its strategy and its tactics, including propaganda, he suggests new policies and new areas for research, he 'interprets' his terms of reference (often exceedingly loosely framed on the advice of the adviser himself)[11] and he, together with other advisers, influences heavily (if he does not wholly determine) the options which are put to ministers.

Nor is this extension of the economist's activities going beyond his proper concern. To instigate research, which may well at a later stage suggest policies, is a central part of his work; to use his creative and imaginative ability to think of and put forward new policies is merely to avoid interpreting his job too narrowly; and in my view he would be shirking his responsibility if he did not also concern himself with the translation of those policies into practice. He must therefore go on to look at both the presentation of policy in speeches, etc., as well as the legal or administrative means by which it might be enforced.[12] Finally, if he is to do his job at all, he must influence both the number of choices and the sort of choices which are put to ministers.

Further, once we have allowed that this active role for the economist exists, and when we relate this to our earlier discussion of the choice of data, of theories, of models and of policies, then it becomes much clearer just how many assumptions the economist must make. Indeed the politician employs him to use his technical skills to do just this, so that in looking at any problem, the *art* of the good adviser – and I use that word intentionally – is on the one hand to select the possible, yet on the other to know when to press for the seemingly impossible.

But nobody has ever claimed that a set of assumptions of this sort is unbiased. (One might be tempted to use words like 'realistic', but that will not do in this context since as we have seen many of his most crucial assumptions are about policies aimed at changing the world.) In addition my view is that it makes no sense at all to talk of an adviser trying to be impartial when he chooses these assump-

[11] This can be justified because the terms of reference often have to be settled in committee and he knows well that such decisions are more easily reached when detail is avoided, and also because he will not wish to have any study too precisely determined from the start as this might jeopardise the possibility of examining policies or facts which at a later stage appeared relevant.

[12] The two can be inextricably connected. From the latter half of 1966 onwards the Labour Party constantly failed to explain adequately the distinction between the fall in people's standards of living which was the result of deflation ('the squeeze') and the incomes policy ('the freeze') which merely affected *money* wages. As a result antagonism to the latter increased and the ability to enforce it decreased.

tions. It is not enough for him to try to incorporate (or interpret sympathetically) the instructions of the politician, he must 'see' the world as they do – not unobjectively since he would then be not doing his job, but sharing their ideology about the kinds of society, of institutions, and of policies which they would view as possible or even desirable. Moreover, I intentionally speak here of the adviser being partial, since that gives him active identification with the party, rather than speaking of him as not being indifferent since that merely implies that one has preferences about the sort of things that one is advising upon. Whereas here these preferences *are* allowed to play an active role in the formulation and choice of policy: i.e. he *is* partial. Finally, he *must* recommend what he thinks should be done because this is the only way in which he can really clarify his own standpoint – and the politicians need these recommendations as one way in which they can learn the economist's preferences. It is only after this interaction is established that they know whether they can accept the recommended 'best buy'.

However, perhaps to many economists working for governments (and even more so for international organisations) this 'active' characterisation of the Economic Adviser's job may sound unfamiliar or even misleading. It would have done so to me during my first few months in the Civil Service. But this is almost entirely because they do not see the results of their actions. They are removed from the political decision by many layers of the bureaucracy, and they probably concentrate on one particular area of economic work which is then combined with others and put to many different uses so that they remain unaware of their influence. (Within the British Civil Service the terms of reference of many lower level committees explicitly rule out any consideration of policy, which reinforces this natural tendency.)

Now, although the influence of any one economist is both more obvious and more important the closer he is to the politician and the more his advice is taken, the total influence remains the same even when spread out amongst many. But when spread out in this way it changes its character in two connected ways. First, the openness of the influence disappears so people's awareness of it decreases and as a result so does their willingness to look for any bias in the advice. Secondly, because no one man's influence is large, then the bias which creeps in, if any, is less likely to be connected with the preferences of any one individual but more likely to be the result of the traditional modes of thought that those individuals have used, or of the ways in which those individuals are combined together in the policy-making process. For example, the recent increase in computers and the increasingly sophisticated models which they have made possible may itself be the cause of bias. An analytic and quantitative approach is essential in economics, but not at the expense of ignoring those relationships where no agreed quantitative estimate yet exists nor at the expense of thinking deeply about the context in which a particular relationship appeared to exist. Yet the work of many economists is now so specialised and many have been so mesmerised by the growth of statistical techniques and the potential of the computer that their time is wholly occupied in preparing data and playing with permutations on it. As a result little or no thought is applied to how their data is collected and what it means, or to the validity or applicability of their results, or to what they have failed to quantify, or to the assumptions which they have built in at all these stages. The computer is capable of being an aid to thought but at present it is often used as if it were a substitute, which is just what it cannot be.

Indeed, one cannot help wondering whether this tendency reflects a deeper misunderstanding about the nature of economics since those who succumb to it are often those most keen to stress the scientific and factual nature of economic advice. An unwillingness to concern oneself with the imprecisions in the subject and the political controversy which surrounds this may lead to misplaced accuracy and a (hidden) lack of realism so that our lack of knowledge can be biased if it reflects a lack of thought. It is an unfortunate paradox that at the very time when the economist can take a detached view, because his own preferences carry little weight, so is he less likely to look for bias because he is less aware of its possible existence.

However, recognition of this difficulty increases the need for objectivity provided we understand the sense in which it is now meant. The economist must try to assess competing theories impartially but he is not impartial in the advice that he gives and you will not get right-wing policies suggested by left-wing economists, nor even unconventional policies suggested by those whose mode of thought is conventional. But it is still no good telling a politician that a policy will work *because* it is left-wing, so the economist still needs to be realistic about those assumptions which are data in our original sense as well as about the tricky dividing line between which of his assumptions are really data and which really policy. Indeed as his identification with the aims of the party increases so also does his need to be open-minded to new evidence and objective about what *is possible* as well as about what *is*.

Economists are not, and never can be, automatic recording devices. Nor can they ever be sure that they have fully discounted their preferences when looking at the world, but they can at least try to be analytic, quantitative and rigorous as well as imaginative, thoughtful, and sympathetic to the attitudes and aspirations of the groups in society they are studying.

These are large demands. Few, if any economists satisfy them, so perhaps I am asking for the impossible. But, if this is the direction in which I want to go then let us at least ask what this view implies about the way in which economics should be taught. An immediate difficulty in relation to teaching is that whatever approach I adopt I cannot during the same period of time be neutral as between that approach and some other. If I believe that economic advice cannot be impartial, that economics is a policy-oriented study and that ends and means overlap then I cannot, unless I am schizophrenic, put the opposite point of view with equal conviction. I can mention that others disagree but ultimately my account must be intended to help my view more than theirs. Of course, which side it *actually* helps may well be very unpredictable as this depends on a complex relationship between teacher and taught. On the one hand I may imply much more scepticism about certain views than I really intend just by my gestures and tone of voice, on the other hand the student may be counter suggestible. But the important point is that even the intended effects of my actions are not neutral let alone the actual ones.

But why adopt one approach? Do I have to take a stand in this way? Can I not just teach economics? Unfortunately not, first because there is a conflict between a number of different approaches to the way in which it should be studied, so that anyone actually teaching cannot avoid taking sides to some extent, and secondly because one of these approaches implicitly requires that one's own position in this conflict should be made clear.

At its simplest the debate is between those who study economising and those who study economies.[13] The former start from as narrow a range of assumptions as possible and deduce what are 'intended to be the principles underlying all economies at all times'.[14] The latter observe sequences of events and then attempt to infer generalisations from them and make further observations to test these generalisations (where these generalisations are limited to certain economies, or parts of economies, at particular periods in time) – and whether observation precedes generalisation or vice versa is a chicken and egg problem.

The first approach is the study and development of a highly

---

[13] This neat distinction is made by M. Barratt Brown in *What Economics is About* (Weidenfeld, 1970).

[14] K. Lancaster, *Introduction to Modern Microeconomics* (Rand McNally & Co., 1969), p.2.

sophisticated logical system. The second can be reduced to saying that there is little if any underlying structure to economics so that economics is less concerned with general laws and more with understanding sympathetically and with political awareness what goes on around us. On this view economic theories are not idealistic creations (the beautiful glass bridge of the engineer) but attempts to explain convincingly the apparent paradoxes in the world. The first kind of economist sees the world as constantly tending towards equilibrium and those events which do not fit his general theory are 'deviations' to be explained away. The second sees instability, uncertainty, change and deviations as the things to be understood. The latter approach is undoubtedly less comfortable, less tidy, less rigorous and some would say less academic. It is also more difficult to teach as it dissolves into history, politics, psychology and sociology. Thus at the outset of economics a choice is involved in the method of approach which is used, and this approach will heavily influence the very questions, theories, and evidence which are considered relevant.

Of course the choice is nothing like so clear-cut as suggested here. There are other colours of opinion and many blends of each. Also each approach extends itself to overlap with the other. 'Special cases' get tacked onto the logical structure as those using it do some empirical work and attempt to come closer to reality, and the claims of those studying particular economies grow in their generality as more evidence accumulates. Indeed when this occurs the feature which distinguishes the two approaches is neither the subject matter nor their generality but the relative importance attached on the one hand to the technical ability to manipulate assumptions in a logically correct way, and on the other hand to the emphasis on getting the assumptions right in the first place. Of course, the choice is further eased since neither student nor teacher need adopt one approach to the complete exclusion of the other.

However, time is not limitless so a question of priorities still remains. Moreover, despite the blurring of the edges, in my view we either have pure theory, which is at once as interesting and yet as empty of the real world as pure maths and questions of neutrality just do not arise, or we have applied theory, which is political economy, and then all the complications of the validity and acceptability of assumptions, of political constraints and of social attitudes, etc., come back into the picture, as do our preferences and the difficulties of objectivity and impartiality. The statement that if total output remains unchanged and more resources go in one direction then less must go in another is obviously logically true, but the interesting economic question is whether output will or will not change. 'More guns, less butter' is a good slogan but contains many hidden assumptions.

If however, we do concentrate on the second approach with its emphasis on the variability of assumptions in different situations and the constant interaction of economics with politics, then there is an obligation on the teacher to make his own position clear and to teach the student to do the same. As Dudley Seers remarked 'before you study economics study the economist; before you study the economist study his historical and social environment' – though he ought to have added 'study yourself as well'. In other words not only is there disagreement on how the subject should be approached, but one approach commits one to making this disagreement clear.

But this approach creates its own problems. First, when should this clarifying occur? There is the danger in doing it too early that the complexity involved will put the student off. Moreover, the stress which this approach lays on recognising 'deviations' from theories may leave the student with no clear idea of what the theory itself says. He may also become cynical too early and with his cynicism weakly founded on suspicion rather than knowledge. Secondly, this approach implies that although there are plenty of theories in the sense of logical proofs, there is an absence of an established body of theory. The result is a conflict between leaving the student to sort it out for himself when he may again end up confused, and on the other hand inculcating him with a set of models which make it more difficult for him to think for himself about new situations as they arise. Intuition and rigour can unfortunately be competitive as well as complementary.

Finally and most difficult of all is the stress which this approach lays on the *context* of economic issues. This raises three kinds of problems. First, the approach can be accused of a bias in favour of the *status quo* – the only allowable knowledge is what we have *already* observed. Secondly, there are no agreed criteria of relevance – the approach assumes that there is little theory which is agreed to be generally applicable, and this, combined with the variability of the context and the many descriptions which can be given to it, means that one genuinely does not know how to decide what is relevant and what is not. Thirdly, this lack of settled criteria of relevance implies that there are no ground rules by which to judge accusations of bias etc. Obviously these problems overlap. Narrow-minded interpretations of relevance would reinforce the first criticism and liberal ones reduce it. But, if liberal interpretations go as· far as Lord Curzon who said 'I do not exclude the intelligent anticipation of facts before they occur', then criticism of bias will be replaced by criticism of lack of objectivity.

Once put in this way, the similarity between teaching and advising becomes more obvious. Exactly as in advising the possibility for unbiased recommendations depended on the interaction between the politician and the adviser, so in teaching do unbiased accounts depend on the student/tutor relationship. In both cases the more they know and share each other's preferences and the more they understand the many implicit assumptions which each is making, then the more can they agree on the way in which problems are to be defined. Perhaps surprisingly both sides of both relationships are involved in a learning process.

However, there are also important differences between what one is trying to achieve in the two situations. First, unlike advising, the aim in teaching is not to arrive at a recommendation, but rather to explore the range of descriptions of any given situation which are possible, and to examine the policies pursued in an attempt to increase one's understanding of an economic system – as well as, of course, picking up certain technical tools on the way.

Secondly, although the student must be taught to be objective (i.e. to check what he is saying against the facts), he also needs exposure to new interpretations and to values different from his own. Thus, on occasion the tutor is justified in adopting a heavily biased position in the sense of deliberately selecting facts to support a particular interpretation, and of course, this may be intricately connected with trying to be devil's advocate for values in conflict with those of the student.[15] But the tutor's ultimate aim must be to leave the student with something at least approximating to an unbiased picture so that the extent to which the tutor puts his weight on one side more than the other will depend not only on how far the student is already well informed and open-minded, but also on the other instruction that the student is getting, as well as on what the tutor himself considers a well balanced picture.

In addition this difference in emphasis between teaching and advising and the changed circumstances surrounding the relationship mean that the possibilities for lack of bias, etc., are different – as are the factors which influence these possibilities. The essence of advising was to select rapidly the policy or policies which were possible and then to assess objectively their likely effects and to put forward a brief unbiased account of these. The likelihood of achieving this increased the more the values of the adviser and advised coincided, the smaller the problem, the more fully it was defined, and the less the theoretical debate surrounding the issue. By contrast in the teaching relationship there is more time available

[15] This will be more difficult the more one has already made clear one's own position.

for looking at alternative views, the student himself can be taught to look for hidden assumptions and to be critical of his own approach as well as that of others, and it does not matter so much if a biased position exists at one point in time. On the other hand, in this looser framework, problems are much less clearly defined, and discussion is often speculative so that there is far greater scope for hidden assumptions. Moreover, there is no presumption that the values of teacher and taught will coincide – rather to the contrary in many universities at the moment – and in these situations students will want to widen the debate so as to call into question their tutor's starting points. Thus how successful the tutor can be at ending with an unbiased picture, *and* one which the student accepts as unbiased, will depend not only on the similarity or otherwise of their values, but also very much on the kind of problem under discussion (How large is it? How well defined? How contentious?) as well as on the kind of contact which they have (Do they know each other well? Do they meet in a tutorial, a class, a lecture?) and, perhaps most important of all, on the context within which they themselves are discussing (Is the atmosphere surrounding the tutorial amicable? Is the tutor looking at those topics which interest the student? Is the tutor open-minded on the assumptions that he is making?). In fact, therefore, we have a series of activities which the economist can undertake (adviser, tutor, writer, lecturer) and a number of variants of each of these. Consider for example the difference between writing a pamphlet for the Fabian Society and publishing an article in the *Economic Journal*. Moreover, there is a spectrum of contexts within which these activities exist – think how different a lecture would sound on the role of the centrally planned economy if given in the U.S.S.R. as compared with the same lecture given in the U.S.A. during the McCarthy era – and think also of the motives of the lecturer.

Whether we are aware of it or not there always exists a relationship between the economist and his audience. Moreover, each party to these relationships has its varying aims and preferences and each relationship exists within a particular historical and social context. Thus how far any given account will be considered unbiased and how far it is considered important that it should be, cannot be answered without fully specifying the situation. Moreover, someone from outside examining such a situation can only reach agreed conclusions on relative bias provided they use criteria which we also accept. We can outline the sorts of consideration which would come into play and we can suggest the varying sorts of conditions under which the possibility of impartiality, or of lack of bias, or of objectivity would be likely to be greater or less, but we can do no more.

Yet although logically the regress is infinite, in practice there is a limiting case for each of us when our own basic values and methods of approach get called into question. One can never be sure that one's approach is not in fact dictated by a chance position in the social structure, nor that one has not made some huge mistake in the interpretation of the evidence, yet one cannot act as if this is so. Economists ought to be imaginative and to have mad ideas, yet it remains unacceptable madness to me to think that one has found the answer, that one's models are reality. How can they be? As Yeats says – 'The particulars are . . . in every man and called by every man his freedom.'

Neutrality and academic values

LESZEK KOLAKOWSKI

Let us try to define neutrality without looking for a concept that would commit us to considering neutral behaviour either as necessarily virtuous or as necessarily to be condemned. Let us admit rather, following common sense and the current meaning of the word, that neutrality may be possible or not, to be recommended or to be regarded as inadmissible, depending on the circumstances of the case.

Neutrality presupposes a conflict and at the same time that the neutral person is not a party to it. Neutrality cannot be conceived, therefore, as a character trait or as an aspect of personal disposition. I can be neutral only in relation to a particular situation of conflict. *I am neutral in relation to a conflict when I purposely behave in such a way so as not to influence its outcome.*

This definition seems to accord with the current use of the word. It implies:

1. That neutrality is always intentional; I am not neutral in relation to a conflict that is simply unknown to me nor if I am merely indifferent to it. Non-involvement through indifference or lack of interest or lack of knowledge excludes the possibility of neutrality. I can be neutral only if the conflict somehow falls within the field of my interest.

2. That I am not or that I do not consider myself as being a party to the conflict. If I consider myself as a party to the conflict, I may (ideally) be impartial, but I cannot be neutral. To consider oneself as a party implies an effort to influence the outcome.

3. That neutrality and impartiality are incompatible with respect to the same situation. I am (or I try to be) impartial if I evaluate the conflict and the rights and the wrongs of both sides by assessing the situation in terms of more general rules that I accept *independently of this particular case*, i.e. without allowing my personal preferences or biases concerning this case to influence my judgement. I am not neutral, however, since 'to be impartial' in a conflict implies intervening in it to try to influence its outcome. The general rules that are supposed to guide my intervention are looked upon as valid irrespective of the case under consideration. They may constitute a civil code (the impartiality of a judge in a civil trial) or logical rules (the impartiality of a scholar) or moral norms (the impartiality of a

72

witness in regard to standards of veracity), etc. It is quite compatible with impartiality to help one side in a conflict against another or to consider both sides as partially wrong. Being impartial I look upon myself, so to speak, as a bearer of impersonal rules that are applicable to the case in question. I may also justify my neutrality by appealing to some general rules; I am not impartial, however, since I avoid any intervention in the course of events.

4. That neutrality is a formal characteristic of behaviour and that no material values are involved in its concept. The concept itself carries no suggestion as to whether or not and in what conditions neutrality may deserve blame or endorsement.

The reason why I am not altogether satisfied with the definition proposed by Montefiore (he defines 'neutrality' as an attitude of helping or hindering to an equal degree all the parties to a conflict; to avoid giving any help or hindrance at all would be the limiting case of this attitude) is because it seems to allow of using the same term for a variety of attitudes which may not only be different, but which may be opposed to each other *both in content and in motivations* in face of one and the same conflict. A certain state may sell arms to both of two states at war with each other; it may do so because it is not interested in the outcome of the war, but only in selling arms; it may also do so because it is interested in the prolongation of the war and in weakening both parties. It may refuse to sell arms to any party because, oddly enough, it has pacifist reasons or because of other circumstances that make peace at this moment more profitable to it, etc. It seems to me inconvenient to treat all these cases as falling equally under the category of neutrality. To sell arms to both sides at war with each other is to be actively involved in the conflict – regardless of the reasons for one's involvement and regardless of whether the help given is equal in absolute terms or proportional to the relative strength of the conflicting parties and aimed at securing a balance of force. In particular, if my neutrality was limited to those cases where I was trying to create an equilibrium of force among the parties to a conflict, it would mean that I was neutral only when giving unilateral help to the weaker side. Either concept of neutrality – that of helping or hindering both sides equally or that of aiming at an equilibrium of the forces in conflict – may hardly be reconciled with the current meaning of the word.

Let us now raise the abstract question of whether neutrality as defined above is a real possibility and what, if so, its moral justification might be.

It is common among political radicals to claim that neutrality is impossible simply because if I avoid influencing the outcome of a conflict, I am already in effect helping the stronger side. This sort of argument is usually based on a simple-minded interpretation of existentialist or Marxist philosophy. An obvious distinction should be drawn, however, between the idea that certain acts may be assessed morally and the idea that such acts are in principle impossible. It is undeniable that if I refrain from becoming involved in a conflict of which the outcome has a moral meaning, my refusal to become involved may be evaluated from a moral point of view, not necessarily as being wrong, provided that I was not simply unable to intervene for physical or intellectual reasons. In this sense neutrality is a choice which is not morally indifferent, if the conflict itself is not morally indifferent and if the neutral is in fact able to intervene if he chooses. This does not mean that neutrality is impossible. It cannot reasonably be argued that a state would be doing exactly the same in offering massive military help to another which was at war as it would in just waiting inactively upon the results of the struggle. There are many cases where it does not depend on my own decision whether or not I am to be a party in a conflict that has already started; in other cases the option for neutrality remains open without ceasing to be an option.

The statement that neutrality is impossible is, however, often an awkward formulation for another idea: namely, that neutrality is always wrong. However silly such a statement would be, it has a latent meaning that deserves attention. I shall argue that neutrality, whether justifiable or unjustifiable, always results from weakness, though that weakness may not always be blameworthy nor always attributable to the person involved, but sometimes attributable rather to certain peculiarities of our culture.

The simplest example is that of neutrality which results from intellectual weakness. I may be interested in the outcome of a scientific controversy and still be neutral towards it because of my incompetence to intervene. To involve myself in it would be to damage a value that I consider important: the requirement that scientific controversies should be decided according to the rules of scientific procedure. My option for neutrality is an option for intellectual values that I recognise. It is justified and my inability to intervene in accordance with the rules of science cannot be condemned, since I cannot be blamed for not being omniscient.

When the issues involve moral or psychological considerations, it is more difficult, if not impossible, to formulate general criteria by which to decide the rights and wrongs of neutrality and which may be applicable to any case whatsoever. It is, of course, very easy to find examples where neutrality is morally inadmissible (for example, if a woman is being raped in my presence). But we are not justified in concluding, by multiplying such examples, that neutrality is necessarily to be condemned. If I considered myself in duty bound to intervene in any and every personal conflict involving other people, I should be an importunate meddler rather than an heroic anti-neutralist; none of us wants other people to intervene in all our conflicts without even being asked to do so. If examples of inadmissible neutrality and inadmissible non-neutrality may be easily invented, to determine a general criterion by which to separate the one from the other seems a hopeless ambition.

More important are the cases where we have reasons to argue that in our option for or against neutrality (certain major) values are at stake that risk being destroyed by our non-neutrality – either because they are incompatible with the values that our involvement is supposed to defend or because of some other causal connections in the world. We can be mistaken intellectually, that is we can be wrong in predicting the results of our options, or we can simply be morally condemnable; but this is not always the case. The Frenchman who in 1939 refused 'to die for Gdansk', or the American socialists who opposed the active involvement of the United States in World War II, were, certainly, wrong in both respects. But only a blind faith in the perfection of history could justify us in condemning a small nation that preferred to be neutral in the conflicts of big powers simply because there is a reasonable risk that it would be swept out of existence, whichever side it took. It can be argued that it may try to soften the conflict rather than to be a party to it; this would mean that it was not neutral (because it would be seeking to influence the outcome). This good advice is, alas, not applicable in all cases. In many situations the only possible way to influence the outcome of a conflict is to commit oneself to one side. This is to be attributed to the nature of the human world and not necessarily to our mistakes. The weakness of the neutral in such a case is the weakness of wishing to exist rather than to contribute to the outcome of a world conflict.

It may happen that any option in a conflict risks destroying something that we have a moral duty to defend. If the values involved are extremely important, we are faced with what is properly called tragedy, that is a conflict in which evil must win in a moral and not just in a material sense. The anti-neutralist who maintains that morally good options are available in any conflict claims that tragedies are not possible in our world – a view that seems to be as comfortable as it is optimistic.

Where may the problem of the so-called political neutrality of the university be located among these distinctions?

The postulate of the political neutrality of the university demands that the university as an institution, which does not of course mean the individuals (teachers, students, administrators) who form it, ought to refrain from taking positions in the controversial political issues under discussion in its society. Against such a requirement it is usually objected:

1. The universities in democratic countries, not to speak of totalitarian ones, are in any case politically involved; they are contributing to war research, they are not free from using political criteria in dealing with their individual members and their teaching, at least in the social sciences and humanities, is often politically biased and conveys the political preferences of the teachers.

2. The neutrality of the university is in any case impracticable since universities are necessarily organs of society, they serve it and – in divided societies – are mostly at the service of the ruling class, etc.

In order to consider the validity of these standard objections other distinctions have to be drawn and the confused character of the objections explained.

I will try to summarise the classical liberal conception of the university. According to this conception there are four main tasks which the university is supposed to fulfil for society:

(a) Higher professional training in a limited sense. (By 'limited sense' I mean that while the university, especially in the social sciences and humanities, is not geared to imparting strictly specific professional skills, it does have to provide its students with the theoretical, factual and logical knowledge and skills to enable them to attain an intellectual mastery of a certain domain of culture and to exploit their skills in different professions, which normally require some additional training.)

(b) The continued transmission of human culture.

(c) The enrichment of our knowledge about the world – this knowledge being defined not only by reference to its content, but more specially by reference to the specific procedures which justify its validity.

(d) The teaching and spreading of certain values that are applicable not only in scientific matters, but in all fields of social life, including the political: these values include impartiality in judgement, tolerance, criticism, obedience to logical rules.

It is obvious – so far as I know, it has never been seriously denied – that there are some values which lie at the very heart of the university; according to the liberal concept, its functioning itself implies certain value-judgements that are, as are any other value-judgements, historically conditioned rather than transcendentally valid. It is equally undeniable that the university has always been an organ

of society and has always been aware that its work has social consequences. For this reason the slogans commonly directed against the
political neutrality of the university – such as 'the university is not
isolated from society' or 'teaching exerts an impact on social life' or
'teachers must be aware of the social consequences that their teaching is bound to have and be responsible for them', etc. – are meaninglessly platitudinous.

In spite of stereotyped revolutionary rhetoric, the difference between the liberal and political (or simply totalitarian) conceptions
of the university does not lie in the acceptance or rejection of a few
trite sentences about the university's social responsibility or the
social meaning of its work. The difference lies in pointing out just
what it is responsible for. The totalitarian conception of the university implies that no human values exist that transcend the particular
interests of one or other of the conflicting political groups. This
principle obviously entails that whatever in the existing spiritual
culture cannot be used as a tool for the pursuit of 'our' political
goals is necessarily a tool for 'our' enemies. The conclusion is that if
the teaching and research that are actually carried on in universities
are politically irrelevant to our victory, they must be at the service of
the dirty interests of some other particular groups (for example, of
Jewish plutocracy in Nazi Germany or of world imperialism in the
pattern of communist thinking) and therefore deserve to be destroyed.

The liberal conception (let us say rather 'open' or 'unbounded' in
order to avoid all the misleading associations that may go with the
word 'liberal'), implies on the contrary that in many domains there
is a continuity of human culture and that some values are not confined to the particular interests of given political groups, social
classes, ethnic, national or racial communities. This belief does
not necessarily imply that certain values are of divine origin or
valid in a Platonic sense; it is perfectly compatible with the acceptance of the historical origin of all values. It implies only that in
some important areas of culture there is continuity in time and
universality in the sense of independence of social and ethnic bar-
riers. This modest philosophy is a latent and necessary condition
for the open idea of the university; but it is at the same time a sufficient condition for it. It means that the totalitarian conception
cannot, unless it lapses into inconsistency, accept the universality,
in the double sense just indicated, of certain areas of cultural
values.

This clash is not, fortunately, based on arbitrary choice alone.
The idea of the universality of values may be open to historical
analysis. It may be shown that some values, despite the shifts they

may undergo throughout their historical vicissitudes, retain an important content that persists intact through the variety of ethnic and social conditions. The belief in the historical continuity and universality of culture (or briefly, the belief in the basic unity of the human species) is not just an arbitrary decision as justifiable or as unjustifiable as the opposite belief that any value is necessarily bound to the interests of some particular social, political or ethnic group. The man who claims that the theory of relativity was based on certain rules of thinking whose application has no specific limitation to Einstein's time, milieu or origin, is in a different cognitive position from that occupied by one who claims that the theory of relativity is a product of perverted Jewish mentality (an opinion apparently abandoned today) or a capitalist invention for the deception of the working class (an opinion also apparently abandoned today).

The reason why I think that the totalitarian conception of the university must give up the idea of cultural continuity is simply because this idea seems to provide a sufficient basis for the claim of those who maintain that the institutionalised form of this continuity is both possible, justified and necessary for society.

The totalitarian claims are, however, not totally without reason, although this reason has quite another meaning from that which is explicitly put forward. This reason consists in the fact that totalitarian movements, by their very existence, produce a situation similar to that which they claim to be 'natural' in any society. In affirming that no cultural values can ever transcend the particular interests which they represent, a totalitarian movement brings it about that any institution based on the belief in such values becomes, simply because it exists, a social entity directed against the particular interests of the totalitarian movement. This immediately means that the university, precisely because it is founded upon the belief in the universality of certain values, is anti-totalitarian, that is, it is not neutral in the conflict between those who aspire to totalitarianism and their opponents. This does not mean that it is non-neutral in the sense of being compelled to a direct involvement in the struggle between political parties; it does mean, however, that since it claims to embody some non-particular values, those who were brought up in the spirit of the university and continue to take it seriously will reject the totalitarian demands. It does not depend on the university whether or not to become involved in this kind of non-neutrality. The situation is exactly the same as when someone suddenly strikes me on the head; I am already a party in the conflict, even if I do nothing to resist him or to strike him back. By the very fact of having been struck, I am already involved in a clash. In this sense, and in this sense only, it may be said that the university is not neutral in the situation created by a totalitarian movement. This kind of non-neutrality has, however, nothing to do with the idea that the university must necessarily be at the service of the particular interests of certain classes, nationalities, races or parties.

In other words, human societies are and probably always will be politically split. In virtue of values that lie at its very foundation, the university is inevitably involved in these splits in so far as these values are at stake. In relation to the conflict between the idea of impartial thinking and the idea that we cannot think except in accordance with the interest of a race or a class, it is not neutral; nor is it neutral in the conflict between those who do and those who do not believe that tolerance is better than police control over teaching.

It follows that the idea of the university is not violated when the university is actively engaged in issues directly bound up with its functioning according to its own basic principles; that the university is in duty bound to react in all cases where such issues as the freedom of teaching, freedom of research, freedom of discussion, opposition to compulsory indoctrination, etc. become the target of political conflict. Even when faced with a political conflict in which these values are involved, a university which defends them cannot be blamed for casting away its neutrality, if it keeps clear the distinction between its endorsement of a social order which provides them with better support and its endorsement of whatever political group represents such an order at any given moment. To be sure, this distinction may often be obscured, especially in moments of violent conflict; it is nevertheless real and not just invented in order to find a casuistic justification for the violation of neutrality – to back or to oppose a certain bill, for example, related to the values that the university is supposed to preserve is not the same as simply to back or to oppose a political party which happens to be committed to the same cause.

It may be argued that since the university has to be and ought to be engaged in conflicts relevant to its basic values, there is no good reason why it should not be engaged in all other kinds of political conflict, provided only that it does not take any stand which may jeopardise its existence as an open university. In other words, if we agree that certain values that the university is committed to uphold are not confined to its own particular interests, why should it abstain from involvement in any political conflict, even if more or less irrelevant or without clear relevance to its basic tasks? The answer is that the neutrality of the university, in contradistinction to its impartiality in research and in teaching, does not belong to the basic values that it is obliged to uphold on pain of running the risk of self-destruction, but is a necessity imposed simply by its own inevitable weakness. The university is and always has been weak in the sense that it has almost no means apart from its own intellectual dignity to defend itself against political pressures which, while trying to destroy its neutrality, at the same time attack its impartiality and other basic values. If neutrality and impartiality exclude each other with respect to the same conflict, as I tried earlier to explain, it does not follow that the converse is true. One *can* be non-neutral and non-impartial at the same time with respect to the same conflict. In the ideal case, I can imagine that I remain impartial in a conflict to which I am a party – such a case is not logically excluded where social conflicts and big social institutions are concerned, though it is excluded for obvious psychological and social reasons. Those who seek to destroy the neutrality of the university seek always something more: to destroy its impartiality in teaching and in research and to harness its whole activity to the service of their own interests. If political neutrality is required, it is not because non-neutrality is logically incompatible with the fulfilment of the tasks of the university, but because social conditions make their fulfilment practically incompatible with non-neutrality. That the university is weak and may be easily degraded is an empirical statement. The political pressure that may be exerted on universities and destroy their basic values through the destruction of their neutrality may be exemplified by many well-known stories of Nazi Germany, of communist countries and of McCarthy's America. The only weapon that the university has at its disposal to defend itself against intimidation and pressure is to proclaim its political neutrality – though as a means, not as a goal in itself. The university that itself deliberately violates its own neutrality, loses all right to resist those pressures which aim to convert it into the tool of some actually ruling political group.

The meaning of this expression 'to be a political tool' hardly needs explaining in the case of the university. The university violates not simply its neutrality, but precisely its own basic values when it yields to the demand to provide information selected according to particular political interests, when it makes use of political criteria in appointing teachers and in admitting students or when it bars or makes impossible free discussion in the name of these interests.

The standard argument put by partisans of the totalitarian university is that all this happens in universities everywhere in any case. Such an argument cannot be used in good faith, however, in order to show the alleged necessity of the university's becoming politically involved in the sense indicated. One probably cannot claim that the highest requirements of impartiality have been met absolutely in any university; it may also be said that no university, even under the worst conditions, has been so utterly corrupted as to leave no element of its teaching or research free from political bias. To infer from this that the difference between the open and totalitarian university is imaginary, or that any difference between them is insignificant ('quantitative only') and so on, is a piece of reasoning very typical of totalitarian crudity. It is possible to say, of course, that the difference between the income of a Rockefeller and that of a garbage collector is 'only quantitative'; one can say similarly that since no one on earth is perfect, no significant difference exists between Saint Francis and Hitler; and so on. There is, of course, a perspective that allows us to consider all the differences in the world as insignificant; but nothing compels us to accept this perspective. Nobody who knows both kinds of universities – open and totalitarian – from his own experience can honestly claim that the differences between them are unimportant or only apparent (it being taken for granted that deviations from impartiality and political abuses are to be found in many open universities and that some honest and unprejudiced research is carried out in totalitarian ones).

The statement that universities are necessarily political tools and that no important distinction can be made between them because, strictly speaking, they are by nature all equally servile, is a totalitarian way of trying to justify the aspirations of one particular group to take over every aspect of intellectual life in its desire for power. To accept this statement is to accept the depravity of the university in all respects, since indeed there can be no reasons for condemning any kind of political abuse if all of them are equally inevitable. The suggestion is that no real ('substantial', 'essential', 'qualitative', etc.) contrast can be found between the Nazi universities that had to act simply as instruments of indoctrination and violently to expel anyone who refused to participate in this work, and the open universities, where, no doubt, some ideological biases may be at work and some political preferences alive, but where discussion is always possible and the teacher's responsibility is not simply to the police and to the ruling party. However imperfect may be the pressure that commands the teacher's acceptance of some universally admitted rules of thinking and makes him responsible before his colleagues, his students and public opinion, the presence of this pressure is always infinitely preferable to the constraints of monopolised political power that claims to possess the solution of important scientific problems before knowing how to deal with them in a scientific way.

We are talking about impartiality as an intrinsic value of the life of the university, not about neutrality, which is not such an intrinsic value, although it has to be observed because of its causal relation to impartiality.

Probably nobody would now deny that any enquiry in the human and social sciences takes place against a background of value-judgements – admitted, implicitly at least, in the choice of categories used and in the hierarchy of importance given to the phenomena under study. This contention may be considered to be well founded in the light of a great number of studies of the subject. It is far from having been proved, however, or even shown to have any probability, that all these values are necessarily bound to the particular interests of conflicting political groups. Neither does the presence of value-judgements exclude impartiality within the broad perspective that they determine. There are a lot of simple technical rules that may be or may not be observed in the course of an enquiry and which determine finally the validity of its results, although we must admit that by themselves these rules do not prejudge the results unequivocally. The research done on the same topic by two scholars with different philosophical backgrounds and differently biased perspectives may differ widely. Their validity is nevertheless defined by the observance of such modest rules as: one must take into consideration all material known to be relevant to the topic; one must analyse all conceptual distinctions that have already been made which may be significant for the material; one must continually ask oneself what possible objections there may be against one's own interpretation and what is or what seems to be valid in them, etc. Such a humble code cannot eliminate disagreement derived from fundamental biases; it can, however, eliminate a good deal of purely ideological or simply dishonest work. To be satisfied with the general assertion that everything in the social and human sciences is purely and simply determined by political preferences and interests – as is common among those who advocate the subordination of the university to political assignments, said to be in any case inevitable – is to deny, against the obvious evidence, the ability of human reason to act according to the rules that it has itself created. This kind of protestant belief in the irreversible corruption of the human mind is, however, self-destructive; it can only avoid the antinomy of the liar if it is supplemented by the belief in another, incorruptible source of knowledge or divine origin, though the advocates of the totalitarian university today rarely seek this kind of assistance.

At the same time the patterns of the attacks against the possibility of neutrality are exactly the same as in the case of impartiality and other traditional academic values. They seek to show that since biases are noticeable in many social and human studies, impartiality is therefore inconceivable in these realms at least; and that no 'qualitative' differences are to be found between their products so far as their fateful ideological involvement or their servile nature is concerned. Apart from the already mentioned fact that the evaluative background to all social and human enquiry excludes neither impartiality nor the spirit of tolerance nor logical consistency, we should conclude, from the totalitarian claims, that there is no real ('qualitative') difference between the scientific value of Marx's *Das Kapital* and Hitler's *Mein Kampf*, or between the studies of Weber and the programme of the Black Panthers. All these would differ simply in the content of their political commitments and the interests they represent, not by the degree of their validity related to the (non-existent or impracticable) rules of enquiry. Exactly the same desire to reduce all forms of social life to their own patterns may be seen in the totalitarian denial of the possibility of impartial justice. Since law and juridical institutions are anyway tools at the service of certain higher social entities – classes, races or nations – there is no ('qualitative') difference between living under a system where the mediating role of law is strongly pronounced or under the most extreme form of despotism; the distinction between the British legal system and a state where the people usually confess under torture to whatever is required and where justice is simply the instrument of the police – this distinction is nothing other than an insidious device of reactionaries. Why should we think that there is any significant difference between those feudal systems where the lord was regularly himself the judge in cases in which he and his serf were the opposing parties and modern legal systems which exclude any such possibility. It is only 'the form' and not 'the content' that has changed, since in every case the legal system as a whole is at the service of the particular interests of the ruling groups.

Discussion with people thinking in this way is hardly useful, because from within their framework of thought whoever defends the idea of impartiality proves in doing so that he is defending the partiality ineradicably hidden in any apparent impartiality. Since impartiality is excluded by definition, one wonders only why its lack is rebuked with such expenditure of moral indignation, which is what usually happens.

I do not maintain, of course, that all those universities which are not involved in totalitarian systems are, in all their aspects, worthy of being presented as models of scholarly impartiality, political neutrality and kindred virtues. I maintain simply that they have a much greater chance of upholding these values and that, despite all abuses, they do in reality uphold them incomparably better than openly totalitarian ones; and, above all, that it is not at all hopeless or nonsensical (as one would be compelled to conclude from totalitarian doctrines) to strive to do better in this respect. The whole of modern intellectual culture would be inconceivable without the medieval struggle of the *facultates artium* against their dependence on the faculties of theology, in reality a struggle for the neutrality of secular thinking in relation to theological controversies. It was the winning of this struggle that made possible the whole spiritual development of recent centuries. To fancy that we can promote further progress by reversing this achievement is on a par with the idea that since we are not perfect while standing upon two legs, we ought to return to crawling on all fours.

I do not pretend to have taken into consideration all sides of the question of neutrality. We must face the inevitable fact that the immanent logic of intellectual development usually does not run parallel with the development of the social needs and requirements that the universities are supposed to meet, and that it turns out sometimes that structures which correspond to the former may be obsolete from the point of view of the latter. Universities have occasionally to experience the crises that result from this kind of inadequacy and which can be resolved only by various kinds of compromises. Such compromises are usually possible without giving up basic academic values. Whether or not we have to cope with a crisis of such a character at the present time, I do not propose to discuss here; such a discussion cannot be meaningful if presented in general terms alone.

One must agree, nevertheless, that in some circumstances the full political neutrality of the university is impracticable. If a general crisis occurs where the whole existence of society is at stake, it would be vain and silly to require that the university should keep itself aloof. It does not, I repeat, betray its own conception in giving up neutrality, as it does in giving up impartial thinking, logical rules and tolerance in scholarly matters. In situations which obviously involve the whole existing structure of society, the neutrality of the university would be an empty slogan. To be sure, we are not able to define exactly the conditions we are talking about or when we may be allowed to state that they obtain. Definitions are here necessarily imprecise, as indeed are all definitions other than those given in the conventional languages of deductive systems (even the definition of a five-pence coin cannot, as has been pointed out, be formulated in such a way as to remove all possibility of doubt in particular cases). But this is not a good reason for giving up efforts to improve them. The need to remain neutral, the impossibility of always remaining

neutral and the impossibility of arriving at absolutely strict definitions of the conditions of neutrality, all these circumstances are
among the results of the same imperfections, imperfections that can
slowly be reduced, but never finally removed.

'Le neutre' and philosophical discourse[1]

LOUIS MARIN
(Translated by Willis Domingo)

Introduction

The first part of this study takes its main inspiration from the article by P. Bourdieu and Monique de Saint-Martin: 'L'excellence dans le système scolaire français'. For our purposes, however, this remarkable paper provides no more than a starting point, itself standing in need of a philosophical justification. For both the meaning and practical relevance of sociological statements and inductions are surely functions of their philosophical foundations, even though we may be brought in the end to recognise that this basis actually consists – *at present* – in its own absence; and even though we may demand that sociology should be established on the ground of evidence already built up by science, a ground that has not yet been laid down and of which it will be the purpose of this paper to draw the negative outlines. Perhaps this empty space prefigures 'le neutre', the very object of our undertaking; perhaps it is 'le neutre' that will provide the very foundations that we are seeking. Hence, as we work towards establishing the boundaries of sociological research – a process whose own nature depends on what are the fundamental presuppositions of sociology – we shall witness a remarkable assimilation of the form of our enquiry to its content and of its syntax to its semantics, or vice versa. Indeed, if a sociological enquiry into the neutrality of the French university educational system leads, if it is

[1] The range of meanings covered by the French word 'neutre' is in English shared between the two terms 'neutral' and 'neuter'. In the course of his discussion Louis Marin moves across the whole extent of this range. In most cases – though not in all – the immediate context makes it clear enough which of the two English terms would provide the normal idiomatic equivalent. Nevertheless, not only the unity but much of the substantial point of what is here at issue would be lost if the question of the continuity of 'le neutre' was to be begged in advance by substituting for it discrete instances of 'the neutral' and 'the neuter'. The substance of these matters is taken up again in Part III, pp. 245 ff. Meanwhile, it has seemed best to leave the French term untranslated throughout, together with its cognates 'neutralité' and 'neutralisation', except in those cases, most of them involving the verb 'neutraliser', where to have done so would have resulted in hybrid constructions of altogether too barbaric a shape.

There is another, rather open set of words which can be translated without much difficulty into almost direct English equivalents, but whose full penumbra of meaning and association is only likely to be evident to readers with some knowledge of contemporary French philosophy. They help, as it were, to set stages on which few English actors are as yet trained to perform or English audiences to pick up the cues. This difficult set includes such words as 'difference', 'closure', 'presence', 'originary', 'trace', 'discourse', etc. Many of them have particular association with the writings of Jacques Derrida and, before him, with those of Husserl and Heidegger; but short of attempting long exegetical footnotes, the simple point may be made that there is bound to be more to them than can meet the eye of mere translation.

to be justified philosophically, to one into the essential nature of 'le neutre' as providing an ontological basis, and if the language and terms of reference of this further enquiry are those of French academic discourse, then one must acknowledge that it has to take itself as an integral part of its own object and that the whole procedure of enquiry is brought into question to the extent that it brings into question its own proper object.

This movement takes place by means of a double contortion, a double turning-back-upon-itself. The first is involved in the position of whoever carries on such academic discourse on the very essence of academic teaching. For this position is itself academic or didactic; the form of language adopted is not that of the novel, fable or myth, but rather that of the university lecture. This is a surprising, meta-linguistic position which, so it may seem, must lead to an infinite regress. Alternatively, and more simply, one may accept that this meta-language, taking itself as the object of discourse, should find expression in its own disintegration and in the 'dislocation' of its own 'facts', thus presenting itself as the language of questioning, that is, as a language that is 'neutre'. This would be the language of a form of discourse that was indeed fully critical, that recognised the myths and mystifications which it embodied and which were embodied even in its own exposure of them. It is a discourse that precedes the discourse of science, that provides the *passage* to science from ideology. It is unstable, as are all transitional formations; yet for this very reason it has to be understood in its essential instability.

The second turning back follows immediately on the first or is internal to it, in as much as the sociological investigation which provides our starting point and which bears for the most part on the neutrality of university teaching in order to expose it, cannot be directed upon its object – cannot be brought so to bear upon it as to break it down – without questioning its own presuppositions, its own neutrality, its own objectivity or its own scientific status. This is not to say that one has ultimately to deny the investigation any scientific standing. But the simple fact that it is possible to question this standing leads the investigation for a time into the sphere of 'le neutre', the domain in which standards of truth and falsity are determined. Indeed, the investigation bears on this very determination and on whatever may guarantee its outcome. It thus becomes itself a part of its own object and, more particularly, of that enquiry into the nature of 'le neutre' which epitomises 'le neutre' itself.

Such is the nature of this second and very radical turning back. To enquire into the nature of man, of society, of images, is to bring each of them into the sphere of 'le neutre' and so to produce in them and in their overall positions certain subtle and radical modifications into which it will be our business to enquire. It is this second-order enquiry into the nature of enquiry itself which lies at the heart of the concept of 'le neutre'. It should not be thought to constitute some kind of neutralisation of 'le neutre', as if beyond the desert region haunted by the ghosts of the rational entities that have been brought into 'question', one had access to a privileged land where reigned some ontological power capable of restoring them to being, of giving to these poor ghosts flesh and blood and life. Nor is it a neutralisation of 'le neutre' in the way in which one position may constitute the negation of another, itself already negative. This questioning of what is involved in questioning itself is the very epitome of 'le neutre' in its empty power of generating infinite repetition; it is the emptiness of all content itself, presenting itself as such to reflection and in which reflection is so drained of its strength that it is able to grasp 'le neutre' only in its figures; for in attempting to grasp it as it is in itself, it would be wholly exhausted.

This infinite repetition is not to be confused with an infinite regress; nor is it a retreat towards some unattainable realm, the unattainability of which is posited as a limit and a goal. It is rather a sort of motionless mobility, a vibration or rhythm unable to move beyond its own pitch. But before we can achieve this grasp of the pure void, which is the foundation that we are seeking, it will be necessary to work through a whole examination of the figures of 'le neutre', figures in which it seems to reveal itself in its true nature, going here under the name of 'objectivity', there 'disinterestedness', there 'authenticity', elsewhere 'justice' or 'independence'; though in fact each of these is but a mystification of 'le neutre' a mystification the characteristic of which is to be nothing but 'le neutre' itself. For it is one of its properties to turn out to be the very essence of dissimulation just when the investigation had seemed to have pinned it down as a dissimulation of being. But 'le neutre' would cease to be what it is, if it somehow took on substance. Underlying substantial being is incompatible with it – if, indeed, such being is even thinkable. Unless, perhaps, it is itself thought of as 'neutre'; not at all as support or ground or base, (in which case one would be faced once again with the problem of foundations alluded to at the outset), but as the field of discourse which provides the passage from one difference to another.

The search for a philosophical foundation for sociological enquiry thus takes on a fundamentally paradoxical character in that to enquire into the nature of 'le neutre' and of 'la neutralité' is to embark already upon the foundation of one's own investigation; for 'le neutre' is this very foundation and any questioning of its nature already partakes of it. When we try, however, to give explicit formulation to this search for a foundation in the context of an investigation into the neutrality of the language of education, we *ipso facto* abandon the zone of foundations and simply fall back into the very language of education into which we are enquiring. In short, our discussion is bound to take forms that are either circular or oblique. The further our object falls out of focus, the closer we may come to grasping it; the closer we come to grasping it through our digressions, the further we may fall beside the point of the question of which we are treating. It is also possible, however, that these allusive or digressive aspects of our discourse should be recognised as belonging as such to the zone of foundations, a zone which they demolish in order to build it up.

In the following text, then, two levels can be distinguished. The first part will be sociological in orientation; the greater length of the text, however, will move on a philosophical level of analysis. We should emphasise that on neither level will the discourse to be developed be academic; or, if it is, it will be only through the direct or indirect use of discourses belonging to other contexts which are themselves academic. It remains the case that distinction is difficult – if not impossible – between the knowledge that we acquire through reading and that which we gain through pure reflection. There are concepts or themes which, although chosen by an entirely arbitrary decision, subsequently turn out to be very highly determined by the positions that they already hold in the cultural field. Indeed, those very concepts or themes which appear to depend on purely arbitrary choice may be among the most strongly determined. They may be compared to the opinions of the common man as spoken of by Pascal. These are at once valid and invalid. Identical in their formulation to those held by men of knowledge, they are in a sense true; but – since their meaning shifts to the very degree that they come under closer consideration – not as true as they may appear. Thus they are also false as a result of their ambiguity or their equivocation; but for that very reason true, if it is indeed the case that natural ordinary language is capable only of ambiguity. In this way our discourse arises from and belongs to the very domain that it will study, the domain of 'le neutre', a domain which belongs in turn to the cultural field within which we have isolated it as a theme and as a concept; it is through its use that we propose to return to this field in order to work out (work through) the new and interminable differences to which our discourse will thus give rise. These sudden passages of learning and ignorance, which will be noticeable throughout its course, are essential characteristics of the game which is played by 'le neutre', that mystified mystifier which our discourse has for its object, a discourse at once learned and ignorant and which will sink deeper and deeper as it unfolds, hoping thereby to mark out its object.

Neutrality and educational discourse

When asked about the role of the university in society, a Head of State once responded by saying: 'The University is neither a foreign body within society nor a national luxury. . . . It is rather that institution which prepares the nation for tomorrow. This implies that the University's role is one of national utility and in saying "national utility" I in no sense exclude culture or disinterested research. All this is part of a nation's greatness; but it is for the sake of the nation that it exists.' In this way Caesar makes two points with respect to the sort of educational discourse which occurs in the context of a particular institution. The university and university education have a social function, *a utility*. It moulds useful citizens of global society, i.e. administrators, teachers and executives who, at a definite moment of their training, can be brought into the machinery of production in order to assume control over the ranks of those forces which are more directly involved in the act of production itself. This is the first end attributed to the university by such political discourse; its other and contradictory purpose, however, lies in the affirmation of the prestige value, the value as a luxury, of the very same institution and the very same educational discourse; thus it speaks of that 'free and disinterested research' which is part of 'a nation's greatness'. The strictly cultural function of the university is affirmed only to be immediately subordinated to its social function, as if it were merely a luxurious and gratuitous bonus of the latter, thanks to which the direct and immediate involvement of educational discourse in the socio-economic sphere may present a façade of independence in order the better to reinforce its very involvement and integration. For disinterestedness and freedom, as the primary forms of a 'neutre' rendered banal by the revelatory platitude of such political discourse, are simply the trade-marks of the interestedness and utility of educational discourse once it has reached a certain threshold of expansion; they make manifest its overall integration. Thus a primary contradiction already appears on the surface of such political statements as a guide to lead us on to others both more compelling and richer in meaning.

In Marxist terminology we could express such a contradiction more or less as follows: Once it became bound to the expansion of modern industrial society, the university, whose cultural function had hitherto been predominant, began to emerge as an institution belonging to the superstructure of that society and relatively independent of its economic and social infrastructure. It recruited its students from certain definite social classes, offering them a kind of knowledge (i.e. the discourse of teaching and of research) whose determination by the economic and social situation was neither immediately obvious nor openly expressed by the political and ideological machinery of the state. Nowhere was this phenomenon of independence and freedom more clear cut than in the Humanities and especially in that discourse which was the crown of all others, namely the discourse of philosophy. In this case the production and transmission of knowledge – i.e. research and teaching – were asserted to be completely free, subject only to the practices and requirements of the scientific disciplines as such and not to the infrastructural necessities of industrial production in all its aspects. Philosophy appeared as universal-abstract knowledge, something distinct from the society in which it appeared and determined only by itself, as an all the more faithful expression of the ideology of the ruling class, both in form and in content, in that it was detached from this ideology, thus becoming its mirror image, its inverted reflection.

From now on the university falls within the realm of fundamental infrastructural contradictions. Having become one social element among others with which it is on an equal footing and having lost its privileged position for the expression, through the type of knowledge that it produced, of pure ideology, the university finds itself directly subordinated to the expansion of industrial society and the reproduction of capital. It has to furnish qualified white collar workers and to respond to a diversified and global demand from the employment market, whose structure, jobs and articulations are defined by the capitalist industrial system. From now on the university's cultural function, the production and transmission of knowledge, is subordinated to its social function, a subordination which becomes more and more pronounced with the growing integration of the whole system. In a sense if the term 'ideology' is taken as designating at least provisionally 'the representation of the imaginary relationships which the individuals of a given society have with their real conditions of existence',[2] that is, the relationship they maintain with existing relations of production, the university ceases to be a purely ideological phenomenon, since its involvement in the economic and social situation and its explicit integration as a moment in the relations of production are now clearly defined.

[2] Louis Althusser, 'Ideologie et appareils ideologiques d'etat. Notes pour une recherche', *La Pensée*, no.151 (June 1970).

It is, on the other hand, the ideological factor which constitutes the resistance to this subordination, a resistance which is made just as explicit as is the integration of the university into existing relations of production and which is expressed in the assertion of the university's independence with respect to any political or economic power. Such assertions are ideological in so far as they express the representation of the imaginary relationship between individuals and the real conditions of their existence, that is to say their economic situation. The coexistence of two contrary assertions, namely that of the involvement of the university in the infrastructural domain of production and that of the university's independence of this domain and of the political power which is one of its determinations, was already apparent in the political discourse referred to above; here it is presented in full clarity in Marxist terminology. The first assertion derives from fundamental political and economic necessities, the second from the ruling ideology. We have now to point out the ambivalent mechanisms of this subordination of the cultural to the social functions of the university; for these purposes we shall follow very closely the lines of Bourdieu's analysis.

The university considers itself and seeks to be independent of society as a whole; it is free, disinterested, 'neutre' in relation to its social context both in space and in time: it is a centre of 'frank and open discussion', which benefits from a sort of extraterritoriality: its teaching, its subjects of research, its methods, its criteria for the selection and assessment of students, its control over their studies are all decided upon by the university itself, its autonomy being more pronounced in the cases in which the disciplines concerned – such as literature, philosophy, the dead languages or history – are in themselves free of all direct social involvement. How could university teaching in disciplines such as these aim at the formation of managers in the middle and upper levels of the machinery of production? Because these disciplines do not aim at forming such managers, this area within the university, these aspects of its course, should in their turn be free from the requirements of the machinery of production. To this extent the university definitively establishes its own independence. This implies that the entire system of teaching within the university and, furthermore, the whole system of the ranking of students and the establishment of hierarchies and differences which appears as the objective side of the system of teaching, rests solely on university values and scholarly criteria. The independence of the university means that the way in which it functions depends solely on itself and that its content and role, i.e. knowledge and the transmission of knowledge, exist and take place within a closed system.

If such are the functions of the university, i.e. the conservation, production and transmission of knowledge, they are accomplished within the framework of an institution, that is, a body of individuals which is subject to laws, rules and structures and entrusted with the production, conservation and transmission of this knowledge in accordance with the rules of the institution. By considering the university as an institution we treat it together with other institutions as forming a nation. In the words of the Head of State already quoted: 'It is not a foreign body within the nation.' On the contrary, every institution has its role in the state, its social function. As an institution, the social function and utility of the university lie in the formation of administrators; and here we return to the other side of our problem. It is at this same point, however, that the 'solution' presents itself to the primary contradiction to which this problem gave rise; for the university is never more determined in its institutional essence, never fulfils more thoroughly its role of a teaching institution, never demonstrates more convincingly its social 'utility' than in its formation of teachers. It is in this very way that the university can also assert both its social utility and its integration as one among all other institutions of global society – namely by fulfilling institutionally its social role and in so doing establishing its independence, its definitive separation from society, in as much as its privileged social function is precisely one of self-perpetuation, self-replacement and *self-reproduction*. Thus one might describe the university as that educational institution whose essence, truth or ideal is to be a system closed both as to its content and as to its form and whose social product is its own self-reproduction and thus the realisation, through its integration into global society, of its own fundamental independence.

The university's 'neutralité' of conduct and discourse depends therefore on the concept of its own institutional independence, and any social function it may have – at least as regards its 'nobler' disciplines – comes about by rebound as a sort of bonus. Indeed, in order to express as perfectly as possible the ideology of the university we should reverse the words of the politician: 'The role of the university is that of free and disinterested research and the teaching of high culture, but this does not exclude its utility or its having a social function . . .'

Nevertheless, within such a self-proclaimed 'independent' society, contradictions begin to appear deriving from deeper contradictions belonging if not to the infrastructure, at any rate to society as a whole. This implies that such an independence is a sort of camouflage or, more precisely, that the assertion of independence is the inverted form of an assertion of strict dependence.

Such contradictions will not be manifested directly, but rather in certain ambiguities where 'le neutre' makes a practical appearance in one or another of its guises. One such ambiguity lies in the tension which exists between teaching and research in the university and which is expressed ideologically in the ideal of making research into a way of teaching and teaching into a form of research. Such a tension or equivocation centres around the difference between the production and the transmission of knowledge. It is obvious that the transmission of knowledge is always and necessarily temporally subsequent to its production. Furthermore, transmission always produces a certain loss of content in the knowledge which is transmitted. This is simpler, more schematic, and more allusive when transmitted than when first produced. Why? Because transmission is always re-production of a message. As Bourdieu and Passeron have demonstrated, repetition has the effect of making the messages repeated homogeneous in order that they may be inculcated more easily, of regularising them and making them routine as a result of their multiplication. In the relationship between the functions of teaching and research there appears therefore a first aspect of 'le neutre', that is, the 'neutralisation' of what has been produced through transmission by way of repetition or, rather, by way of a necessary reproduction of messages affecting the very content of the messages in question.

Moreover, knowledge is only re-produced if it is in one way or another socially legitimate and its transmission equally so. Hence the neutralisation of what has been produced as knowledge (i.e. the results of research carried out in the university) by its reproduction as part of the discourse of teaching is merely one aspect of the de-neutralisation, by making it socially legitimate, of its transmission. Its content – as content – is neutralised in its transmission, but the forms of transmission are themselves far from neutral, for the simple reason that they are bound to rules of legitimatisation which are actually the value requirements of some social class, society or group. This point calls for an exact analysis along the lines established by Bourdieu and Passeron, an analysis which would enable us to see how the transmission of any knowledge whatsoever by means of established discourse necessarily requires the authority of an institution which manifests itself externally by means of standards, supervision, programmes or schedules. This institutional authority is in turn projected no less necessarily onto the teacher as if to consecrate him in his role. As the functionary of an institution he is endowed by that institution with a certain authority just as any other functionary of any other institution. It so happens, however, that his function is the transmission of knowledge (a knowledge which, as authorised knowledge, is itself legitimised by the institution). As Bourdieu so powerfully expresses it: 'The authorisation of this knowledge by the institution gives to the teacher the authority of knowledge itself.' In other words, 'the authority of the teacher already has a secure foundation in the institutionalisation of the knowledge that he has to pass on: consequently he has no need to justify it at the moment of its transmission, for the public has already been converted.' Bourdieu goes on to quote Durkheim: 'The "master", like the priest, possesses recognised authority because he is the organ of a moral authority which goes beyond him.' Such a primitive institutionalisation is necessary because the teacher does not produce knowledge in the act of teaching, but merely reproduces it. He is the author of a discourse which is bound to escape from its paternal origin and yet it is he and he alone who transmits it. Since he does not create his knowledge as he transmits it, but has inevitably to transmit it within and through an institutional framework, he is necessarily dispossessed of his discourse at the moment of its utterance, being able to regain it only in his role as a functionary of the institution.

Hence arises the psychologically understandable attempt to re-neutralise the transmission of knowledge in the university by what Bourdieu calls the complementary ideology of the master against the teacher. The institutional functionary whose position is that of a university teacher denounces the institution within which and thanks to which he exists as a teacher by taking up a non-institutional position from which he can assert his independence from the most obvious or outward requirements of his institution such as its curricula or its discipline . . . The knowledge which he transmits from such a standpoint may seem to recover a tentative 'neutralité' with respect to the teaching institution. 'The teacher can place himself at a distance from his institution because he is already endowed with the symbols of authority which are attached to his role as teacher: . . . these symbols are essentially constituted by certain ways of speaking . . . and by various codes of rhetoric characterised by their own particular premisses, figures, mannerisms and styles.' This is an essential point and we should consider it more closely. The teacher's craft is exercised through the spoken word; his function is an essentially discursive one with a very special relationship to language. His position in and with respect to the institution of the university is one of discourse. It is perhaps a peculiarity of language in general, of discourse in particular and especially of the discourse of teaching that, in its very utterance and at the moment of its expression, it should cause its listeners to *forget* the situation of its utterance and the position of the individual expressing himself. Such discourse is able to realise the topological paradox of being simultaneously *within the (teaching) institution*, because such a 'teacher' speaks within and through it, and yet *outside* and independent of that same institution, because a teacher will be considered all the more brilliant and all the more 'a teacher' to the extent that he acts more like a 'master', i.e. someone who speaks from outside and even against his own institution (even though it provides him with a place in which to speak, an audience, and even the matter and ends of his discourse). The discourse of such a teacher will be defined primarily by its content and will necessarily conceal any of its other functions in favour of this content's transmission. In this style of language, that is, in the discourse of teaching, we may perhaps grasp the reason for the necessarily interested gratuitousness, the indentured 'neutralité' and dependent independence of the transmission of knowledge within a university framework. To the extent that discourse takes the form of one designed for the transmission of knowledge it must necessarily conceal its place of utterance, the respective positions of speaker and audience and the highly elaborated codes set in play by the messages it transmits. Bourdieu speaks of a rhetoric of educational discourse whose function is to symbolise institutional authority, i.e. to express and at the same time to conceal such authority behind the autonomous and independent play of language with itself. But is it not a peculiarity of language in general that it should be unable to speak of itself at the same time as it speaks of something else? Can it ever be simultaneously language and meta-language? There can be no doubt that not only the codes, but also the functions of the sender and receiver of a message are identifiable only at the level of meta-language. In so far as educational discourse is one by which already produced knowledge is then transmitted, it cannot take itself as its own object. Essential to its presentation, therefore, is the fact that its origins, ends, ways and procedures are hidden or masked. Once analysed, however, it is these very origins, ends and procedures which would reveal the involvement of this discourse in global society and its dependence on the 'values of the ruling class' of such a society. It is precisely because educational discourse – and perhaps all discourse – necessarily disguises its figures, its system of enunciation and the positions of those involved in its utterance that its very independence and 'neutralité' function as means utilised by the class, group or society from which it proclaims its independence. As Bourdieu writes so convincingly, 'This is a very special way of making it serve external (i.e. social) ends . . . The educational system never fulfils so effectively its social functions nor its ideological functions of concealing its own social functions, as when it appears to pursue exclusively its own ends.'

In other words, while 'neutralité' as independence is 'overtly' a process of rejecting certain ends, it is 'immanently' the index of a logic of such ends and one which aims at their realisation. We must here emphasise as clearly as possible that such dissimulation is not simply an inert screening off of a deeper reality. It is, rather, a means to an end, a means possessed by an end for its own self-realisation. It is the mark of a force aiming at a goal, a mask of the violence of this force or, in different terms, its 'reactivity'. What is this force and what are its goals? It is the force of class domination aiming to ensure as completely as possible the domination of the ruling class.

Just as Bourdieu's analysis has shown, therefore, that it is natural and necessary for the practice of education that it should dissimulate and repress its own theoretical consciousness (for the reasons which he gives himself, but also, and perhaps more fundamentally, for those which stem from the very essence of discourse), so the problem we are obliged to face is that of producing within the very practice of educational discourse the theoretical and critical consciousness of the conditions of its reproduction, i.e. of its dependence on the values and requirements of the ruling class. If, however, it is characteristic for the practice of education to censure and repress this consciousness *within such practice itself*, are we not then obliged to step out of this practice (that is, out of the university and out of any position within such an institution) in order to accomplish our criticotheoretical work and thus to produce as a separate form of consciousness that which this practice effaces in the discourse belonging to the transmission and reproduction of knowledge? But where is this 'standpoint outside the university' from which that other discourse on discourse itself will have to take place, that discourse which – in so far as it does take place – will perhaps necessarily collapse once more into the object of its own critique? This circle, into which all critical reflection on discourse and more specifically on educational discourse seems doomed to enter, may perhaps be the scheme (schema) of that neutral (neuter) foundation which we are seeking and whose terrain we hope to map out.

Proposals for a pure analysis of 'le neutre'

As a point of departure we shall propose an abstract definition of 'le neutre' (etymologically ne-uter, neither one thing nor another) which, grammatically speaking, being neither masculine nor feminine has no gender and being neither active nor passive is non-voiced. Thus in the realms of botany and zoology we call 'neutre' those flowers or insects or indeed any plants or animals which are

deprived of reproductive organs, which have no sex and which are therefore unable to couple or to reproduce. Similarly those verbs are 'neutre' which are intransitive, which express actions in themselves, such as marching or dying, and to which it is impossible to assign a direct object. Such verbs express an action which is to be attributed to the subject, which does not impinge on any object and of which the subject is not in some sense the source. This intransitive quality of 'le neutre' has a double meaning: in the first place, it appears as the expression of a pure action, in which sense any verb in the infinitive is 'neutre'; in the second place, it is the closing off of a subject enclosed within itself and whose actions are the passions of a subject which is its own object, in short a form of self-consciousness. The first case is one of an indeterminate action without subject or object, a 'thinking' or 'speaking' without any indication of who speaks or about what, of who thinks or about what he thinks – a pure virtuality which is the ground on which language will piece out its figures. In the second case, however, 'le neutre' is no longer the insignificant ground from which meanings are elaborated only to detach themselves from and to obscure it. It is rather a divided being which introduces distance into itself only to blot it out again in presence and whose acts burst out of themselves only to return immediately to their source, a self-consciousness which cannot yet be counted as *consciousness* of something, but which all the figures of consciousness will preserve for the sake of anchoring themselves in the active reality of a subject, though they will forget it for the sake of finding themselves embodiments in the world. The game of grammar, as we have sketched it, clearly designates the zone in which 'le neutre' is circumscribed at the very beginning of the movement of dialectically double negation of two opposing sides – circumscribed but non-determined, as Aristotle forcefully points out in *De Interpretatione*. Thus, basing ourselves on such grammatical considerations, we may give the following two definitions in which the concurrence of the two negations and the distance taken with respect to that conjunction can be read simultaneously as if 'le neutre' were to be found in some other place (neither the One nor the Other), but also as if it were other than any place at all – that non-place or nowhere (utopia) which, according to the verdict to be rendered by the tribunal of history, is the place of all true 'neutres':
(1) *In chemistry* we call those bodies 'neutre' which are formed by the chemical combination of an acid and a base in such a way that certain properties are reciprocally annulled. In this case 'le neutre' is the bare empty residual matter left over from the mutual destruction of its qualities, the substratum of all formal compositions, which is only perceived thanks to such a destruction: neither base

nor acid, but 'neutre'.

(2) *In politics* we call 'neutre' he who takes no side in a debate and in particular he who does not take sides between parties who are at war with each other. This latter definition is difficult, the difficulty it presents being that of the indeterminate or non-determinate itself. For while 'le neutre' does not take sides neither is he or it completely foreign to the conflict nor without any relation to it. With respect to that towards which he is 'neutre', therefore, 'le neutre' must sustain a relationship which cannot, however, be considered as binding him to the conflict or to the war. In the same way that which is 'not-man' is non-determinate, not non-determinate in general, but rather non-determinate of 'man', constituting its pole and anchorage in determination. It is the non-determinate in relation to 'man', which thus admits, in a form devoid of content, a first determination which will in turn permit – and ground – all the others.

Our preliminary glance at dictionary definitions has already given us an outline of the pure analysis of the notion of 'le neutre'. It can accordingly be defined in relation to a dynamic totality whose constituent parts are in opposition to each other *in a position of marked difference*, such a relationship having, however, the peculiar characteristic of placing 'le neutre' itself outside the totality in question and in a position of difference with respect to the system of internal differences which constitutes the totality. 'Le neutre' thus gives rise to the paradoxical idea of a part of the whole which is somehow outside of the whole, a part which is, as it were, supplementary to the complementary parts of a totality which is itself fully accounted for by their sum. In other terms we might call it the difference which may be added to the closed system of differences. Just as relative non-determinacy, so this too is an idea which is difficult to think. But is it really impossible to find a way of thinking it? Could we not perhaps attempt to grasp it as the transitory and fleeting term which allows us to pass from one opposite to the other, which acts as the mediating term of these opposites, but which can so act only because it possesses the characteristic of being neither the One nor the Other in relation to the 'One and the Other'. We may, for example, see how it functions in the logic of myth (Lévi-Strauss, Greimas) as the instrument and constant repetition of the originary contradiction and its displacement in view of the final conjunction (which is both its term and its goal). How else might one pass from forbidden to prescribed sexual relations? Hence to speak of a term that is 'neutre' in this sense is to substantialise or ontologise a process, a movement, a passage from sameness to otherness. The neutral term will be, then, the One which is no longer the One without yet being the Other; it is a sort of logical attempt to say (to

rationalise) the passage between the two in such a way as to overcome the impossibility of saying 'le neutre' (*legein* = gather together) which is, as it were, the surplus of the system in the double
sense of being a supplement to it, while nevertheless belonging to it.
Equally, if 'le terme neutre' functions logically as an instrument for
the conjunction of opposites, then it is on its basis and around it that
these opposites will find an equilibrium in their opposition. As Jacques Derrida has pointed out, 'le terme neutre', placed as it is at the
centre of this structure, acts as its principle of organisation, as the
rule of its coherence, in that it allows for the substitution of elements
within the overall form. It is the term which, at the moment that the
conjunction between opposites is accomplished, designates this
very process. It ontologises this movement as a synchronic opposition which it henceforward orders and controls. It is thus 'le
neutre' which constitutes the principle of the conjunction of opposites; it is precisely that relation which joins them in their very opposition. It is the sign or mark of their opposition and of their being as
opposites controlled by their relation of opposition to one another;
in this way it both dominates and binds them together. It is the
oppositeness of opposites which sets and holds them in their relation of opposition to each other and in so doing escapes from this
relation of which it is the ground. One of Pascal's political *Pensées*
might help to illustrate this movement of thought: 'Great and small
are liable to the same accidents, the same annoyance, the same passion, but one is at the top of the wheel and the other near its centre,
and thus less shaken by the same movements.'[3] The axle of this
wheel is the king himself, the motionless centre around which turn,
more or less rapidly according to their remoteness from it but all
turning with the same motion, the great and small of the realm, the
interchangeable and replaceable elements of the state, subject all to
this circular dynamic, ruled and organised by its own centre which,
while belonging to it, yet stands itself outside the circulation that it
governs. We should understand, however, that there is a difference,
at once indiscernible and all-embracing, between Derrida's indifference which grounds the play of differences and the difference
which is added to the system of differences as a supplement
excluded from it. For the centre of a wheel is both within and yet
outside the wheel itself, a paradoxical situation of which that of the
unthinkable supplement of a difference to the system of differences
is the reverse. But such a reverse situation, such an inside–outside
inversion, is essential; through it alone does it become possible to
produce, to bring to light, *that which is other than the royal position*

---

[3] B. Pascal, *Pensées*, tr A. J. Krailsheimer (Penguin Classics, no. 705) (ed. Brunschvicq
Minor, no. 180).

of mastery and domination, that which is other than the violence of the central adminstration of the whole structure, that other which consists in the uninhibited liberty of the play of differences or the open infinity of their production – all this may be brought about only though the introduction into the system of differences of a further gratuitous difference that causes the rules of the system to break down. Such an inversion, however, is just as difficult to think as was 'le neutre' in its role of supplementary difference. One of the most effective ways of thinking it, therefore, is negatively, that is by means of the critical thought of 'le neutre' as the intransitive centre of the structure, a centre which is nevertheless brought back to the purely verbal position of a term that links two opposites.

'Le terme neutre' thus appears between two opposites as being neither the one nor the other, but rather as the still missing yet awaited third term. 'Le neutre' is not itself this third term; it is rather its weakest form = 0. It is the zero degree of synthesis, that is, the synthesis of opposites, a synthesis which has been reduced to a state of pure virtuality. If the synthesis of opposites itself consists in the simultaneous cancellation and preservation of both terms, then 'le neutre' marks the empty slot waiting to be filled. In itself *neither* term, it awaits the being of *both*. It is the emptiness which calls for the plenitude of the organising centre, the dispenser of order in which both opposites will recognise the figure of their higher unity, their master.

From this point we can take a further and fundamental step in our pure analysis of 'le neutre'. The centre occupies a position of potential reference for the two parts of the totality which are in conflict with each other; the existence of the centre means that the conflict is no longer a mere confrontation, but carries with it the possibility of a new beginning. This position is tied to the opposition of opposing parts reciprocally neutralising one another in a state of tension, which Kant, writing against Leibniz in his *Essay on the Concept of Negative Magnitudes*, has identified as 'a real zero of opposition'.[4] In other words, the position of the third term as 'neutre' (neither one thing nor the other) is somehow the projection of the dynamic 'neutralité' of the forces in conflict, of the magnitudes or values in opposition. It marks the point of equilibrium in the tension between these forces, while receiving its own force from the forces in conflict. These forces in their state of reciprocal 'neutralisation', these parts of the totality in the tension of their conflict, *neutralise each other in the neutrality of 'le neutre' (se neutralisent dans 'le neutre')*, of which their tension is the negative mark. The third term, 'le neutre', first points to this tension and then regulates

[4] As opposed to 'a logical zero'.

it. Here lies the source of that which we called above the paradox of 'le neutre', which is both within and outside the totality. Once 'le neutre' is made into an object of thought it can be seen as making manifest the 'neutralisation' of opposites or, to put it another way, their opposition as the reciprocal annulment of their forces. 'Le neutre' is that which presents to thought this movement of mutual annulment as such; it makes it appear as a theme in itself before returning to the conflict from which it, 'le neutre', arose and over which it will henceforth assume its authority as judge and arbiter.

This analysis of the reflection of the conflict in the third term, 'le terme neutre', allows us to come closer to the 'juridical' force of 'le neutre' over the forces in opposition. The real zero of opposition, which characterises dynamic equilibrium, confers upon the third term a force $= 0$ which gives it the *right* to intervene. This force $= 0$, which is by no means an absence of all force but rather the location in a third term of the real zero of opposition, plays in this case on the articulation of force and law. It is a force of right or law, a regulatory force which appears in the real and reciprocal annulment of opposing forces in a state of tension; in other words, it is an *effect* of the 'neutralisation' of the conflict.[5]

These analyses may be given generalised expression in the opposition of the binary and the ternary. Polemical opposition is characteristically binary. It is a contrast of symmetrical, egalitarian and infinite exchange, of conflict without end. The third term creates in such a structure an assymetry in which we may note, together with Lévi-Strauss, the conditions for the possibility of hierarchy, of institutions and of the state, which presents itself as the arbiter between different groups and the judge and moderator of the class struggle and thus as the 'neutre' occupant of the paradoxical position of this third term, at once part of and outside the totality. It is perhaps this that is the essential function of 'le terme neutre', namely to create the possibility of a hierarchy in which it will denote the empty slot. Lévi-Strauss cites in this respect certain zero type institutional forms, forms which have 'no intrinsic property other than that of establishing the necessary conditions for the existence of the social system to which they belong; their presence – in itself devoid of significance – enables the social system to exist as a whole'.[6]

From the state that is 'neutre' to discourse which is 'neutre', we can see how, through a desire to overcome oppositions in conflict through the product of some synthesis, there is reproduced a kind of

---

[5] We shall refer later on in what will appear as a somewhat naïve passage to this recourse, by way of 'neutralisation', to 'le neutre', a recourse which confers on this latter a force of right or law, that is to say, a force which possesses the reality of the zero of opposition.

[6] Claude Lévi-Strauss, *Anthropologie Structurale* (Plon, Paris, 1958); *Structural Anthropology*, tr. Claire Jacobson and Brooke Grundfest Schoepf (Penguin Books).

juridical force, a kind of authoritative speech which, while subduing the conflicting parties, is yet no more than their 'hypostatised' reflection. It is as if the opposing parties saw bearing down upon them the unrecognisable mirror image of their own opposition and took such fright that they abandoned themselves to it as if it were a principle of transcendent justice and law, a justice and law which is perhaps no more than the disguised reflection of their own force. 'Children, who are scared of the face they have daubed, are just children . . .', and Pascal adds, 'but how can someone who is so weak as a child become really strong when grown up? Only our imagination changes . . .'[7] The same misunderstanding is at work in childhood and in the founding of an institution, of justified force, one of the figures of 'le neutre'.

Three paradigms of 'le neutre'

Each stage of our pure analysis seems first to offer the possibility of a general definition, which then turns out to be merely one determinate figure of 'le neutre'. Each of these figures does embody certain possible relational aspects of the essence of 'le neutre', which seem to exist in a coherent unity up to the point at which the development of our analysis brings to light new relations and the first figure is displaced by another and different one. Approaching 'le neutre' thus becomes a process of continuing displacement and essential instability. This is another form of its indeterminacy, indicated through the contradictory play of the figures thus presented for reflection.

   We propose, therefore, the direct study of three paradigms of 'neutralité', whose concrete character will better illuminate the essential traits of the figures which are intertwined, grounded and linked together in the field which has been opened up by our pure conceptual analysis: the referee, the judge and the father. All three paradigms do indeed occur as 'natural' examples of 'neutralité' in the various discourses, be they psychological, sociological or analytic, which take 'neutralité' as their subject.

The referee. What, then, is the position of the referee in a game or sport? What is his peculiar status in relation to the players? The usual answer, which will serve as point of departure for our descriptive analysis, is that in a competitive sport the referee represents the rules of the game. This answer presupposes, indeed, that the two sides recognise the rules as valid for the game they are playing. If not, either they would not be playing at all or they would be playing a different game. Such a recognition naturally reflects a decision,

[7] Pascal, *op. cit.*, no.779 (no.88).

both personal and collective, to observe the rules and to submit to them in the course of the game. These rules define the limits of the competitors' freedom of play and of their mock combat. In this sense they prohibit a certain range of acts or moves, but at the same time circumscribe – negatively – the acts and moves permitted, that is to say the relatively indeterminate field of action in which acts occurring during the competition may be considered lawful. 'It is forbidden to hit below the belt' signifies negatively that all blows above the belt are legal. By what they forbid the rules give focus to the struggle; the competitors must strive to win within the field defined by the rules of the game, which thus close it off, giving it a relatively determined and systematic form within which they are free to act as they choose. There is, of course, a constant danger of the rules being broken – the latent risk that the players may be carried away and their desire to win become stronger than their original commitment to observe the rules defining their participation in the game. The risk involved is, then, that one side might win without observing all the rules. This is the paradox of the cheat who wins a different game from the one that he is playing to the extent that he chooses deliberately and consciously not to play game G as defined by a set of rules n, but rather game G as defined by sets of rules n-1 or n-2. As long as the gap between n and n-1 . . . passes unnoticed by his opponent, the victory of the cheat is assured, his only risk being that his opponent might eventually discover the 'misunderstanding' and refuse to go on playing with him with the result that the cheat can no longer play and win.

The referee, as we have said, represents the rules of the game. By his presence he incarnates the pure form of the *agon* by which his particular game is defined. We could conceive of a 'pure' referee (such, for example, as an electronic eye that would immediately and automatically register all transgressions), who would in a sense be the rules in themselves as they give form to the whole set of actions constituting a 'match' by closing them off in a system of play. The referee can and must be no more than the rules as pure form; otherwise he would cease to be a referee. No doubt 'subjectively' he may have his own feelings and emotions, his desires that one side should prevail rather than the other; but in this he is no referee. This he can be only if the representation of the rules of which he is the signifier and his own 'subjectivity' are effectively kept apart from each other. If not, he would *qua* referee be homologous to the cheat *qua* player. If he sides with either x or y, he ceases to represent this set of rules to become the representative of another. The representative of the rules as pure form, the pure signifier of these rules, such is the position of the referee who is 'neutre'.

In this way the referee is both in and out of the game. In the game he is the figure of its limits and its norms, i.e. the personal presence, or figure, of an impersonal set of rules which 'has no regard for persons'. At the same time, however, he is the power of intervention to which either side may have recourse; he is the force of the rules in so far as they are recognised by the players by simple virtue of the fact that they are the players. As the figure of a limit the referee also occupies a position of force, a force which exists only through the previous recognition of the rules by the players. Hence the space which has been enclosed and mapped out by the rules is organised around their representative, the referee. It is in this sense that he is both in and out of the game as the figure of its limit, for the limit belongs *neither to the figure nor to the ground*, but rather to the mark of the pure difference between figure and ground, 'le neutre'. In phenomenological terms, the *limit-force* is not of the same order as the forces brought into play by the competition. It is a force whose 'origin' is elsewhere, but whose point of application is indeed the ·space of the game. The force of the rules, of which the referee is the depository and the instrument, stems from the fact that the opposing sides both 'recognise' the rules which 'structure' their actions; it appears as the resultant of the mutual repression that the players impose upon their actions in order to play the game. It is reactive in the sense that it is born from a subordination of the polemical forces in play to the rules of the game. Thus, the structure and limits of the playing space are simply that which has been traced out in advance by the force of the rules, which, because it regulates the game and defines it as such, precedes both structure and limits. At the same time, however, this force of the rules exists only by virtue of the polemical action of the forces of the players, that is, only because those forces confront one another within the framework and according to the schema outlined by the rules and, ultimately, only because *the game is played*. If there were no actual game, if it existed only as the possibility of play, there would be no need for a referee.

Thus the 'neutralité' of the referee can be characterised as a potential reactive force of zero value. It constitutes the third term between one team and the other, while favouring neither; by its presence within and yet outside the game it signifies to both teams the rules which they have previously recognised in order to be able to play. At the same time (and in a negative fashion since the referee does not himself play) it gives order to the game and hierarchy to its space by intervening as a limit force not to be transgressed, a force which exists only through the laying down of prohibitions and the possibility of their transgression.

The judge. The paradigm of the judge is presented to us in the apparently naïve text of La Fontaine's fable about the cat, the weasel and the little rabbit. The plot of this miniature drama is familiar enough. The weasel has taken over the rabbit's dwelling place and justifies his actions by the principle according to which the land belongs to the first comer. The rabbit demands that the weasel leave, justifying his right to the property on the basis of custom and tradition. The resulting situation of conflict is insoluble, for although the weasel has superior force on its side (weasels kill rabbits), the rabbit can offset this superiority by appealing to 'all the rats in the land'. The consequent equilibrium is reflected in the weasel's suggestion and the rabbit's agreement that the two sides have recourse to the judge, the cat. The end of the fable is well known. Raminagrobis [Grimalkin], the judge, brings the opponents to agreement and resolves the situation of conflict by devouring both of them. Perfectly 'neutre', since he has favoured neither the one side nor the other, the judge brings the situation to a 'definitive solution'.

In this story the weasel and the rabbit exemplify the clash of two forces in an equilibrium of sustained tension. The weasel, of course, appeals to the law of nature, while the rabbit turns to civil law. The civil law, however, carries with it the potential force of the rats, which counterbalances the natural and immediate power that the weasel possesses over the rabbit. This conflict between Nature and Culture, that is, between primitive force and the force of law, presents us with homologous yet inverse regressions on the part of both protagonists. In referring to a judge the weasel subordinates natural violence to the law by its decision to accept its authority. In its appeal to a superior law, that of the judge, it abandons the law of nature, which is the law of force. Yet this law it abandons only because it does not believe itself capable of holding Janot the rabbit's burrow by force alone, since all the rats in the land are on Janot's side. For its part the rabbit asserts the force of civil law, but, as a result of a similar evaluation of the relative force possessed by the two sides, agrees to submit the social law to a court of higher appeal, that of the judge. La Fontaine here points out with disturbing precision that the state of nature and civil society between them define a situation of conflict of forces. It is not force that is opposed to law or nature to justice; if that were the case the conflict would *ipso facto* be resolved by the triumph of the weasel. But we know very well: 'Right without might is helpless . . . Right without might is challenged because there are always evil men about . . . . Right is open to dispute, might is easily recognised and beyond dispute . . .'[8] The conflict is assessed by the real zero of opposition only because

8 *Ibid.*, no.103 (no.298).

the right of the rabbit is 'fortified' by the rats.

> 'Well', she rejoined, 'a truce to talking,
> Let's lay the case before Grimalkin.'[9]

The basis for this assessment is expressed in the reciprocal recognition on the part of both the weasel and rabbit of a superior law, whose only force lies in the continuing absence of any outcome to the conflict. The conflict thus enters the phase of recourse to 'le neutre', which has literally been brought about and created by the real zero of opposition, but which is also *justified* by moral and intellectual guarantees. Such recourse brings 'le neutre' into the conflict as a term which both transcends the opposition and is created in its transcendence by it; herein lies its original strength or force, which is indeed simply that of the forces of the weasel and the rabbit as they are opposed to and reflected in each other. It is this force which will be justified, according to Pascal, by the morality and the adroitness of the cat.

> This was a sanctimonious Cat
> Who dwelt recluse in pious meditation,
> Well-liking, rich in fur and fat,
> And famed for skill in arbitration.[10]

It is this superior law, which derives its strength or force from the opposing, inferior forces, that in a single gesture is to resolve the conflict and bring the opposing powers into the integrated unity of a synthesis. 'He makes their peace' is a formal judgement which realises the aims of the weasel and the rabbit in their joint recourse, but does so only by 'crunching one and t'other'. The 'neutralité' of the judge, the fact that he belongs to neither party, is completed and fulfilled – or, to put it more precisely, turns back into a synthesis of both. By annihilating both sides, by his transitive negation of them both, he discovers and reveals the roots and foundation of his own 'neutralité' through a reflection of the opposing sides. At one stroke, the cat has simply become both sides; he has absorbed them both. This is the stage of the positive and real resolution by 'le neutre' of the double negation of opposites by its discovery, in the institution itself, of the violence of judicial synthesis. This violence is the hidden face of judicial 'neutralité'; it is, however, posited at least potentially in the very position of 'le neutre'. If 'le neutre' was thus posited, it is because it (or he) was in a sense required by the opposing forces of the weasel and the rabbit, enslaved as they were to the higher law.

[9] *Les Fables de La Fontaine*, tr. Sir Edward Marsh (Everyman, London, p. 161).
[10] *Ibid.*, p. 162.

The judge is indeed the representative of the law in its 'neutralité' just as the referee was the representative of the rules of the game. The law may transcend the conflict; it nevertheless possesses the force to intervene in this situation. Such a force remains, however, secondary. It is the reflection of the primary opposing forces in their mutual equilibrium – the reflected force=0, which constitutes its judicial transcendence in relation to the conflict. Thus the 'neutralité' of the judge as the representative of the law is the reproduction of the real 'neutralisation' of the opposing forces in a situation of conflict. It is the symbolic reproduction of that tension itself and rises up with unparalleled violence to suppress or subdue it and so institute the order of law.

The father. The third paradigm, that of the father, is presented to us by one of Alan Montefiore's examples earlier in this volume. He defines neutrality in terms of an agent whose aim is to help or to hinder to an equal degree two parties in a situation of conflict. In the course of discussing this suggested definition Montefiore takes an example to illustrate the case in which the parties to the conflict are very unevenly matched, namely that of a dispute between two children, one much stronger than the other. They appeal to their father. Would the father not decide in such a case to give greater help to the weaker child in order to re-establish the balance of equality? Can he then be qualified as neutral? It would seem that there must be cases in which neutrality would consist in acting in favour of one party to the detriment of the other; or, alternatively, where strict neutrality is impossible.

I do not believe that Montefiore's example was constructed for the sake of illustrating his 'case'. I take it, rather, to have a special place in the study of 'le neutre' and, to a certain extent, to govern the paradigms of the referee and the judge which we have discussed above. It is noteworthy that in the example chosen the conflict between the two children is defined in terms of force and that they have recourse to their father in a situation where their conflict is, as it were, asymmetrical. This implies (in the sense that it is presupposed by the analysis) that on the one hand the father's status as referee in the children's games is given before this particular conflict breaks out and that it is natural for them to choose him as judge; and on the other hand that his presence in the conflict appears as a source of complementary force aiming to balance the conflict rather than to resolve it. In this sense the *position* of the father in the structure of the conflict differs from that of the judge analysed above, even though his *function* is homologous. In this example the father does in fact appear as a power of 'neutralisation'. As a result of his intervention in order to complement the force of the weaker child, the conflict will tend towards an equilibrium of opposing forces. His aim is to create the real zero of opposition in which our analysis has discovered 'le neutre'. But this he can do only because he already occupies a distinctive place in the children's eyes before the conflict breaks out, namely that of judge and referee. It is as if the recourse had already taken place potentially before the outbreak of the conflict which serves as its actual occasion. That is to say, the father occupies this particular position at the moment of our example only because he is *naturally* caught up in the position of the 'third' (contentless) term in a more fundamental situation. Hence his intervention (in the example) consists indeed in the paradox of 'working' in favour of one of the conflicting parties to the detriment of the other in order to arrive at the state of 'neutralisation' (la situation 'neutre') in which recourse to a judge is logically justified. This is the reason for his preliminary activity of practical intervention undertaken for the sake of a 'neutre' that is to come and justifiable only by reference to it. In other words, 'le neutre' is here defined as a power of 'neutralisation', whose aim is to neutralise ('neuteriser') the opposing parties, a 'neutre' which receives its force from an 'originary' position in a situation of dual conflict.

To pursue the analysis we must turn once again to the 'grammatical' 'neutre'. Neither masculine nor feminine, 'le neutre' designates that which cannot be classified with respect to sex. If there is any classification, therefore, which should leave neither remainder nor residue, this is it. Any such remainder would be ab-normal, a monster. There are, then, two kinds of monster, the one complex, the monster which is both masculine and feminine, the androgyne, and the other 'neutre', that which is neither masculine nor feminine, the castrato. 'Le neutre' is thus the neutralised difference between the sexes; it is the 'neutralisation' which suppresses their difference, but only by suppressing the very reality and mark of this difference. The role of such a 'neutralisation' in the constitution of the law and in its internalisation as the third term, the superego, is well known. In this case 'neutralisation' is castration and appears in the relation which establishes the law. When we ordinarily speak of 'neutralisation', however, we mean a process involving something active and something passive, a subject and an object, a neutraliser and a neutralised ('un neutralisant et un neutralisé'). 'Le neutre' possesses the remarkable power of displacement all along the relation of castration and occupying either successively or simultaneously both active and passive positions in this relation.

When situations of conflict arise in the dual relationship of mother and child, the power of 'neutralisation' appears at first as the negative pole, the pole of absence. The third term is recognisable in this pole, the pole that is 'neutre', but it remains a negativity in which are concentrated all the elements that are lacking in the dual relationship. It is an empty zone which the third term will eventually occupy in its positive form. It is from this standpoint that we may define the Oedipal triangle, characterised by the ambivalence of the child's feelings towards his father. As an object of both love and hate in the eyes of the little boy involved in the full Oedipal situation, the father constitutes for him an admired being, the source of power, authority and law with which he seeks to identify himself. At the same time, however, and for the same reasons, he sees the father as a source of prohibition and punishment, and – in so far as the father forbids the child's incest with his mother – the threat of castration as well. The little boy admires – and identifies with – the power of 'neutralisation' and yet he fears it. He is ready to become this power even at the price of submitting to a partial 'neutralisation' himself; to become a neutraliser ('neutralisant') he must agree to be neutralised ('neutralisé'). In order to become a father he must accept the prohibition against possessing his mother. He can fulfil his genitality only at the price of relative castration.

Freud describes this dialectic by means of a myth: the murder of the father by his sons. This murder is the 'neutralisation' by castration of the father in order that the sons may gain possession of the father's women and yet the effects of this crime rebound on the murderers themselves with the institution of the prohibition of incest, which is nothing else than their own partial 'neutralisation' resulting from the 'neutralisation' of the father. It is in this way that the law is established in the ego, by the return of the dead father who, by neutralising me ('en me neutralisant'), assures me of my neutralising power ('ma puissance neutralisante').

With the anguish of being 'neutre' ('neutralisé') the child enters the period of latency. The superego is formed, whose outward manifestations will appear as the imperatives of the moral and religious consciousness. Why is there such an anguish of 'neutralisation'? Both its effect and its cause are to be found in the prohibition of the maternal object. Only because the maternal object is forbidden, however, can the little boy become a father in his turn, i.e. that neutralising power ('cette puissance neutralisante') to which he himself has had to submit in the anguish of 'neutralisation'.

Thus the paradigm of the father, as described in this rapid, psychoanalytically oriented sketch of the myth of castration, brings to light the fact that 'le neutre' or 'neutralisation' is to be defined along a 'semantic' axis of 'neutralisation' conceived as a process whose semes can be labelled neutralising/neutralised ('neutral-isant/neutralisé') or active/passive and seen as the poles which the axis holds together. The position of 'le neutre' occupied by a succession of actors (successively or simultaneously both active and passive) is displaced along the length of this axis.

This paradigm points to the foundation and 'origin' of that force which is one of the essential elements in the pure definition of 'le neutre', that force which turns back upon itself in a kind of self-reflection. Its origin lies in human desire itself as inseparable from its own prohibitions and repressions, a desire which can be fulfilled only if a prohibition is laid down, only if there is a sort of partial 'neutralisation'. It seems to be this displacement of 'le neutre' from position to position along the semantic axis of 'neutralisation' that allows us, even in Montefiore's example, to understand that paradoxical 'neutralité' whereby the father intervenes in favour of one side against the other. When this example is deciphered (and it is surely not a wholly innocent one), the neutral–neuter father appears as neutralising ('neutralisant') his sons; he renders them 'neutre' in balancing their conflicting forces through his intervention. Hence the position of 'neutre' is occupied first by the father who neutralises and then by the elder son, the stronger child, who is neutralised. In other words, the positions are reversed; 'le neutre' is marked by the absence of separation from an object, which is given to or taken by the other who, in turn, gives the object back. This is the law of exchange of 'le neutre' whereby something which belongs to one, something with which one identifies oneself and which is yet detachable from oneself is lost in exchange for something which is foreign, but by which one's self is formed. 'Le neutre' as neutraliser/neutralised ('neutralisant/neutralisé') is this exchange itself, this empty zone, this in-between in which 'le neutre' is accomplished; it is here that that which is mine is taken from me or disappears to return as something quite different, something by which I myself fulfil myself. Hence 'le neutre' allows us to lay bare the link between desire and law which our analysis has shown to be essential. Only that which becomes an object of desire is forbidden; and it is the strength or force of the desire that measures the force of the prohibition. The two forces are *the same*, the one being simply the reflection of the other. 'Le neutre' is, then, the zone of this reflection; it is the space of the process by which such reflection is fulfilled and turns back upon itself. 'Fate', as Hegel observed, 'is consciousness of oneself, but as of an enemy.'[11]

To conclude this stage of our analysis, the description of a simple

[11] G. W. F. Hegel, 'The Spirit of Christianity and its Fate', *Early Theological Writings* (University of Chicago Press).

game will provide a perfect illustration of the displacement of 'le neutre' and of its essential instability. There is a child's game played in France called the 'jeu du furet' or 'ferret'. One of the players is placed in the centre of a circle formed by all the others, who are linked by a piece of string which they each hold behind their backs. Attached to this string in such a way that it can run along its length is a metal link called the ferret. The player in the middle has to guess which of the players in the circle has the ferret and to stop it before it can be passed on; if he succeeds, he exchanges positions with the player whom he has caught. The point of the game, therefore, is *not to have the ferret*, that is, to be 'neutre'. Each player in the circle becomes 'neutre' in his turn as he gets rid of the object which would mark him out as different from the others. Thus, thanks to this circular movement of exchange, all the players in the circle are 'neutres' and yet none of them is, since each has the object for only an instant. They are neutralisers-neutralised ('neutralisants–neutralisés'). The player in the centre is another and more definitive 'neutre', since he never has the object, never receives it and never passes it on. In other words, it is he who openly bears the mark of absence. Hence his position in the centre. It is thanks to and around him that the object is exchanged in a continual movement of gift and counter-gift. He is the motionless 'axle' of the exchange, the presence and the fixed point within which the game finds both its origin and its limit. His is the only position in the game at which nothing takes place, because nothing goes by. Within the limits of the game the player in the centre finds himself placed differently from the other players; he finds himself placed as if out of the game.

At the same time, however, the player in the centre occupies a commanding position and serves as the game's point of reference, since he is the one who can put a stop to the movement of substitution and circulation. He has the discretionary power of marking a player by the presence of the object, not by giving him the ferret, of course, but by indicating the moment during which the ferret marks the player. At that moment he stops the exchange and suspends the game. The player in the centre himself is never marked; he is, rather, the marking power, which simultaneously produces the difference, exhibits it on one of the players and definitively condemns all the others to a state of being 'neutre'.

Because one of the players possesses the object, however, and finds himself designated as its possessor, he is marked out as different and hence *punished*. He has lost the game. This means that he must lose the object which he possessed and submit to 'castration'. He has received the mark (the object) only to lose it immediately, but very differently than by way of *exchange*. Indeed, he has to change places with the player in the centre; he becomes the centre himself. Thus marked out and neutralised ('neutralisé') in accord with the rules of the game, he becomes the centre of 'neutralisation'. He is exiled to the centre as a neutralised neutraliser ('neutralisé, neutralisant'). In this exchange, however, the player who was in the centre takes the place of the player in the circle who has been caught and now finds himself in the centre in his turn. He receives the object. He is indeed the one who neutralises (castrates) his opponent, but only to return into immediate play the object of which he had despoiled him, thus setting off the exchange once again. The game of ferret is the game of 'le neutre'. That which is desired is forbidden and that which is forbidden is desired. Everyone desires the ferret, but *no one* may possess it and as soon as anyone does possess it he is immediately punished by being deprived of it. Thus a process of infinite substitution is established within the closure of a system of determinate positions. Is this not, however, a possible definition of games as such? Is 'le neutre' itself the game – that game in any case which is introduced into a system by presence, absence and default?

'Le neutre' and philosophical discourse

We must now turn once again to discourse itself and to the possibility of its 'neutralité' and more specifically to that particular project which can be pursued only through discourse, philosophical research. What does our analysis of the problem of 'neutralité' imply for philosophical discourse? What is the status and position of 'le neutre' in such discourse? The guiding thread of our enquiry can be found in a passage from the First Book of Plato's *Republic* which alludes directly to the paradigms of 'le neutre' that we have just been discussing. This text provides the starting point for a type of philosophical research whose development centres around the area where we initiated our own enquiry, namely, the area of overlapping relationships between politics and philosophy, between force and knowledge. In this passage Thrasymachus has just argued that 'The fate of the unjust is happier than that of the just.' Socrates counters this claim with the opposite assertion that the fate of the just is happier than that of the unjust and asks Glaucon, 'And you, Glaucon? Which side do you take? Which statement do you consider the truer?'

'I think that the life of the just man is more profitable.'

'Have you heard', writes Socrates–Plato, 'the list of blessings which Thrasymachus has just assigned to the life of the unjust man?'

'I have', he said, 'but I am not convinced.'

'Then shall we convince him, if we can possibly find a way of proving that his statements are untrue?'[12]

We have here two perfectly opposed theses; the question is, which of them is true. The answer is of more than merely passing interest: for it would appear that morality, politics, the destiny of the individual and that of the state are all involved. Hence the obligation to persuade the other that he is in error and to bring him into the realm of truth and justice in individual and social conduct.

What means of persuasion are employed, however? In the following key text, put into the mouth of Socrates, Plato embarks, ideally at least, upon philosophical discourse:

'Now if we match ourselves against him and give speech for speech, enumerating the advantages of justice, and he speaks a second time, and we speak yet again, then we must add up and measure the advantages enumerated by each party in each speech, and *we shall need a jury to decide between us*. But if we follow our previous form of enquiry, arguing till we come to an agreement, then *we shall be at the same time jury and advocates*.'[13] In this passage Plato contrasts two methods just as previously he had contrasted two theses. It is no longer a question of content, but rather of the form of discourse; more precisely, it is plausible to suppose that, by proposing a method of approach to such problems which makes explicit reference to tribunals, judges and referees, Plato already enters into the very content of the theses under examination (such as the relative utility, advantage, force or power of action of the just as against the unjust). This means that the positions of utterance in philosophical discourse implicitly determine the positions of problems and the content of such substantive assertions as may be made in this same discourse. Hence the attention that the philosopher gives to these positions: for in questions of the nature of justice and force, of power and of truth is involved the force of justice and the power of truth possessed by philosophical discourse itself.

Is there a means (a *dunamis*) of persuading Thrasymachus that he is in error? Will we find a force of truth and justice in philosophical discourse that may triumph over the argument that justice lies in the interests of the stronger? In Pascal's terminology, the problem is to 'fortify justice' by finding a mode of discourse on justice that will carry weight. Thus two themes are intertwined from the very beginning of Book I of the *Republic*. The first is that of 'content' (What can we conclude about justice and force?) and the second that of 'form' (How much force is possessed by true discourse, i.e. the discourse which is to describe the proper relationship of justice and

[12]   Plato, *The Republic*, Book I, 377e–348a, tr. A. D. Lindsay (Everyman edition).

[13]   *Ibid.*, 348a–b.

force?). We have therefore to realise that the interventions in the dialogue of one speaker or another, their standpoints in the discourse which constitutes this opening presentation of the Platonic theory of 'politics', are themselves positions of political force. Furthermore, does not Plato's entire philosophico-political *techne* consist in dissociating the force of discourse from discourse on force and in the skilful transformation within language of Thrasymachus' *discourse on force* (which confines itself to naming as 'justice' what are no more than naked relationships of force) into a *force belonging to discourse*, i.e. a conclusive demonstration of truth. The entire problem is to be found in this beginning or 'overture' which at bottom turns on the notion of a force of judicious language – that is, in all essentials, a force of speculative (theoretical) and practical truth. We can thus see how it is that he who *gives verbal expression to force*, but does so incompetently because he is himself in fact a pure force, finds himself bound *as a slave* to a secondary force, namely that of a rigorous discourse that expresses the truth. Thrasymachus (the etymological meaning of his name is 'Brave Warrior') will be reduced to silence, a silence from which he should never have emerged, and Glaucon – the brilliant, the luminous – will be the one to reduce Thrasymachus' thesis to ruin by means of *discourse*, thus offering Socrates the picture of an adversary henceforward subjugated by a force which he had not sufficiently appreciated, the reflective (reactive) force of philosophical discourse.

The discourse of knowledge

Thrasymachus' subjugation is presented in the *Republic* in two stages of which the text quoted above is the second. The first stage comes when Socrates condemns himself and thus Thrasymachus to the discourse of knowledge by stating boldly that *he does not know* what to conclude about justice and force. Not only does he not know, but he says that he does not know and that he is in any case unable to say what he does know, because he is confronted by a person of authority who does not allow him to speak. By the same token, it is for Thrasymachus to *speak of force*, because he does possess the *knowledge of force* and such knowledge is itself a form of authority or force. Socrates' artifice of disqualifying himself, whether in good or in bad faith, forces Thrasymachus to displace his position of utterance from one of a discourse of force to one of a discourse of the force of knowledge. The trade-mark, as it were, of his ruse in the discourse of the dialogue is his constant posing of questions. Thrasymachus is well aware of this and yet falls confidently into the trap set by the Socratic method and the tactics of ignorance:

'If you have a genuine desire to know what justice is,' he says, 'don't confine yourself to asking questions, and making a show by refuting any answer that is given. You know that it is much easier to ask questions than to answer them . . .'

'. . . The task, I fancy, is beyond our powers (*dunameis*)', replies Socrates, 'and, therefore, you clever people' (clever or terrible ones = *deinoi*) 'should rather pity than scold us.'[14]

Socrates' refusal to respond and his taking refuge in asking questions (a subtle indication, an artful avowal of ignorance) forces Thrasymachus to hold forth with the authoritative discourse of someone who knows what he is talking about. This discourse, furthermore, fails to persuade Socrates and so reveals itself to be a discourse without force:

'I am not convinced', says Socrates; 'give us satisfactory proof . . .' Thrasymachus is astonished. 'Well', he said, 'how am I to persuade you? If you are not convinced by what I have just said, what more can I do for you? Am I to take the doctrine and feed you with it [by force]?'[15] Too late Thrasymachus discovers the ruse and the displacement it has provoked. He believed that his was a discourse of force and all he could present was a discourse of the knowledge of force, a discourse which, he discovers, is itself without force. As Pascal writes, 'Right is open to dispute, might is easily recognised and beyond dispute.'[16] Socrates' guile consists in making Thrasymachus present a discourse of knowledge rather than a discourse of force. Hence, in Pascalian terms, Thrasymachus is simultaneously contradicted and accused.

Henceforth Thrasymachus is prepared to submit to philosophical discourse, a sort of discourse, however, which is to be not so much discourse as such as a series of questions, or, rather, an interrogation. It is the method which will enable Socrates to 'persuade' his opponent. But how? In its discursivity discourse is the presentation of knowledge. One begins to speak because one has knowledge to impart; and one does not finish until one has said what one knows. Hence the attitude of the listener–receiver of a discourse of knowledge; he is the one who learns something as yet unknown to him from someone who knows; 'I am condemned to learn', as Socrates says. In the sort of discourse in which knowledge is displayed and demonstrated it acts as a punishment and a repression. It is a neutralising power ('une puissance neutralisante'), it makes display of a means of imposing obedience, that is the authority that knowledge gives to him who possesses it over whoever does not.

14   *Ibid.*, 336c-e.

15   *Ibid.*, 345a-b.

16   Pascal, *op. cit.*, no. 103 (no. 298).

Hence power and knowledge are mutually implied in discourse and are the source of its force.

As far as Socrates was concerned, however, we have seen that such discourse lacked force, because a different thesis, a contrary opinion, was presented against him in a sort of discursive conflict. How is he to escape from this conflict of discursive forces and from their polemical opposition? This is the question which Socrates puts to Glaucon; it allows of two solutions, of which Socrates adopts one while setting the other aside. But something is presupposed by the question itself, namely, that it is possible and even necessary to overcome the situation of discursive conflict and, going beyond the clash of opposing opinions and claims to knowledge, to attain the unity of a knowledge which is firm, convincing and accepted. It is both possible and necessary to arrive at an agreement; it is both possible and necessary to resolve the tension of opposites. War must give way to friendship – *discors* to *concordia*. The dialectic is already implied in this presupposition. Thus Plato defines a situation of discursive conflict as a contest that takes place on the level of language and this contest he assesses in terms of force and quantity. The rival discourses are set against one another as opposing forces to be weighed up and assessed for what they may respectively contain of what is just and good. Finally, this reckoning up, this measuring of opposing arguments, this double-columned balance sheet of conflicting considerations must be drawn up by a referee or a judge who will settle and debate and, in separating the two opponents, award to each one his due.

Thus we return to the situation analysed above in quite general and abstract terms, *but this time on the level of philosophical discourse*. The opposing forces of discourse submit themselves to the evaluation of an external power which they recognise and which they invest with the energy of their own reflected force. This external power, born of the tension between the discourses in opposition and which then subjects them to itself, is none other than the third term, 'le neutre' ('neutre' and impartial), that is, the pure and empty possibility of synthesis. It is easy to see what is implied in this sort of approach, which Plato suggests only to set aside. The judge or referee is the grand calculator; it is he who draws up the final balance sheet of the discourses in opposition. He assesses, geometrically and arithmetically, the difference between the positions. But if he is capable of so doing, it is only because he has first of all rendered homogeneous the elements involved in the two series, in the two opposing discourses. He has neutralised them. The referee and the judge, to whom Plato refers, neutralise the elements of the discourses that conflict with each other; it is the power of 'le neutre' that makes it possible to judge between the two adversaries. This reduction to a state of homogeneity brings identity into the confrontation and the indifference of sameness into the original difference. There is no longer an opposition of same and other; the problem is no longer posed as a choice between alternatives. 'Le neutre' is precisely neither the one nor the other in the sense that it is a reduction of both to a sameness, of which the token is in its turn the reduction of the difference to a simple quantitative gap.

The objection will be made, however, that Plato explicitly sets aside any reference to some third man or impartial 'neutre' who would submit the discourses to his adjudication. Is not the third man – the human figure of 'le neutre' as third term – characteristic of sophistical discourse, which is by definition competitive and seeks a good, that is to say a favourable, decision from the judge before whom the opponents present their arguments? No doubt, and we shall have to turn in the pages that follow to that other figure of 'le neutre' proposed by Plato – interrogation. If we read 358d and 367b, however, we shall see that, at Socrates' instigation, Glaucon turns to the solution of the conflict which Plato had set aside on 348ab, and 'apes' Thrasymachus to the best of his ability in order that Socrates should defend the opposing argument. The two discourses are opposed to one another in a struggle to the death – but only on the level of representation (in a mimesis of a struggle to the death), since it is one and the same person who maintains the one discourse while believing in or being persuaded by the other.

Questioning

The problem remains, nevertheless, of how to overcome the force of discourse, of how to escape from the power of the discourse of knowledge. The first solution lay in having recourse to a judge on the basis of antilogies which had been carefully neutralised by the judge himself. The second solution will be to turn to the method of questioning in search of an agreement or homo-logy. This solution lies in the recourse to 'le neutre' in search of 'neutralisation'. In both solutions, however, two henceforth abiding ideals are written into the origin of philosophical and educational discourse. These are the ideals of knowledge and of questioning, of science and interrogation; and it is through them that the implicit power of 'le neutre' will become manifest.

It is, of course, to questioning that Socrates turns in order to confound Thrasymachus' force and reduce it to silence throughout the first ten books of the *Republic*. Furthermore, the discussion of the alternative (proposed on 348ab) between antilogies and dialogue suggests the outline of a theory of questioning. For the questioning which constitutes the dynamics of the dialogue does not result from a conflict of claims to knowledge, but from a certain discursive practice which aims first at the progressive establishment of partial agreements between the interlocutors and ultimately at total agreement. This sort of process presumes that at each stage both interlocutors simultaneously generate and evaluate the quality, depth and extent of their own agreement. Within this perspective of infinite totalisation and harmony in truth, the question can be seen as the perpetual reopening of the discourse, the rupture which compels it to continue in the search for a new equilibrium. What then is the question within this framework of face to face dialogue that Socrates proposes?

The question – every question – presupposes an admission of ignorance on the part of the questioner, i.e. an expression of not-knowing something or other. It is because I do not know where X's house is, for example, that I ask a passer-by. At the same time my question implies my implicit recognition that the person to whom I put it will have an answer; but there is always, of course, a risk: that the other will reply 'I don't know'. The very essence of a question lies in this ambiguity of turning to someone else recognised as the source of some knowledge which the questioner does not possess at the same time as he, this other, is characterised by the essential possibility of not-knowing. Otherwise there would be no need to pose a question; I should simply request the other to teach me something of which I was ignorant. Asking a question puts my interlocutor into a position of 'neutre'; I do not know whether he knows the answer or whether he does not. Between the two possibilities of knowledge and ignorance, the knowledge of the other is, at the moment I put the question to him, in a state of instability – 'neutre'. It must equally be understood, however, that the subject of my question – be it X's house, justice, the directions I need or God – finds itself in the same ontological state – that of 'neutralisation'. To ask the question 'Where is X's house?' leaves me open to the reply 'But X never lived here', or 'Who is X that he should have a house in this district?' The question in our example merely asks for something's location, not for its being. Yet it places its being in brackets while waiting for the other's response, just as it takes the other for the moment simply as a source of knowledge, the origin of an answer. The circle of this dialogue will be practically closed when we note that in posing a question concerning the location of X's house I place myself, as poser of the question, in the position of a 'neutre' 'between' knowing and not-knowing. For how would I be able to pose such a question about X's house if I had not already certain indications as to the possibility or probability of finding it somewhere nearby, that is, if I did not possess some 'previous' knowledge, which was nevertheless incomplete in respect of the essential information (or at any rate that information which is essential to me today when I have to meet X at his house) – an incompleteness as a result of which all my knowledge turns into ignorance.

The play of 'le neutre' between the positions of neutraliser ('neutralisant') and neutralised ('neutralisé') is already apparent in this simple example. In a sense, my question neutralises the object concerning which it is asked, just as the lack of the facts, which gave rise to the question in the first place, neutralises all my knowledge at the very moment of waiting upon the other's reply in which my own neutralising Ego is neutralised; for now the other, hanging in the balance between an answer and a non-answer, between knowledge and non-knowledge, appears as a power that is 'neutre', as I myself am with respect to the object in question. Thus the circle, the sphere of 'le neutre' uniting questioner, questioned and question, is closed. Moreover, a precise, positive response to my question would change nothing in regard to this closure in the instability of being of 'le neutre'. For it has already been constituted as such at the one decisive moment at which I asked someone else a question about something. From then on, all the positive discourse which may be offered in reply will do no more than cover up to consign to oblivion this zone of the closure, the zone which lies in fact at the foundation of such discourse and in which the three poles of meaning are bound together in a reciprocal, anonymous 'neutralisation'. For this closure can always be reconstituted and reappear elsewhere; the questioner can always question anew the answer he has received from the other and neutralise in its turn the positive response that is offered to him as an object of knowledge. This philosophical dialogue, of the sort that is conceived, inaugurated and realised by Plato, will consist, therefore, in the constant conversion of 'le neutre' of the question into positive response, 'le neutre' which is nevertheless a necessary condition for the discourse ever to begin or then to progress to a point where it may receive an unquestionable reply, an unquestionable reply to a pure question: that is, the 'neutralisation' of 'le neutre' itself in the positivity of the infinite *telos* of philosophical discourse, the 'neutralisation' of 'le neutre' and its origins by the *telos* of the Good.

Henceforth the problem of philosophical discourse is posed as the problem of its point of origin, the problem of the question of principle which presides at the inauguration of philosophy as first philosophy and which may be taken to designate as 'neutre' the point of departure for all philosophical inquiry, that point of initial questioning in which all subsequent questions will participate. 'I do not know; I state openly that I do not know and I do not believe that anyone knows as of yet. I do not believe that a knowledge of the answer exists previously to my question.' And any reply that may be offered will be seen as a piece of knowledge to be displaced towards 'le neutre' of that which is unquestionable. As we may reread at the end of Book I of the *Republic*: '. . . the result of our conversation' (of this process of questioning) 'is that I know nothing. For when I do not know what justice is, I am hardly likely to know whether it is a virtue or not, or whether he that possesses it is happy or unhappy.'[17] The method of questioning, taken as posing a question *ex arches*, provides the negative contours of the region or space of 'essence', that is to say, the space in which will appear the wholly positive goal of the dialogue, whose attainment will work to its conclusion on a note of harmony and assimilation of opposites.

'Le neutre' as foundation

But does philosophical questioning really provide a point of departure that is 'neutre'? Can the sort of philosophical discourse which proceeds in the interrogative mode pose an absolute, that is to say, an absolutely original question? If this were possible, philosophy would give to itself its own radical point of origin and, in making itself articulate, would include its own foundation in itself. This has, of course, been the ambition of philosophers from Plato to Descartes, from Hegel to Husserl. The problem is at the same time that of 'le neutre'. When philosophical discourse finds its point of departure in a question of principle which is preceded by nothing, this means that the origin of its mode of speaking is to be taken as 'neutre'. This is in general the source of that powerful striving towards 'neutralisation' which is to be found in the first book of the *Republic*, in Descartes' first *Meditation*, in Husserl's *Logical Investigations*, etc . . . – the attempt to constitute by means of doubt, dialectic or eidetic reduction a space that is 'neutre' and empty and from which the owl of Minerva can take off and spread its wings; all such presuppositions, all such prejudices, everything that already exists as 'implicit knowledge' is to be brought to light by the process of questioning and put into question in order to find its originary 'ground', 'le neutre'.

Are we to believe with Thrasymachus that the philosopher is an imposter, that he really knows the answer to his question while, through some crafty dialectical ruse, pretending not to know it? Is

[17] Plato, *op. cit.*, 354c.

the 'neutralité' of the point of departure sought by the philosopher a mere 'aping' of non-science? Is he just disguising his knowledge so that behind this mask he will be able to realise his ends, exercise his force and so persuade the other of his truth? It may be, however, that while the philosopher really believes (as Descartes believed, in Husserl's opinion) that he has attained the 'neutre' and radical zone in which philosophy has its foundations, in fact his pure question is actually over-determined by the cultural, psychological, affective or metaphysical influences which may affect *the particular thinker* through whom the logos finds its way, the *voice* that he borrows from the past, the *language* that he uses, his *listeners*, the direction in which his thought will take him and the reception of his discourse in a particular time, group or class. By means of their successive sedimentation such influences may likewise establish a philosophical tradition, and so overload the question of principle as to reduce it to the consecrated banality of didactic discourse.

The problem is then whether it is possible to pose a pure question? This question is directed not towards a questioned object, but to the very possibility of questioning itself and to what lies at its foundation, as if truly radical philosophical questioning could signify its own foundation – even though 'le neutre', which this questioning seems to reach, consists in the very absence of all foundation. The philosophical swindle would consist, therefore, in presenting as foundations, first principles or *archai*, what is and must be – given the questioning discourse of philosophy – merely the unveiling of the absence of foundation. 'Le neutre', however, which philosophical discourse *takes* as its point of departure, ground and origin, is both the figure and the mask, the manifestation and the dissimulation of that other 'neutre' which is always prior to 'le neutre' of philosophical discourse, because such discourse is forbidden ever to speak it, or again, because speaking it would necessarily bring it down to the level of a figure. Seen in this light, questions appear as a roundabout form of knowledge. It is this necessary deviation that constitutes 'le neutre' of the question as a form of 'neutralisation' and which points figuratively towards that absence of foundation which is presented therein, in however hidden a manner. Such is the insidious violence of 'le neutre' in the asking of philosophical questions. Unless, indeed, the philosophical question takes itself as its own object, thus neutralising itself in its own 'neutralité' in an effort to point towards the foundation which is an absence of any foundation. It may be, however, that such an indication could no longer derive from discourse, be it by questioning or by dialogue. To have any chance of pointing at 'le neutre' instead of figuratively concealing it, philosophical 'discourse' would have to constitute itself as a non-discursive indication, a mere silent gesture with one's finger. 'The god whose oracle is at Delphi does not speak and does not dissemble. He points.' Yet because we must speak, because the philosopher's destiny is speech (the logos), he can designate the absence which grounds his speech only by the intervals between his words, the silence which will melt into their gaps. The modes of such a speaking or 'le neutre' will therefore be the fragment, the *pensée*, the aphorism. Its logic will be the oblique logic of digression, its function that of a criticism which neither grounds nor enhances, but rather dismembers knowledge by chipping cracks in its edifice.

We can make the same problematic observations with respect to the aims and ends of interrogation. Plato indicates such a possibility in the text quoted above by the term *anomologia*, which means progress toward agreement by climbing the steps of partial agreement towards the totalising harmony of the *eidos*. The aim of such interrogative discourse is that of the progressive annulling of differences, the cumulative reduction and 'neutralisation' of opposites in the recognition that it is truly thus and not otherwise. Truth here appears in the discourse which takes it as its *telos* and produces it within itself as a process of 'neutralisation'. It is a truth of the one as a not-the-other, that is, of the one as the negation of the other as other, of the one as the negation of that difference which radically forbids the *homologia*, just as it had radically forbidden any sort of foundation by positing it as an absence.

It may be, then, that this progressive reduction of differences in the unity of a totality could be both the converse and the figure of the 'discourse' to which we referred above, that is, a sort of discourse which has been shattered into fragments and which presents in its very texture the affirmation and maintenance of the difference as such. Philosophical 'discourse' in this sense would be the reductive 'non-neutralité' in which truth appears through the separation of opposites. The itinerary of questioning is here more clearly revealed; not as the 'neutralisation' of opposites (for in that case it would be the swindle of a positive doctrine seeking itself in its own dissimulation), but rather the displacement of a non-limitation *through* and *in* discourse – another way of speaking of difference within sameness, of truth in separation.

'Le neutre' as difference: the utopia of philosophical discourse

This account of 'le neutre' in philosophical discourse, by which it is defined as that which is other than 'neutralité' is thus a very difficult one. 'Le neutre' as pure possibility, as the zero state of synthesis, stands opposed to 'le neutre' as the sustained separation of opposites as to its antitype. 'Le neutre' itself is neither the one nor the other, but rather a sort of pure difference between the two by which they are contrasted and distinguished. The problem of philosophical discourse is thus the following: how can this separation be maintained? How can philosophy *maintain itself* in the separation of the difference? It is not a matter of philosophical discourse seeking to establish itself on the foundation of a centre that is 'neutre', a fixed point from which all differences may be perceived, explained and understood; that would be a position of utterance without any position. Is it not, however, the fundamental claim of philosophical discourse that it is produced from no particular place because it aims at finding the truth of differences through their systematic reduction? The very project of reduction goes with the installation of such discourse in a region located 'outside the circuit', but from which discourse concerning differences may be carried on and taught – and of which dogmatism is the banalised and impoverished form. But is it possible not to establish philosophy in such a spot? Are we able in this day and age to escape such a position by means of philosophical discourse? Is it not already implied by the very fact of engaging in philosophical discourse? We have already alluded to the difficult alternative between a silent pointing of one's finger and a form of speech which can find its way only in the detour, digression and fragmentation of its own continuity. Perhaps there is no tenable position of utterance from which it might be possible to assert and maintain the separation of the difference not only at the origin of philosophical discourse, but also throughout its development. A separation at the point of origin would signify that such discourse constantly precedes its own rationale, a separation in its development that the continuous thread, the chain by which the transfer of evidence from principles to consequences is accomplished, is yet continually broken.

Let us, nonetheless, stake out a few marking-posts of this untenable position. The first can be found in sophistry, or rather in a certain type of sophistical discourse. This is not that type of discourse which is so totally subordinated to its concrete performances that it aims only at judicial or political success, hence forcing on the opposing discourse a confrontation that is to be submitted to the judgement of a superior authority, 'le neutre'. (This is the sort of discourse that Socrates sets aside in the passage from the *Republic* which we used as a pre-text.) We have in mind, rather, sophistical discourse in general, or, more precisely, the philosophy of such discourse in so far as this philosophy presents itself as a *game*, a gymnastics of the spoken word, and in so far therefore as it is eminently teachable. This is a philosophy of *antilogies*, in which one learns to be *both* sides, one after the other, in order oneself to be neither one nor the other, and thus to speak from the position of the gap between them both without ever reducing it. If value in its diacritical essence were to be defined as a difference or opposition between elements, then sophistical speech may be taken as aiming at the accomplishment of certain values rather than at establishing the truth; for such discourse detaches value from any adherence to Being. 'For the means by which we indicate is speech, and speech is not the real and existent things; therefore we do not indicate to our neighbours the existent things but speech, which is other than the existing realities. Thus, just as the visible thing will not become audible, and *vice versa*, so too, since the existent subsists eternally, it will not become our speech; and not being speech, it will not be made clear to another person.'[18]

Such philosophy presents itself not only as a discursive game, but also as the tragedy of such a game, since nothing is communicated through such discourse, which simply develops in pure difference from Being. It is true that the philosopher speaks; but he does so only to uncover the contradictions in all the statements that he utters in his efforts to explain reality. Philosophical discourse is self-defeating by very definition. But if this is so, it becomes henceforth necessary to act – taking full account of the irreconcilability of the extremes, and to act in a way which is as tragic as the discourse itself. As against a philosophy of discourse, so to act is to spring something new and unexpected upon the discourse, something illogical and irrational and taking the form of its concrete working out. So we find ourselves faced with the brutal choice (*kairos*) of one of two irreconcilable opposites, whose force will turn back on the neutral judge or referee to seduce, persuade and enslave him by means of *apate* or *peitho* to an irrational truth.

The other marking-post which we suggest to indicate the whereabouts of this untenable position of utterance lies in a text by Pascal, in which he writes that human grandeur consists not in the idolatry of truth, but in occupying and maintaining oneself in the in-between area of the gap between opposites. 'We show greatness, not by being at one extreme, but by touching both at once and occupying all the space in between. – But perhaps it is only a sudden flash of the soul from one extreme to the other; perhaps greatness only ever lies in a single, as in a glowing ember? – Maybe, but at least that shows how agile the soul is, even if it does not show its range.'[19] This text is written in the form of a dialogue and the very position of the speaker is one which is divided between the one and the other; neither one nor

---

[18] Gorgias, *Treaty of Non-Being* (Sextus Empiricus, 84–5, Loeb, Vol. II, pp. 35 ff.)

[19] Pascal, *op. cit.*, no.681 (no.353).

the other, but rather an exchange between one and the other in the discourse of the dialogue. Pascal speaks from within the distance of the exchange, maintaining himself in the gap between the protagonists between whom his own thought and discourse is distributed. He likewise begins a discourse in the first person: 'I do not admire the excess of a virtue like courage unless I see at the same time an excess of the opposite virtue, as in Epaminondas. . . .' His position is that of an 'I' who speaks of the grandeur of man as a synthesis and totalisation of opposites, extremes and excesses. This position of discourse, however, which corresponds directly to its own content and which, on another level of analysis, *is* its own content, will eventually disintegrate not as the result of any external objection, but because of the widening gap within the position itself; not in the face of some thesis opposed to that maintained a few lines above ('grandeur consists in totalisation'), but rather in that of the other of this thesis ('grandeur consists indeed in the synthetic totalisation of extremes, but such a totalisation is merely the figure – the exhibition and the veiling – of a point of instantaneous movement, the rational figure of a paradox of the infinite'). The distance between the two extremes is occupied by a point displacing itself instantaneously (i.e. with infinite speed) from one position to another. But this same inassignable distance appears in Pascal's own discourse as 'the indiscernible of silence', which breaks its continuity in order to deliver it over to exchange, an indiscernible that may be marked by mere punctuation or by some brief word, and which is itself the position – a position of standing apart – from which Pascal speaks. Of what, then, does this other speak in the inassignable distance of 'le neutre'? Of a grandeur of the soul which is not to be defined in terms of magnitude, extension or of the accumulation of knowledge, of extreme and intermediary virtues, of value and benignity and of all that is in between; but which is to be defined in terms of *agility* – a movement so pure and so rapid that it seems to be at rest, or rather to have sketched a continuous line just as when in the darkness one pokes the embers of a fire and in so doing draws a motionless circle of light. This trace, which is empty if one tries to grasp it at any given point, but which is full when one looks at it against the background of the night, is the very figure of 'le neutre': 'le neutre' which allows itself to be seen only in the figure by which it is concealed. The displacement and fragmentation of the position of utterance which separates itself from itself in order to place itself in its own distance-from-itself is necessary if one is ever to grasp (obliquely and in the form of a hypothesis, of a mere glimpse of a suggestion) the infinite motion of the point – 'le neutre' as pure difference and as the play of the difference. For this movement is a game, a dance, in which the agility of the soul takes the place of its own apparent magnitude.

There is indeed a need for agility, if one is to maintain oneself in the pure infinite difference of extremes – that agility of the soul which will in a single instant traverse the distance between them in a continual displacement of their middle point, the exact middle, the region which is fixed outside space, as the organising centre of that space from which philosophical discourse is uttered. 'Le neutre', which Pascal's text-fragment has enabled us to glimpse as the distance of exchange and as infinite movement, is the non-place, the absent foundation of philosophical 'discourse'.

This, in a word, is the utopia of philosophical discourse: not the nostalgia for a fixed centre, but its other in the gap of the difference.

Neutrality in the university

CHARLES TAYLOR

Montefiore's paper raises the central issues of neutrality in the university: is it really possible, or is the affectation of neutrality rather a sham on the part of liberals, behind which is hidden an unavowable commitment to the *status quo*?

I want to say that neutrality is in one sense possible, and I think desirable, but that in another sense it does repose on commitment, and hence is always relative. I don't really know whether in this I am in disagreement with Montefiore or not. I want therefore to argue, first, that there is no absolute neutrality, and that therefore the goal of a university which is not politically aligned must repose on certain commitments; and secondly, I shall try to outline very briefly what these commitments are; thirdly I shall try to show how they are challenged by many of today's *contestataires*.

Neutrality and value-commitment

Absolute neutrality is impossible in virtually any predicament where neutrality is meaningful, because we need a background of value-commitment (or if 'commitment' is too voluntaristic a word, we need some accepted value background) to give neutrality a clear application. This is not to make the relatively weak and uncontroversial point that we need some value background to *justify taking up* a neutral position relative to any conflict; it is rather the much stronger thesis, that 'neutral' has *no unambiguous sense* without such a background.

I think this is the point which actually emerges from Montefiore's discussion of his key examples. Let us take that of the referee in the football game. In calling a penalty kick against side A in the last moments of the (tied) game, he is obviously in one sense helping B. But this does not suffice for us to accuse him of lack of neutrality, something we would only do if his call were in some way suspect. For he is applying the rules impartially, which means that he is awarding penalty kicks only where fouls are committed.

Now superficially we could argue that there are two ways of describing what he is doing here: 'applying the rule without any favour' and 'giving B an extra chance to break the tie in the dying minute of the game'. Under one description his action is identified as quite in keeping with neutrality, under the other it is identified as highly partial. But the question evidently doesn't rest here; we in fact choose the first description as the relevant one for adjudging the neutrality of the referee; what does it matter that this applying of the rules turns out to win the game for B? That's A's look out; their forward shouldn't have tripped the opposing player.

But why is this description privileged? The answer that this behaviour is what is prescribed by the rules will really not do here. We have here to do with a codified field of behaviour, the game of football, but this only superficially answers our question. We can see this by unpacking further what is implied in the answer. Football is defined by its rules, it is the game it is in virtue of its rules. Thus, to do away with all foul rules would be to transform it into another game; the contest would no longer centre around what we now think of as good football performance, but rather around the ability to kick, trip, manhandle the players of the other team.[1] We would similarly transform the game if we called players for running faster than a certain speed; this would rightly be thought an outrageous thing to do, for we would in effect be penalising one of the elements of what is recognised as good football performance.

Thus we privilege the description 'applying the rule', and judge the referee's performance as neutral because it is of the essence of this being a game of football that he apply these rules. But this doesn't mean that his being neutral is just a matter of stipulation; rather it is that we are operating here against the background of an overriding common interest in the game which is presumed of all who engage in it. Part of what is entailed in that common interest is codified clearly in rules, but it is not the codification which provides us with the background for judging the referee's neutrality, but the presumed common value of the game.

This should be clearer if we look at cases where the rules are not appealed to: there are a number of rules in any game which may not always be adhered to strictly. Or else there are rules which require judgement on the part of the referee which in the nature of things must be exercised within large bounds. Thus a referee can apply strictly or leniently a rule against rough playing. In certain circumstances, the referee may be lenient because otherwise there would be too many stoppages in play and the game would suffer. Let us say that his leniency is impartial; but as a matter of fact, one of the teams is on average more robust, shrinks less from jostling contact with the others, and hence has a slight edge as a result of this greater

---

[1] In other words, to use terms introduced by John Searle, the rules in question here are 'constitutive' of the activity which is playing football, and not simply regulative. Cf. his *Speech Acts* (Cambridge, 1969), pp. 33–42.

leniency, since the members of the weaker team have just a marginal hesitancy at tangling with their opponents, and this means that they often lose possession of the ball. Now in this case, we would in all likelihood agree that the referee was neutral, even though it was rather a shame for the lighter team, and even though we might feel that they may have lost the game because of this. We would still consider that the referee has not sinned against neutrality because we see that he did it for the good of the game, and there were some defensible reasons for his judgement that the game would be improved by this leniency – even if we might not agree with this judgement. We would not feel this way, of course, if we knew that he had done it for no other reason than to make the lighter side lose the game.

Thus our judgement of neutrality reposes on a background of valuation; here a supposed common commitment to the game. Some of what is involved in the game's being played is codified in its rules, and the common interest requires therefore rule-following; but not everything can be expressed in the rules, and we may have to go beyond simply citing the rules, and point to our sense of what a good game is, to justify or identify a referee's performance as neutral. But this background not only justifies the referee; it also provides the context within which the word 'neutral' is given a sense. It establishes certain descriptions of his actions as the crucial ones for the question of his neutrality, while others are simply irrelevant.

This reference to a background seems to be present wherever we use the concept of neutrality. This is because granted two parties in a conflict, and a third which is in actual or potential interaction with them, there are almost bound to be ways in which this third can rightly be described as helping one rather than the other. Thus even poor Belgium found itself invaded in two world wars because its geographical position made Germany's task of invading France much more difficult. Just by being there it was helping the French side. Probably the only way to avoid any such intrication in a quarrel is to have no relation whatever, actual or possible, to either party. In this sense, the inhabitants of Alpha Centauri were 'neutral' in the Vietnamese war. But the inappropriateness of the term here shows that we wouldn't want to use it where the very possibility of alignment was out of the question. But if some party can be aligned, then his non-alignment can always be interpreted as helping someone, e.g. the side which is now winning and will go on doing so unless the balance is tipped the other way.

Now in order to resolve disputes about neutrality we often have in practice to resort to rules; and in the world of international conflict there are such rules, even as there are in football. International law establishes what a neutral power must do and not do to remain neutral. But the mere existence of rules doesn't answer the question why we should accept these as criteria of neutrality, even though in obeying them a power may in other respects be *de facto* helping one side. Why should obeying the rules be given precedence over the *de facto* help? We can answer: that's just what is meant by 'neutrality' in international law. But then the question can return in another form: why is there such a status as neutrality in international law, when in fact all states are *de facto* helping one side more than the other in any conflict? And the answer is that there is a felt sense of overriding common interest in there existing at least the possibility of limiting conflicts, so that all disputes between men don't degenerate into universal wars. This is why we have a set of rules which single out certain types of help rather arbitrarily, it might appear, over others, and stipulate that giving help of this kind constitutes belligerency, while being of help in other ways does not. In the light of this interest in international order, it is right and justifiable that Belgium should not be considered in violation of neutrality just because the deployment of troops made it imperative to sweep across her territory; whereas armed attack on Germany would have been considered such a violation.

The appeal to rules is thus never enough, unless we are just interested in the legal or stipulative question. Otherwise a judgement of neutrality reposes implicitly or explicitly on a background of valuation which selects what is relevant to the judgement, and rules out all the innumerable ways in which the neutral may nevertheless be helping one side.

A background of this kind is also what justifies us in refusing a claim to neutrality, even though the action was in conformity with certain rules. This is what we see in the case Montefiore discusses of the doctor and the Nazi. In order to make the case as dramatic and absurdly extreme as possible, imagine that Hitler is victim of a road accident in France sometime in 1943; a French doctor is called to his side urgently. He knows that Hitler's death will in all probability shorten the war, reduce the German will to resist, in short cannot but produce good. Let us add, quite implausibly, that he knows about the S.S. extermination plans, so that he knows that every day of shortening the war counts. In addition, he has simply to introduce the wrong drug in place of the anaesthetic for Hitler to succumb, and he has a sure-fire escape route.

Perhaps more than half of the world would judge today that he certainly should in these circumstances go ahead and kill Hitler. No plea of neutrality on the basis of the practice of medicine would be accepted by those who think in this way. What is involved in this position? This we can see by setting out what this position denies. The argument for treating Hitler as a normal medical case reposes on the ethic of medicine, the neutrality of the doctor in his purpose of healing which in turn reposes on an overwhelming common interest and commitment of mankind: that the art of healing be used for healing and not for assassination. Clearly it would be a much worse plight if those charged with healing spent as much time killing their enemies as they did curing their friends. The considerations which lie behind the recognition of the status of neutrality, and the status of non-combatant individuals in belligerent countries, weigh similarly in favour of the ethic of the Hippocratic oath with the implied neutrality of the doctor.

But those who would urge our imaginary French doctor to do away with Hitler would argue that this case was exceptional, in that we are dealing here with a man who has declared war on all the values of civilisation which underlie the medical ethic, a man dedicated to destroy the neutrality of medicine and science, and who would respect no neutrals. Hence in this exceptional case, the very considerations which normally weigh overwhelmingly in favour of the neutrality of the doctor should incline us to break the Hippocratic oath. The exception proves the rule, as it were. Obviously, this is a dangerous line of argument; and as the memory of the horrors of Nazism sinks into the past, we will probably find that fewer and fewer people would approve of our French doctor's doing him in – unless, of course, the very values underlying medical neutrality disappear, a possibility not to be too lightly discounted.

But dangerous or not, this argument is clearly understandable and even persuasive. And its persuasiveness rests on its redefinition of the background of valuation against which neutrality is to be judged. Just because medical neutrality, as any neutrality, is not absolute, but assumes a background of overriding common commitment beyond the struggle, there can be cases where, since what is at stake in the struggle is precisely the object of these common commitments, neutrality of this kind is no longer a valid plea; in these cases we are dealing, in the old natural law language, with 'enemies of Mankind', an appelation to be used sparingly, but which must sometimes apply.

The value background to university neutrality

All of this applies to the problem of neutrality of the university. But before examining in more detail what the value background is here, it might be well to answer a possible objection to our language: perhaps the word 'neutral' is badly chosen, implying a kind of disinterest in the conflict concerned; but the university should be vitally interested in the political life and struggles of the society in this sense, that its political scientists, sociologists, philosophers etc. ideally should be concerned with this political life, and many of them will as individuals be actively engaged in one way or another. But if 'neutral' is an unfortunate word, we have to find some other here like 'non-aligned', for instance, following a well-known precedent and for some of the same reasons. For we want to make the case that the university as an institution cannot be engaged on one side or another of the political struggles of society. In other words, though university people, students and teachers, will and should be concerned with and involved in political life as students and/or participants, the university as an institution must not determine or restrict the form or direction of this concern or involvement. There are obvious limitations to this general principle, touching such things as chemical research for a programme of bacteriological warfare, which no member of a university should be allowed to do; but these will be the exceptions which will relate to the general rule very much as the case of the French doctor called to Hitler's side related to the general medical ethic.

This relation, as we saw above, can only be stated in terms of a background of valuation; what is this background in the case of university non-alignment? I should like to set out two related parts of what I think this background is.

The first covers ground which has been well trodden by John Stuart Mill: truth, particularly important truth, can be found, or in cases where we cannot speak in such clear-cut terms, truth can be approached, only where different beliefs, different theories, different manners of seeking truth are allowed to dispute with each other. The necessity for intellectual polarisation is fundamental and inescapable, so that even where one is sure that one theory or approach is superior to its rival, one nevertheless loses by prohibiting this rival because the acuity and depth of one's perception of that truth one sees declines when it is no longer forced to define itself against rivals.

This is, of course, a liberal belief. It was powerfully stated by J. S. Mill in his 'Essay on Liberty'.[2] But it is also a considerably older doctrine: it is implicit in the view that the truth can only be approached through dialectic, that we rise towards it only through the negation

---

[2] When the truth cannot be challenged by free discussion, he said, 'instead of a vivid conception and a living belief, there remain only a few phrases retained by rote; or, if any part, the shell and husk of the meaning is retained, the finer essence being lost'. Everyman Edition, p. 99.

of half-truth and error. This view is as old as philosophy, as Louis Marin shows in his contribution to this discussion.

We might usefully apply this thesis to our subject itself, and define this value background further by showing in what ways it may be negated, what it is therefore opposed to. There are in fact two major challenges that have been levied against it. The first is the more fundamental one, which questions the value put on the discovery of the truth. Granted that the more abstruse refinements of truth about man and the world can only be approached through dialectic, should we therefore retain an open field of opinions even though this in some way distracts from the struggle for betterment or social transformation? Of course, it can be challenged whether the suppression of free discussion really does contribute to betterment, or more realistically, in what conditions it really becomes necessary for the general good; but leaving this challenge in abeyance for the moment, we can see the makings of a case against the value background of university non-alignment whose basic thrust is that the kind of approach to truth which goes dead in the absence of dialectic is a luxury. It is indecent to want to maintain it when it is at the expense of the meeting of crying needs of the many and/or the universal betterment of mankind. If university neutrality is in fact helping to maintain an oppressive system, why should we cavil at sacrificing the arcane joys of the search for truth through dialectic in order to liberate mankind?

This is a view which has cropped up a number of times in the past in different forms. The Russian nineteenth-century radical Chernyshevsky came to consider the cultured life of the minority an expensive luxury which was indefensible in the face of mass poverty. As long as men were in misery, one should be willing to trade the works of Shakespeare for a pair of boots by which the barefoot might be shod.

The second challenge to this background is one which accepts the value of truth but holds that we have now discovered it. The truth being clear, it is the worst form of dalliance with reaction to permit the continued propagation of old errors. Free discussion can only be permitted within the limits set by the established truth. This is a stance which draws its strength from one strand of the tradition of the Enlightenment, the belief that we have finally surmounted religious, metaphysical, confused or ideological forms of thinking and founded a clear and unambiguous science of man, society or history. This belief has been continued after the eighteenth century not only by positivism, but also by the Marxist tradition, or strands in it. The belief by itself doesn't automatically bring about the dogmatic stance above, but it does provide the basis for it.

These two challenges can, of course, be combined. There are certain fields of enquiry where the optimistic enlightenment claims seem to have some grounding, viz., natural sciences. Even here a defender of the value of dialectic would point out that while routine 'normal' science (in Kuhn's phrase) would not be adversely affected by the foreclosing of discussion, those innovations would which involve the questioning of further definition of the underlying principles which are never fully formulated in the way that theories and observations are.[3] But one could in focusing only on presently available technological applications argue that all 'useful' knowledge was clearly and unambiguously available without dialectic; and that what wasn't so available should be classed as an unpardonable luxury, a secret vice of the few.

Another part of the background which should briefly be mentioned here underlies a great deal more than simply university neutrality. This is the personalist view that freedom of discussion of doctrines is part of and inseparable from the freedom of the person. In those areas in which our beliefs are closely tied up with our commitments, our values, our identity, the suppression or restriction of a belief is inseparable from the oppression of persons. Hence even if, by hypothesis, a belief is known to be wrong and pernicious, there are grounds for opposing any restrictions on it. Of course, this personalist view is generally closely interwoven with the dialectical view we have just examined, so that there will rarely be a case in which we can speak of beliefs of this range – about the nature and meaning of human life, man's relation to nature, history etc. – as simply wrong or simply right. Rather a personalist will tend to see our intellectual predicament as one in which any important truth is differently refracted in different lives; it is something inherently hard to define, precisely because we can only come at it through our life and life-situation. Hence the only hope to achieve somewhat more adequate definitions lies in the sensitive confrontation of ours with others.

The personalist view thus meshes closely with the dialectical thesis above. It adds to it another range of supports: important truths are difficult to define because they are bound up with the self-expression and identity-formation of diverse human beings; the only approach to more adequate formulations thus lies through the confrontation of different views, and any restriction of this confrontation can only make truth less accessible. But this personalist argument is a recent addition to the long history of the dialectical view.

---

[3] In fact this seems generally recognised: even in countries where there is a severe restriction on political and ideological discussion, like the Soviet Union, natural scientists have considerably greater leeway, in spite of occasional spectacular lapses like the Lysenko saga.

Contrary to the belief of some contemporary radicals, it is not part of the tradition of classical liberalism, but comes to us from one of the great reactions to the Enlightenment, the Romantic anthropology of self-realisation, which in other forms also underlies Marxism and modern nationalism.

Now it might be questioned whether this personalist view has anything to do with the question of university neutrality; this question will be raised by those in the academe who hold that such deep and fundamental beliefs, which are the stuff from which *Weltanschauungen* are made or identities are formed, have no relation to the search for truth as it should be carried on in a university – unless it be as objects of this search. This because such beliefs are thought to lie beyond an epistemological pale, to be too murky, uncertain and undecidable to be objects of serious concern to the serious student of man, nature or society. That this temper is well represented in the modern university can hardly be doubted; indeed, it seems to be easily dominant in university departments dealing with the science of man and philosophy in the Anglo-Saxon world. One of its paradigm expressions is the belief in value-free sciences of man, whereby questions of 'value' or fundamental commitment are thought to be separable from those concerned with scientific discovery. Properly understood, the former are thought to be matters of personal choice, and not decidable the way the latter must be by intersubjectively valid reason – although, of course, that certain value choices are made can itself be a fact deserving of study.

We will look briefly later at the question to what extent the spread of this temper has helped to obscure the value background of university neutrality which those who share it strongly desire to defend. But at the moment I should just like to say that this attempt to separate questions of value commitment or *Weltanschauung* from those amenable to science is fundamentally misguided. Rather the basic approach we take to the study of man is inseparably bound up with certain major issues separating different *Weltanschauungen*. One need only look at a doctrine like mechanism, which underlies a family of approaches in psychology, politics and so on, constitutes a family of traditions in philosophy, and is closely bound up with views about man and his capacities which enter into the definition of our value commitments. The dispute over mechanism is interwoven, indeed, into the debate over moral reasoning which opposes the proponents of *Wertfreiheit* and their adversaries. In the light of this, it would appear to be a kind of empty posturing to go on claiming that one abstracts from such fundamental questions in one's scientific work in psychology, sociology, politics, or whatever.

If this is correct, then the personalist view is also relevant to university neutrality. Our grounds for defending the unrestricted choice of option by university people is not only that the interests of truth demand it, but that this freedom is bound up with their self-realisation as persons – and this, of course, even where their positivist prejudices make them incapable of admitting the connection between their basic beliefs and their intellectual work. But it is obvious that this personalist consideration has relevance far beyond the walls of the university.

What are the possible negations of this personalist background to neutrality? Parallel to our earlier discussion, there could be a negation which rejected the whole idea of self-realisation, such as might be put forward by a positivist heir to the Enlightenment. But, for two reasons, this is not likely to arise: first, the positivistically-inclined heirs to the Enlightenment are generally defenders of neutrality in our day. This is not necessarily or always the case; we saw earlier how one strand of the Enlightenment tradition, its claim to have founded a certain science, can justify the banishment of past 'error'. But in our day, the threat to the university has come so much from other ideologies – communism, fascism – that the mainstream of the Enlightenment has been on the defensive. But secondly, the anthropology of Romantic self-realisation has become so widespread and deep in modern civilisation that it infects everyone, even those who have little place for it in their philosophy. Thus even positivists feel a sacred horror at the repressive restrictions which stop people from doing their thing.

Hence the more common challenge to the personalist background comes from within the Romantic heritage; it accepts the language of self-realisation, but holds that the shape of this self-realisation is already clearly revealed, and that men must follow it. Those who stand out with different opinions cannot but be either blind or ill-willed. It is a dalliance with the continued enslavement of human potentiality to tolerate them. This objection to the personalist background to neutrality thus brings us back into the issues raised by the dialectical view: how can the truth be made clear? It is these which we can expect to see arising in the current contestation of the non-aligned stance of the university.

The challenge to university neutrality: 1

This discussion of the background of value underlying university neutrality should help us in examining the challenge to this neutrality implicit in much of today's student contestation. We saw in the first section how an understanding of background enabled us to distinguish an irrelevant challenge to neutrality, such as that which would tax a referee for helping side B when he calls the penalty kick, from one which builds on the background, such as we would make to our French doctor should he plead medical neutrality in order to save Hitler's life. These two can both be distinguished from the kind of challenge we looked at in the last section, where the background itself is called into question.

Now we cannot treat present day contestation as presenting *a* challenge to university neutrality, for in fact there are several strands in it. Most notably, there is a not too clearly marked but nevertheless very important line between those who challenge the university for not living up to its vocation of neutrality and hope to return it to this vocation, and those who point to the alleged or real lapses from neutrality as proof that the ideal is misguided. The line may be hard to draw, for both kinds of contestation pick up the same issues, the one to achieve the abolition of certain practices and institutional ties, the other in order to show the inner contradictions of an institution which is constantly in violation of its own constitutive values, and which is thus on the road to suppressing itself according to the dialectic of history.

It is with the second, more radical type of contestation that we shall mainly be concerned here, since the main aim is to examine the grounds and limits of the goal of university neutrality. But we shall constantly have to identify this more radical challenge in relation to the less radical. Both, as we said above, come in the form of pointing to real or alleged lapses of neutrality. These can perhaps be fitted roughly into four categories:

(i) The university departs from neutrality in being involved in war research. Considered purely as an area of research in which some of its members engage, war research might not be thought to impugn the neutrality of the university as such. Rather, we can imagine the plea that the very neutrality of the university forbids its interfering in the freely-chosen research projects of its members. To which many of us would reply, as was suggested in the case of bacteriological and chemical warfare above, that this is one of the exceptions which must be made, which 'prove the rule', that is, which are based on the very background value which underlies the neutrality in question, like the French doctor case.

But the problem for university neutrality is not posed by the research projects of particular individuals, but rather by the institutional tie-up which generally goes with military research. The university or some of its departments becomes increasingly financially dependent on the military, and this ends up having a noncoercive but real influence on the orientation of research taken up by its members in the future.

But more fundamentally, it is argued, the university in accepting these ties is placing its valuable expertise at the disposal of whatever project the military are engaged in, and this is a flagrant breach of neutrality; it is in fact direct alignment with one side.

(ii) Similar arguments are made about research tie-ups with industry ending up distorting the university budget and/or such tie-ups themselves constituting alignment with one side. But in addition, the university serves the economy (iii) and by extension those who dominate it, by forming competences needed in the economy. The obligation laid on the university to do this, either by government in return for budgetary support, or by private industry itself, can be objected to in the same two ways: as a distortion of the normal balance of university studies, or as a taking of sides.

(iv) At a more profound level, the liberal university is accused of creating the ideological justification of the system. The very notion of value-free social science is seen as a barrier to a critical study of the society. A radical critique cannot be received since its conceptualisation would cut across the fact–value dichotomy. At the same time, it is alleged, the supposed value-free picture of reality which we are given by mainstream sociology, political science, and so on, propagates unavowed definitions of normalcy, according to which radical challenges to the *status quo* are at best misplaced if not actually symptomatic of pathology.

This last criticism is obviously at a different level from the earlier ones, and so I should like to handle it separately. There are, however, a number of common issues to the first three which justify taking them together.

We saw that in connection both with military research, industrial research and the training of skilled personnel there were two criticisms made. The first was that the university's balance is upset or distorted by the goals imposed on it by the supplier of funds, military or civil, private or public. But what defines the 'normal' balance, against which this distortion can be measured? There are two possible answers to this question. One is to say that the normal is the state in which members of the university choose their field of research with the minimum of external interference or limitation. It is the possibility of disinterested research which is being defended here, and the ideal sought is the old one of autonomy of the university.

If this is the standpoint from which the criticism is levelled, then it is obviously firmly based in the value of neutrality, and its aim is to realise this neutrality more fully, to defend it against encroachments. For the ideal autonomy is grounded in the same background of value as neutrality, that the options made in the pursuit of truth should be maximally free from restrictions and limitations. But once we state this ideal we can see that it can never be totally realised. Since the university always has been and will have to be paid for by society, it will always have to, and has always had to, come to some kind of *modus vivendi* whereby it fulfils some of society's goals as well as those defined by the research goals of its members. The crucial questions concern the degree of this autonomy and the scope of disinterested research which society will support; and there are very decisive differences here in the historical predicaments of universities. But the goal of a university community without any obligations at all with regard to research and training to its society or any outside institution, this is a chimera. Certain favoured portions of the university community can enjoy this status, but never the community as a whole – as long as it must rely on resources made available to it by society. The only totally free university in this sense would be one operating as a self-sufficient commune – not a model likely to become general in our world of fat-cat dons and well-fed students.

Thus those who object to servicing industry by research or training *per se* cannot be arguing from the standpoint of the previous paragraph. Our present predicament does indeed call for a struggle to extend university autonomy and a vigorous defence of that autonomy attained. The western university is threatened by the growing power of the giant corporation. It is both in danger of being lured into a subordinate role by the corporation's growing control of social wealth, and of being bludgeoned into line by government in the service of the dominant values of corporate capitalism. The university's vocation must lead it to oppose these values, and the opposition will become sharper as affluence increases. For inherent in the values of the university is the aspiration to use increased social wealth to liberate more people for study, thought, research and creation; and this means a university which doesn't just serve as training ground of one age group, but which people can enter and ˙leave more than once, and at very different stages of life. For the contemporary corporate system, on the other hand, increased wealth must serve the ends of increased production in a never ending circle, and university expansion, as any other kind of investment, can only be justified by this goal.

But the very nature of this struggle by the university to be true to its basic purpose, concerning as it does the conditions and extent of its access to social wealth, presupposes that the university come to a *modus vivendi* with society. An objection to there being *any* tie-in and servicing of whatever kind with the outside cannot really be grounded in the concern for autonomy, or only at the expense of

ignoring the most fundamental conditions of the university's operation. The objection here seems generally in fact to be based on
another idea of normalcy, not that of disinterested research and
autonomy at all, but rather that of the servicing of other institutions
and forces.

But this brings us to the second criticism made of these tie-ups
with military and industry, that they constitute *per se* alignment. Let
us see what underlies this criticism. Clearly, when it is a matter of
helping the Pentagon to develop new arms, or devise 'counter-
insurgency' strategies, we are dealing with a very clear case of alignment, and the demands of neutrality are that universities break
these ties.[4] Similarly, in the case where a department of industrial relations is retained by a firm to cope with its employees; or where a
university feeds information to employers about its students without their knowledge or consent. But how about cases in which geo-
logists do exploratory work for oil or mineral extraction companies,
where this is in conformity with the development policy of the
country concerned? Or cases in which universities do research for a
military establishment which is set up to fulfil international peace-
keeping missions under the U.N.? And how about the training of
engineers, doctors, lawyers, as such?

A global objection to all of these and other such, as long as the
university operates inside the present system, is equivalent to saying
that there is no such thing as non-alignment because our entire historical predicament is one of radical struggle in which no institution
nor mode of activity can be neutral. For instance, if we think of geo-
logists doing exploratory work for mining companies as abandoning neutrality, it can only be because we think of these companies as
being participants in a state of war of a total kind, one in which their
enemies are striving to hamper all their activities, so that any help in
keeping these activities going is an intervention in the struggle. Analogously, we would have thought of a geologist helping the Nazi
government to find additional sources of war-required minerals in
occupied Europe as giving aid and comfort to their side in the war.
We should note that this kind of total war is not synonymous with
the class war of Marxist theory. A Marxist geologist might easily
undertake exploration for mining companies since the struggle is
not over whether or not to develop natural resources, but rather
how, for whom, under whose control. Nor will the issue be decided
by whether or not the activity of development is sabotaged or man-
ages to carry on, but rather by the mobilisation of political power

---

[4] Although the inefficacy of 'counter-insurgency' advice, owing to the escalating gap between pretension and actual achievement in social science, probably makes it on balance objectively helpful to insurgents; at least the money isn't being spent for something genuinely
harmful like napalm.

against the present regime of ownership and control. Hence while there are circumstances imaginable in which it would be tactically useful to deny the companies the possibility of exploration, the notion of class war does not usually entail the attempt to prevent ongoing economic activity; rather this is distinguished from the system of private appropriation which is made the target.

The notion of total war in which all forms of collaboration with industry or any kind of military is a breach of neutrality only makes sense if we hold not only that there is a class war whose issue must be the overthrow of the present system, but also that this war has reached a final show-down in which all ties must be broken: the kind of situation in which we might call for a general strike to initiate the revolution.

It would seem that many student contestataires believe that something like this is at hand, and this is their ground of challenge to the supposed neutrality of the university. But it is clear that in a situation of this kind university neutrality is an impossibility. For we have seen that since the university is paid for by society it cannot refuse all forms of servicing of that society. The university can only make this kind of global refusal by ceasing to exist.

Now in a genuine situation of show-down the university would no doubt go into abeyance; and this of necessity. And to the extent that this abeyance was chosen and not just imposed by the civil war situation, it would be justified as a kind of rule-proving exception, a temporary abandonment of the search for truth in the name of the values underlying it. But in fact, of course, our situation is far from being one of show-down in the usual sense. If it is a show-down, it is rather one which is to be drawn out over decades and perhaps longer, and thus really a situation of an entirely different kind. So that the demand to break all ties with the system is not a call to temporary abeyance, rather it is an invitation to the university to die gloriously as a martyr in a struggle which it cannot live to see victorious; to make a sort of Paris Commune of the university community as a whole. This is what is involved in the 'critical university', in the sense of one which is aligned in total war against the existing system.

It should now be clear that there are two very different kinds of critique, mutually incompatible, underlying the challenge to the university's tie-in with military and industry. One is in the name of autonomy and hence wants to realise the value of neutrality by cutting certain ties, and creating a *modus vivendi* which maximises the university's autonomy. The strategy needed here is to find allies in the society which will support the goal of an autonomous university. In capitalist society, universities need to struggle particularly vigorously against the encroachments of large corporations, and in the United States, of the military as well. The other challenge is rather in the name of another total alignment; the strategy called for is a fight *à outrance* against the system, which involves cutting all ties; and the invitation to the university is to die with honour.

Now in the context of a real show-down in which the abeyance of the university would be short-lived, we can understand university people responding to this appeal as a rule-proving exception. But when the struggle is seen to be one of decades, then we must be making a more radical choice. And in fact what often seems to underlie this stand is what we identified as the first negation of the value background of neutrality, a depreciation of the kind of search for truth that can only be pursued in a free university or some analogous institutions as a luxury that we cannot decently afford. This position thus seems to be based on a rejection of the value background of neutrality, rather than on a plea for a rule-proving exception. The search for truth is a luxury enjoyed by the few while the many go through the agonies of exploitation and repression; if we need to sacrifice it to carry on the struggle, we should be glad to do so. Thus no matter if the university will go under in taking a stand of total alignment with the revolution; to the extent that this sacrifice helps the cause, it will be justified; ours not to count the cost.

The position here is one of moral concentration which we are familiar with in revolutionary thought. By that I mean that all moral questions are concentrated in a single issue. No independent value is allowed to stand. To the extent that this is at stake in contestation today, then the university's neutrality is effectively challenged; for its value background is denied. But then whoever is right, a certain kind of neutrality is no longer possible, for the university cannot be neutral towards *these* aspirations. The demands of university neutrality are that it opposes this image of its vocation uncompromisingly.

The challenge to university neutrality:2

Thus the first negation of the background to neutrality underlies one form of critiques (i), (ii) and (iii). I should now like to show how the second negation underlies critique (iv). This, it will be remembered, challenges the university as the fabricator of justifying ideologies for the society. In particular the notion of a value-free science of man is seen as an obstacle to a radical critique, while the content of this science is full of unavowed concepts of normalcy supportive of the *status quo*. I want to grant these two accusations against mainstream social science, in part because I agree with them, but mainly because getting this argument out of the way enables us to bring out clearly what the standpoint is from which the criticism is made.

Now here, as in the above discussed criticisms, there are two not always separated but very different standpoints. One arguing from the background of neutrality, the dialectical and personalist views, is strongly critical of value-neutrality and the kind of science of man built on it and related notions. But another strand argues from the impossibility of value-freedom (*Wertfreiheit*) to the unreality of neutrality of the university. It calls instead for an aligned science of man, aligned with the forces of progress. And this is evidently a very different thesis.

The first strand, in other words, responds to the ideology of *Wertfreiheit* as an unconscious support of the *status quo* by a critique of it as ideology, i.e. as thought not fully conscious of its underpinnings and hence of its content. The point of this critique is to bring certain fundamental issues to discussion which are buried under the false pretence of value-freedom, issues centring around the premisses about man, society, explanation etc., which underlie this science and its unavowed valuations. So the aim of this critique is not to do away with a given school, but to enlarge and deepen the confrontation with it; the critique is pre-eminently based on the dialectical thesis. Thus the critique, while denouncing the supposed neutrality of theories and findings in human science, requires absolutely a neutral *context* in which this confrontation can take place; and it is the university's vocation to be this context.

By contrast, the second strand responds to the ideology of *Wertfreiheit* as an enemy to be defeated and replaced. That there is no neutral science of man is taken not as grounds for a deeper confrontation between views shorn of their specious claim to lie beyond the battlefield of world-views, but rather as a call to make a radical choice and to do away with pernicious theories supportive of an intolerable *status quo*. But this is of course incompatible with there being any intellectual confrontation which is more than a sham. But on the dialectical view presented above, this must mean that our search for truth will suffer, that our grasp on it must atrophy, even assuming that we have opted for the 'side' which is nearer to the truth. So that those who call on us to choose in this way must reject this thesis in one way or the other, either by the claim that truth doesn't matter, or by the more direct negation of this view, that truth is clearly accessible without dialectic confrontation with error or with its less adequate formulations. In so far as the claim is to a *science* of man aligned with the revolution, the plea cannot be the first, that truth will be unattainable but unimportant; rather it is the second, that the truth can be clearly and unambiguously grasped by a new science outside all dialogue with the old. Thus on this view, the university cannot be allowed to be a neutral context of confrontation. It is not now, because it is dominated by the ideology of *Wertfreiheit*; nor should it be so in future, for our task is not to create a genuine confrontation, but rather, accepting alignment as inevitable, to shift that alignment.

There is a disturbing convergence between the proponents of *Wertfreiheit* and their most violent critics. Both confound equally this issue with that of the possibility of a neutral university, so that both these are thought to stand and fall together. And the convergence is not just a chance one. Rather the unconscious dogmatism of the *Wertfreiheit* ideology has contributed to discredit the very ideal of university neutrality, and has made it appear inextricably linked with an unavowed defence of the *status quo*. This must be so as long as the two kinds of neutrality are confused.

The confusion reaches the point in some statements of the radical position where it ends up accepting the substance of the belief in a value-free science. The model on which these base their view of the sciences of man is provided by the natural sciences, where findings which are neutral in the sense of lending themselves to a number of uses, are taken up into technology and given a use through social policy. Thus the findings of nuclear physics are neutral between peaceful and warlike uses; it is public policy which decides. The notion of a 'policy science' as used by Lasswell reposes on the same picture: there are findings of human science which are neutral in themselves, but are applied to various policy ends. A policy science is the selection from among the neutral findings germane to a certain end. Those who are critical of value-freedom naturally regard this claim to achieve value-free findings with the scepticism it deserves.

But we often hear radicals who attack social scientists for lending themselves to such projects as the development of a counter-insurgency policy. Social scientists who engage in this kind of thing obviously think of themselves as having something of the status of chemists and physicists doing war research. In fact, of course, the comparison is ludicrous, as events continually show. Now one can certainly claim that the intentions of such social scientists are blameworthy, but to blame them for actually giving help to the Pentagon and its imperialist schemes is to take their scientific claims seriously; it is to allow that there really is a neutral science of insurrection and hence by extension historical change available to all regardless of option, as there is unquestionably such a science of nuclear physics. But this is precisely what should be questionable for those who are sceptical of *Wertfreiheit*. There is in fact no understanding of historical change which is in purely neutral terms, and those who would try to treat it in such terms will inevitably misunderstand it grossly. One can understand it only if one can become sensitive to the aspirations at stake which can of course be done without sharing them but cannot be done from just any option. Thus the criticism which puts political scientists working on counter-insurgency into the same bag as chemists working on germ warfare is confused. They belong in the same category as to intention, but in no sense as to the real role they play. To put them in the same category is to accept the substance of the *Wertfreiheit* ideology. It is a simple call to change employers.

We can see the confusion in the call to behaviour scientists to cease working for counter-insurgency and turn their talents to aiding the cause of insurrection if we consider it in the light of an orthodox Marxist view. From this perspective, there is held to be a deeper understanding of historical change available to those who have broken through the ideological limitations of bourgeois social science. But this new understanding is not of neutral fact, it is inseparable from an understanding of the moral necessity for revolution. Bourgeois behaviour scientists working on counter-insurgency are thus bound to fail because they lack the understanding of the problem at the depth required to affect the course of events. The call to such scientists must thus not just be to change their employers, but to alter as well their definitions of human science.

The confusion of some contemporary radical statements is that they both want to make a rather grossly simplified Marxist claim to a superior science based on the revolutionary perspective, *and* want to blame bourgeois social scientists for putting their expertise at the disposition of the Pentagon instead of the peasant guerilla. But if the first claim is right, then it cannot in a crucial sense be the same expertise which is available to both, and indeed, that available to the Pentagon is highly suspect. The desire to take sides against bourgeois social scientists has pre-empted a dialectical understanding of bourgeois social science. The 'critique' of social science which arises from such radicalism is naturally a pretty thin affair.

What I have called the dialectical view above is closer to Marxist than this type of 'radicalism'; but it is separated from dogmatic Marxism in that it supports no claim to a pre-eminent perspective which has gone beyond all ideology. Rather it sees all perspectives as amenable to an ideological critique from their opponents, and hence no one of them can be accorded the right to sole possession of the field of human science. The radical challenge to university neutrality, on the other hand, seems to repose either on a crude version of the dogmatic-Marxist claim to transcend the history of thought in a 'scientific socialism'; or, even worse, on a simple call to take sides in a radical show-down which ends up swallowing wholesale the crucial intellectual pretensions of mainstream social science.

This latter refers us back to the first line of challenge to a non-aligned university which we discussed above in connection with the university's relation to society, the military and the economy. Putting this together with what we have gleaned from the critique of the university as the fabricator of ideology, we can identify one strand of the contestation in the university which involves a total rejection of the background to neutrality. This is based partly on a simplified Marxism and partly on an apocalyptic reading of the historical predicament as one of absolute rupture between opposing forces, the total war of the final show-down, but which can be of indefinite duration. This could require the university to break all links whatever with the existing order and work with total commitment for those forces which are interpreted as opposing this order. In its view of the intellectual life of the university, this strand hovers between two notions: one which accepts the substance of the value-free definition of the findings of social science, but insists that these be put at the disposal of the revolution rather than the system; and the other which is founded on a cruder version of the Marxist belief in a science which utterly escapes ideology. On the first view, we are called upon to go on practising the same kind of science but under the direction of a different set of extra-university goals; on the second view we practise a different kind of science but without any contact with the earlier kind. In neither case is there any confrontation of perspectives.

Finally, we cannot expect the system to tolerate this kind of total opposition, and so we must look forward to a glorious martyr's death for the university whose legend will stand like that of the Commune until the ultimate triumph of the Revolution. There is no way in which the university can be neutral towards this critique. This challenge defines one of the limits of non-alignment: the university can only oppose this vocation uncompromisingly.

The challenge to the university itself

This discussion has illustrated the thesis that there is no absolute neutrality, that the concept to be meaningfully applied requires a background of value commitment; and this background while defining and enjoining neutrality in some contexts, forbids it in others, i.e. in those where the background values are themselves attacked.

The western university today appears to face two such challenges, towards which it cannot be neutral. The first is that of a society dominated by what can be given the shorthand name of corporate capitalism. This pushes the university towards an increase in numbers, but begrudges the investment required to increase the number of those who can effectively study, think and develop. For this would require not only a greater investment per student, but also a radical reorganisation of career structures permitting people to go to university at the moment in their lives when they want to rather than at an arbitrary point in the life cycle, without paying a penalty in their future career. The resultant explosive growth of the university as a training institution has put a tremendous strain on it, and this has helped to set off the second challenge which has arisen within it.

But this challenge, whose scope we cannot measure now – it is much more intermittent than that of the corporate system – surely links up with deep strains, and even threatened breakdown, in our civilisation. The university has been the locus where a more widespread malaise can most easily find expression. In this sense, if in no other, the theory of the 'weakest link' has a validity. Whatever its origins, important strands of this contestation of the university are based on a complete rejection of its constitutive values.

These two challenges feed on each other. Contestation is provoked by the pressures of the corporate system; and the more destructive actions of contestataires are grist to the mills of law and order which would bring the university back to its 'function' in society. This mutual reinforcement of its enemies points to tough times ahead for the university. But it should be clear that in face of these options no neutrality is possible.

Before a student is admitted to the University of Singapore, he has, like students entering all the other institutes of higher learning in Singapore, to obtain a Certificate of Suitability from the Ministry of Education to prove that he is not politically subversive. Once in the university, he will be under a Vice-Chancellor who is, at the same time, a senior Cabinet Minister for Science and Technology, and the Chairman of the ruling People's Action Party. And in 1969 all first-year students, together with some Students' Union leaders and the lecturers in the departments of philosophy, political science and so-ciology, appeared before the Prime Minister to be warned against being influenced by their teachers, especially foreign or expatriate teachers, into adopting postures and attitudes which are irrelevant to Singapore. Students were told to think for themselves, but they soon learnt that there were severe limits to what they should think, for their leaders had also been further warned that if they stepped beyond certain limits (which were left ominously vague) and caused trouble, they would be sent back to Malaysia if they were Malaysian citizens, and be put in National Service if they were Singapore citi-zens. Soon after this meeting with the Prime Minister, some students on government bursaries and reading philosophy, political science or sociology, were told by the Public Services Commission to switch over to other courses of study or lose their bursaries. The ostensible reason given was that these three subjects do not provide as good job opportunities as various other subjects, or that the students con-cerned showed a greater aptitude for other subjects. But many stu-dents, including those directly affected, did not of course take this paternalistic concern over their welfare at its face value. For the notice to change courses of study came rather late in the university's first term when no such changes were normally allowed. Those who switched courses at this stage would be quite severely handicapped as they would have missed a great deal of work. Again, the only lec-turers invited to the Prime Minister's talk were those teaching the three subjects, and the non-citizens among them had also been threatened with deportation if they interfered with local issues by making snide remarks to students. It seemed quite clear that the Public Services Commission was intent on taking away some students from the corrupting influences of these teachers. After all these events, few students would be under any illusion that politics and education are rigorously kept apart.

The conflicts between academics and the government which have led to the imposition of the Certificate of Suitability, the appointment of a Cabinet Minister as Vice-Chancellor, the harassment of students, and the warnings given to both student leaders and lecturers, centre round three main, interrelated issues: the dangers of communist subversion of institutions of higher learning, the role of foreign teachers in the University of Singapore, and the general social and political attitudes of teachers and students. I shall briefly discuss each of these.

A democratic system of government in this part of the world is somewhat fragile. Firstly, there are no deeply entrenched critical traditions which respect dissent from established views. Those running the government were the nationalist leaders who galvanised mass support against colonial rule, and who came into power after political independence in a blaze of popularity. They are not used to criticisms from their own people, and are likely to be very sensitive and intolerant of these, attributing the meanest of motives to their critics. Secondly, there is the danger that one racial group would dominate over the others, or that racial antagonisms would be so strong as to lead to the destruction of any ordered government. These racial problems are not wholly internal matters. Neighbouring countries have similar problems involving similar races, and events in one country are causally linked with those in another country. Singapore in particular would feel the impact of external pressures most strongly as it has a predominantly Chinese population (over 75%) in a region where the Chinese elsewhere form large, and not very well liked, minorities. Thirdly, and this is what I would like to discuss at greater length, there is the threat of communist subversion of the democratic system.

In Singapore, the efficient way in which the government approached social and economic problems has minimised communist exploitation of these issues. But communist subversion can take another route by politicising education. Some Chinese secondary schools were, at one time, thoroughly penetrated by communists. Singapore's other university, Nanyang, whose main medium of instruction was Chinese, was at one time virtually run by communist students, who freely intimidated staff and fellow students. By appealing to youthful idealism, and strong chauvinism towards the Chinese language and culture, the communists made a significant impact on students. When the University of Singapore, whose medium of instruction is English, began to admit a limited number of Chinese school students, the government, while welcoming the move, felt that there should be some safeguards against the entry of communists into the University. It wanted the Vice-Chancellor to take into account political considerations of this type in the selection of Chinese school students for admission. The government was also concerned with the alleged communist penetration into a radical left-wing student political club. The dispute between the government and the then Vice-Chancellor about what should be done to keep the university free of communist influence led to the government threatening ΄to withdraw financial support from the university unless the Vice-Chancellor resigned. The Vice-Chancellor, who had the support of a substantial number of the academic staff and the majority of students, subsequently resigned. That was in 1963. Later, in 1964, the Certificate of Suitability was introduced, and this provoked strong protests from the students and from some teachers. The protests were renewed each year until they reached a climax in 1966 when large demonstrations were held in the campus. The students criticised the government for trampling on 'academic freedom' and 'university autonomy'. The government replied that students and their teachers were politically naïve and unaware of the dangers of communist subversion of free institutions. The bitterness of the dispute hid the fact that both students and those teachers who opposed the Certificate of Suitability were against communist subversion. In part their differences from the government can be explained in terms of their lack of personal experience of such subversion of educational institutions, an experience which only the Chinese-educated had. This inexperience, combined with the government's claim that the threat of communism in Singapore was well under control, and the fact that there were already considerable powers of detention without trial of suspected political subversives, led to a genuine doubt among many students and academics about the necessity of the Certificate of Suitability. The conflict between the students and the government was aggravated by the fear of many students that the Certificate of Suitability was intended not merely to check communist subversion, but also to exclude candidates whose political views were radically opposed to the government's. Unfortunately a rational examination of honest differences of opinion and interpretation of events was avoided because government spokesmen highlighted *ad hominem* arguments pointing out that some of the prominent student leaders were not Singapore citizens but citizens of neighbouring Malaysia, and were therefore not in a position to tell a foreign government what to do. The students were also taunted with their lack of ability to organise themselves as compared with their

Chinese-educated counterparts, and this provoked them to concentrate on massive displays of strength at the expense of a more coherent statement of their case against the Certificate of Suitability.

The second series of conflicts between academics and the government arose out of the government's resentment of the conduct of some foreign teachers in the University. The most publicised of these was 'the Enright affair'. In 1960, the professor of English, D. J. Enright, made some critical remarks, in the course of his inaugural lecture on 'Robert Graves and the Decline of Modernism', about the government's anti-'yellow culture' campaign. The government regarded this as an interference with local politics, and wrote an abusive letter to Professor Enright threatening to withdraw his professional visit pass. Before this, the government had also strongly objected to an expatriate law teacher giving solicited advice on constitutional law to an Opposition Member of Parliament (there was then a parliamentary opposition in Singapore). This too was construed as interference with local politics. Again, in 1968, the contract of a young and articulate lecturer in English was not renewed on expiry. No reason was given, but it was widely believed, though perhaps wrongly, that it was because the lecturer had, on several occasions, made some critical comments in public about government policies.

Apart from these instances in which individuals were accused of interfering in local issues, there was also a more general hostility towards the expatriate community. The Prime Minister summed up his own attitude when he said: 'Newly independent nations are held together by the strong impetus of nationalism. This can find expression in the life of the university only if those who run the university understand and feel strongly about the future of the nation. Expatriate staff inevitably talk of internationalism – a philosophy to which they must subscribe to rationalize their own existence in universities in foreign countries.' Soon after these remarks were made, a group of local academics, some of whom had close connections with the government, started a new Staff Association whose membership was confined exclusively to local academics. The inaugural meeting of this association was held in August 1964, and in a Memorandum presented for discussion at the meeting, the sentiments expressed by the Prime Minister were echoed: 'The continuing misunderstanding between the expatriate dominated Senate and the elected representatives of the people of Singapore have made it obvious that by and large the expatriate teacher, no matter how well-intentioned, is incapable of understanding the aspirations of our people and the part that the university must play in the service of the people. The expatriate don encumbered with his so-called "liberal" ideas is concerned first and foremost to keep his job and to rationalise his presence in our country by upholding internationalism as against nationalism. Our very survival depends on welding a multi-racial society into a national whole and this can be done only by the impetus of nationalism.'

Expatriate teachers have also been accused of being bad influences on their students. In this they do not stand alone, for the government also believes that the values and attitudes of some local teachers are equally undesirable. The third main area of conflict between government and academics relates to the nature of these values and attitudes, which seem to spread over a very wide range of issues. Some of these are clearly political. The government feels that academics are out of touch with 'political realities' and generate unrealistic attitudes in their students. Their alleged failure to appreciate the dangers of communist subversion of higher institutions of learning is a case in point which I have already referred to. The government has also been very concerned about the recent racial clashes in Malaysia and their effects on Singapore. It believes that university teachers and students are insufficiently aware of racial problems in Malaysia and Singapore. The Prime Minister once referred to a Political Science student who had commented that the separation of Singapore from Malaysia in 1965 was caused by a clash of personalities. He thought that the student could only have arrived at such a silly view from his lecturers. The Prime Minister has also castigated expatriates for 'poisoning' the minds of students with the pernicious doctrine that they belong to an international community, and that patriotism and nationalism are parochial and outmoded. And those sympathetic to the government have complained again and again that academics lack 'commitment', though no great details have ever been given about the nature of this commitment.

The government's dissatisfaction with the attitudes and conduct of university teachers and students even extends to activities which are not normally regarded as political in nature. In one of his speeches the Prime Minister held academics partly responsible for a panty raid conducted by students: '. . . for this particular community, faced with dire problems of life and death, to think that they [the students] have the leisure to afford this frivolity is an indictment not just of the student, but, I think, an indictment of the teachers and also of the political leadership that has failed to bring home the urgency of these tasks, the acuteness of the problems to the students and give them the lead and thinking and inspiration.' That was in 1966. Panty raids have since then gone out of fashion. But more recently, in 1968, a newspaper report about the appointment of the present Vice-Chancellor of the University of Singapore revealed that apart from the many academic problems the new Vice-Chancellor would have to solve, there were also non-academic matters calling for immediate attention. It went on to say that some Cabinet members were disgusted with student 'beatniks' who went to lectures in pyjamas. The report added: 'One or two members of the teaching staff have also been known to turn up in shorts and slippers. All these are going to be stopped.' Soon after the new Vice-Chancellor assumed office, the staff were informally told to be more formally dressed: shorts were prohibited; and shoes which exposed the toes were not permitted etc.

The government is also worried that students here, urged on perhaps by some of their teachers, would imitate the tactics of student radicals abroad. But so far at least there have been no real signs of such imitation.

After more than ten years in power, some of the Cabinet Ministers are no longer young by Singaporean standards. There is much talk among them of preparing a second echelon leadership to take over when the time comes. The government naturally thinks that the universities are among the important sources of the country's future leaders. It has quite definite ideas about how future leaders should behave, and does not want the energies of young men to be deflected by student unrest, hippie movements, panty raids, and talk about the abstract and universal rights of men.

The government's solution to the problem of inculcating politically realistic attitudes in academics is for them to spend a period on secondment to some government or statutory body, or at least to work part-time in various public committees. A number of academics have also been appointed as Ambassadors and High Commissioners. The hope is that, firstly, these selected few will become 'men of the world' instead of ivory-tower scholars, and thus be better able to assume political leadership. Secondly, when they return to the university, their presence will change the atmosphere of the ivory-tower for the better. A sense of realism, relevance and commitment will be introduced into otherwise abstract thinking. This solution applies of course only to citizens. With expatriates, the safeguards against bad influences on students are of a different type. Clear warnings about the dangers of meddling in local politics will be issued from time to time. Expatriates will also have a rapidly diminishing say in the decision-making processes in the university.

The position of Malaysian academics in the university is slightly ambiguous. When I joined the University of Singapore in 1964, Singapore was still part of the Malaysian federation. As a Malaysian citizen, I was of course regarded as a local, and not an expatriate, teacher. But Singapore was separated from the rest of

Malaysia in 1965 and Malaysians and Singaporeans then belonged to two different countries. They continued to have identical contracts of service with the University. In this respect Malaysians are different from 'expatriates' who, for example, receive an additional $2,400–$3,240 (Singapore) per annum. But in the end citizenship seems to be the decisive factor in the classification of academics, and the government intends its warnings against non-citizens interfering in local politics to apply to Malaysian academics as well.

I have given an account of the conflicts between the government and academics, and it is against this background that I shall now examine issues concerning the political independence of the university and the value of academic objectivity and impartiality. I accept Montefiore's helpful analysis of the concepts of independence, objectivity and impartiality. However, it is, I think, sometimes important to insist that an objective and impartial presentation of a subject should go beyond attempting to state rival views in the way that those who hold them would state them. The advocates of a particular view may not have given as good an account of their case as could have been done. A liberal teacher should try to give the best possible exposition of this view, even if it means putting forward a far more persuasive account of it than any of its actual advocates could have given. I shall also extend the concepts of objectivity and impartiality to include not merely the exposition of rival views, but also a fair-minded critical analysis of these views which draws attention to their relative strengths and weaknesses. This means that objective and impartial teaching need not be neutral, for some views may, after discussion, emerge with very little respectability left. It also means that an objective and impartial teacher is not precluded from stating and arguing for definite positive views of his own.

I shall argue that the political independence of the university has a special importance in Singapore.

Singapore is a democratic country in which the democratic opposition parties are extremely weak. The strongest opposition to the government comes from the pro-communists who, however, refuse to participate in parliamentary elections. The result is that in the Singapore parliament all the seats are occupied by the ruling party. The state-controlled radio and television give a great deal of publicity to government views, but seldom to views critical of the government, and the newspapers are not well known for their courageous stands against the government on serious and controversial issues. The result is an excessive degree of conformity and intellectual timidity among the people. Even within the university, few academics will talk frankly on political issues in front of fellow academics known to be members of the ruling party. The majority of students are also very cautious about anything they say or do which could have a political significance because many of them believe that some of their fellow students will report on their political views and activities as well as those of lecturers to the relevant authorities. I do not know whether there is any real basis for this belief, but there is little doubt that many students share it. In such a situation there is a danger that the ruling party will increasingly dominate the social and political life of the community. Whatever measures the government regards as vital to the sustenance of democracy and to the promotion of the general welfare will then remain unquestioned. There is already a tendency among some party members to use notions of the 'national interests' and the 'common good' in a manner that is descriptive of particular government policies, so that those who disagree with these policies are regarded as being against the national welfare and the common good. The idea that different people's notions of what the national interests demand may vary fundamentally is hardly acknowledged. Those who disagree with the government will withdraw from participation in the political process, and government leaders will run an increasingly greater risk of moving within the closed circle of their own men, ideas and reactions, when they tend to get the sorts of reports and comments which they like to hear.

What is clearly missing is a tradition of public rational discussion of important issues. No amount of private discussions within a political party can replace this tradition, for party members will be partly influenced by internal pressures and loyalties, and there will in any case be individuals who do not agree sufficiently with the party leadership to work with it. The presence of a tradition of public rational discussion will inspire a constant interaction between the views of the government and those of the general public. At present the government pays quite serious attention to the task of explaining and justifying its policies to the people, but there is a virtual monologue, and no fruitful dialogue can emerge unless the views held by the people are not wholly parasitic on the government's views, but are formed in fairly substantial independence of them. What are needed therefore are independent feed-backs of the effects of government policies, and independent assessments of the value of these policies, and these will very likely only arise in the presence of politically independent organisations and institutions. To some extent organisations like trade unions and bodies of professional men can provide the necessary independence. But they cannot, without distorting their essential character, make comments on a wide variety of political issues. For they are not political parties but bodies of men with certain more limited shared interests. Moreover, their comments on those government policies which affect these shared interests, though independent, are not likely to be more objective and impartial than the government's.

In this context I believe that the university, if it is a politically independent institution, has a very important contribution to make. The university as such should not set itself up as an opposition group presenting partisan points of view aimed at embarrassing the government. It should instead be an institution where individual academics feel free to express objectively and impartially, both inside and outside the classroom, their views on relevant contemporary issues falling within their area of study and competence. Thereby students and the general public could be stimulated by considered and independent opinions. The organisation of the university could help in developing a greater willingness on the part of academics to participate in such rational discussions, though of course it cannot guarantee that the discussions will be forthcoming. A few academics will need no encouragement to participate, but many will seek assurances that renewals of contracts, promotions, study leave and other benefits are not dependent on the acceptability of the individuals concerned to politicians. In this respect it is to be regretted that the Vice-Chancellor of the University of Singapore should also be a Cabinet Minister. It is conceivable that a Cabinet Minister is so clearly objective and impartial that no one would feel that purely political considerations will ever warp his judgement on academic matters. But such a man is very rare indeed, and though many may strive to attain this ideal, they are not likely to reach it in the eyes of those over whom they have the power of effective judgement. It takes little for people to believe that injustice has been committed, whereas justice, if done, will not be easily seen to be done. And in these matters it is not what you are, but what you are seen or believed to be, which influences the behaviour of others.

Granted the need for independent universities, it would be naïve to think that this independence can only be endangered by government intervention. The communist tactic of penetrating and subverting non-political organisations and institutions is well known, and as mentioned earlier, some educational institutions had, in the past, been so subverted. A liberal academic should certainly be under no illusion that the values of objectivity, impartiality, and political independence would be respected under communist rule. He should, therefore, in principle be prepared to support measures which are designed to curb communist subversion, and are effective in doing so with the least possible sacrifice in freedom and other important values. He would also insist that any sacrifice of freedom and other values should be fully justified, and would not be satisfied with appeals to blind faith in the knowledge and good intentions of the authorities.

In certain extreme situations, a liberal academic must even be prepared to consider temporarily sacrificing the values of objectivity, impartiality and political independence. Thus some politicians have argued that in 1963 when the democratic system in Singapore was gravely threatened by communists, all academics who believe in democracy should have joined or publicly supported the People's Action Party which was the only democratic force in Singapore capable of fighting successfully against the pro-communist political party in the elections. It was essential to maintain the solidarity of the democratic forces, and objectivity and impartiality might lead to criticisms of some aspects of the policies pursued by the ruling People's Action Party, and thereby indirectly help the pro-communists in the electoral struggle. Even neutrality was not good enough since the ruling party needed support to win. A liberal academic's response to this argument would depend on his assessment of the situation. How great was the risk of a pro-communist victory? What were the likely effects of his own actions or intended actions? What was the exact goal for which his help was sought? These are some of the questions he would ask. Consider, for example, the last question. I think that a liberal academic is more likely to accept a goal for which there are fairly clear criteria of achievement. Ensuring the victory of the pro-democratic party in one election is clear enough, whereas containing communism within reasonable limits is not, and may call for indefinitely prolonged partisan support. Again, some goals demand far too much sacrifice of liberal values. For example, the goal of completely eliminating the threat of communism is not likely to be achieved without resort to totalitarian powers. But I do not think that any very clear rule can be formulated to guide action. A certain reluctance to sacrifice liberal values, and to resist accepting assessments of situations as ones of crises involving such sacrifices, is itself a measure of the depth of one's commitment to these values. But an absolute refusal to make any sacrifices under any circumstances is more likely to be a sign of dogmatism and ignorance.

What about the role of expatriate teachers? Should any qualification be made to their participation in the rational discussion of issues which fall within their area of study and competence? This is an important issue in a developing country like Singapore where, because of the shortage of local personnel, a large proportion of the senior appointments in the universities were held by expatriates.

When the new Staff Association, which excluded expatriates from membership, was formed in the University of Singapore in 1964, one of the chief complaints about expatriate teachers was that they did not have a sufficient understanding of local problems, or a sufficient degree of sympathy for national aspirations. This gave rise to the widely accepted view that expatriates should not interfere in local issues, particularly those which are political in nature. But this view is not usually clearly formulated. It is surely not meant to exclude expatriates from commenting on local issues, for a great deal of what is taught in the social sciences relates to local problems. 'Interference' implies more than mere comment, it implies unfavourable comment. But unfavourable from whose point of view? The obvious answer is: the government's. No expatriate has been reprimanded for commenting on local issues in ways that are favourable towards the government, even though unfavourable towards other local groups. The local issues which could be regarded by the government as having political implications are numerous, and not always easily predictable. The cause of objective and impartial treatment of problems will not be advanced if expatriates fear reprisals for making critical comments on government policies. It is surely not desirable that teachers should steer clear of controversial local issues when these are quite relevant to the topics under discussion. Creative teaching will be badly hampered when this happens, and teachers will tend to withdraw into a world of inoffensive research and publications. Even if, as in some cases, expatriate teachers are not intimidated, the view that they should not interfere in local political issues still impedes rational discussion. It encourages the use of *ad hominem* arguments in which general accusations about the nastiness, mischief or plain incomprehension of expatriates are made. These will tend to replace the attempt to rebut specific arguments. The interests of rational discussion demand that expatriates should not only be allowed to comment on local issues within their area of study and competence, but also that this area should be widely interpreted so that no man need be inhibited from a full participation in discussion by the fear of stepping beyond the narrow confines of his subject.

It may, however, be objected that expatriates do not have a stake in the country. They are, as their critics have often said, 'birds of passage' who do not plan to stay permanently in the country they are now in. It is further alleged that they often do not make responsible comments since they need not bear the harmful consequences of whatever bad advice they may give. Citizens, on the other hand, have a greater sense of responsibility since their own future is tied up with the well-being of their country. This argument is too simple. Many local academics have good mobility. In fact it is generally the case that the better academics have greater mobility than the others, and if mobility diminishes responsibility, then only the less competent local academics are qualified to comment on local problems. But the point may be that whereas expatriates *want* to move on, citizens can, but generally do not wish to leave their country. However, this also means that expatriates have a lesser need to court the favour of the government than local teachers, and can therefore afford to be more frank in their comments. It is in any case an unwarranted assumption to think that those who do not intend to stay very long in a country will not care for it, or that there is typically an 'expatriate point of view' which is different from that of dedicated local academics. The expatriate academic community is not a homogeneous group. It includes citizens of America, Canada, Britain, Australia, India and Pakistan, and consists of men with a diversity of backgrounds and experiences.

I think that the expatriate teacher should have the same degree of freedom as the local teacher in commenting on local issues within his area of competence, widely interpreted. There will occasionally be expatriates whose comments are crude, insensitive and irrelevant, but this is a small price to pay for an increase in intellectual liveliness.

Finally, an important function which the universities here are expected to fulfil is the moulding of the future political leaders of the country. In this respect government leaders seem particularly dissatisfied with the behaviour and attitudes of students in the University of Singapore. It is a common complaint among them that both students and teachers lack 'commitment' to their society, and are unrealistic in their attitudes, and that students are furthermore immature, frivolous and irresponsible. Earlier, I have given a few more specific illustrations of these criticisms. I do not want to dwell on them, but I do not believe that leaders with initiative, imagination and self-reliance will be produced by stamping out the playfulness and spontaneity of some student activities, and by trying to harangue students to full respectability and responsibility. Perhaps no great leader was ever born in a panty raid, but it is difficult to show that any great leader was lost in one.

I also do not think that leaders are very likely to emerge if both teachers and students act as if every step of education is a preparation for future leadership. Consider an analogy. It may be true, as many have claimed, that sports promote goodwill among people. But the goodwill may only come about as a by-product of spontaneous and full-hearted participation in sporting activities. Therefore if people took part in sporting activities simply in order to promote goodwill, they may not succeed. Their lack of interest in the intrinsic attractions of the activities will prevent a full and free participation. There may, in other words, be desirable consequences of activities which can only be realised if these activities are pursued for their intrinsic value, and not with the conscious overriding aim of attaining the consequences. Education seems to me to be one such activity. The immediate aim of those who teach a subject should not be to produce leaders for society. It should rather be to initiate students into a tradition of enquiry which has its own internal demands. There are of course different techniques of initiation, and one such technique is to start, whenever possible, with problems which immediately engage the student's attention because they are problems with a direct practical significance, or which arise out of ordinary experience. But once students have been so initiated into a particular form of enquiry, they would be caught up by it, and the issues which suggest themselves for discussion would to a great extent depend on their significance as issues within that tradition of enquiry. These issues would include, or spill into, issues of contemporary social and political relevance, and priority would naturally be given to the problems of the society in which a university is located. But it would be educationally unwise to insist that other issues, which are not of this category, and which appear to be abstract and remote from the daily concerns of social life, should be avoided even if they have an important place within that tradition of enquiry.

If a teacher could teach his students to think deeply, clearly, objectively and impartially about the issues under discussion, he would have inculcated habits of mind which are valuable to all men, including political and intellectual leaders. A university which provides the environment where such teaching can flourish would probably contribute more to the emergence of good political leadership among students, than one which has a highly politically charged atmosphere where aspiring leaders are too busy thinking of becoming leaders to be able to learn much.

As for 'commitment', I think that the university as such should not be politically neutral between the democratic system and the communist system in so far as this relates to Singapore. I also believe that continued racial tolerance is crucial to the stability of Singapore, and indeed to its very existence as a united nation. There is enough evidence from the tragic racial and tribal conflicts of other countries to warn any racially pluralist society of the dangers of racial intolerance. The university should therefore be prepared to pursue academically acceptable policies which promote, and not weaken, racial tolerance. If by 'commitment' is meant commitment to democracy and racial tolerance, then indeed the university as such should be committed to these values. But even so, the university should, I have argued, be politically independent so that indi-vidual academics, and even the university as such when an issue affects it directly, can make independent assessments of facts and judgements on policies designed to sustain a democratic and multi-racial society. For even here there are surely issues over which reasonable and sincere men would disagree, and it is desirable that such disagreements should be voiced.

The importance of the political independence of the university becomes even greater when discussion is centred not on the general framework within which a society is to develop, but on the many substantive issues which any society has to decide. Here, what is dis-puted may well be the ends to be pursued, and not simply the best means of attaining given ends. The idea that the university should be 'committed' to society, if it involves the mere passive reflection of the dominant social and political views in society, cannot be accept-ed. Academics who in the course of their teaching can, but diligently refuse to, subject any of these views to objective and impartial analysis and criticism, would have shirked one of their important responsibilities.

The acuteness of some of these problems arises, no doubt, out of the peculiarity of Singapore as a small city-state. Its size makes it more vulnerable than larger states to what are considered as unde-sirable influences. Again, the newness of the nation, and the differ-ent racial and cultural groups that compose it, are reflected in the emphasis on the search for, and the evolution of, a focus of loyalty and a Singaporean identity. Unless there is success here it is felt that the very basis of the survival of the nation cannot be entrenched. These considerations should have been given more prominence for they help to explain, and to some even justify, the impatience and in-tolerance of the government to expatriate teachers and others whose views and styles of life are said to threaten the viability of the nation. But the openness of Singapore as a commercial centre inevi-tably subjects it to many of the influences that are thought to be un-desirable, and by comparison the part played by university teachers was negligible. In any case there are enormous dangers of other kinds in imposing restrictions on expatriate teachers. Views and styles of living that are merely irritating and distasteful to some influential and loyal members of the ruling party come to acquire a wider significance, and may even be seen as threatening the safety and integrity of the nation.

The dominance of the ruling party and the pervasive intellectual timidity is also shown by the fact that to an increasing extent the primary concern of many people, when considering any important issue, is how the government would react to it, and not what are the intrinsic features of the issue. Where there is disagreement with the government, it is hoped that someone else would voice the disagreement.

In emphasising the importance of maintaining the independence and liberal character of the university, I have argued that this involves in part the willingness to take measures against organised attempts by communists to subvert the university; and I have claimed that the university should not be neutral between the democratic system and the communist system in so far as this relates to Singapore. But in not elaborating on these remarks, I open myself to a number of misunderstandings. First, lack of institutional neutrality in this sense does not mean that individual academics or students who merely hold communist views, but who do not constitute a threat to the freedom of the university, should be penalised in any way. It is important that a centre of free enquiry should have a place even for those who do not believe in free enquiry, so long as they are not part of an effective effort to destroy freedom. The alternative policy of enquiring into the political views of members of the university will not merely encourage hypocrisy and timidity, but will also lead to a serious undermining of civil liberties. Secondly, lack of institutional neutrality may be confined to the limited area of maintaining the independence and integrity of the university that I had in mind, or it may be extended to include a positive and direct role in combating communist influence in Singapore generally, in so far as this influence is hostile to democracy and freedom. If it is granted that the university can only establish itself as a centre of free enquiry in a relatively free society, then it may plausibly be argued that the university should be prepared to help directly in preserving and strengthening such a society. However, though there is certainly a function here for individual academics, the university is too fragile an institution to be cast in such a role. The university will not normally be able to withstand the pressures on it to adopt the government's view of what it should do, and will rapidly lose whatever independence it still has. Even if the university stands up to these pressures, the resultant divisiveness among academics over a wide range of social and political issues only very indirectly related to academic goals will create an atmosphere unconducive to the pursuit of these goals. It is only in situations where the university's contribution can be shown to be decisive in preventing the destruction of a free society, that it should abandon institutional neutrality in the wider area.

Finally, my paper may appear to many to betray an excessive and obsessive fear of communism. The bogey of communism has of course been raised frequently. But in the peculiar circumstances of Singapore, the dangers of communist subversion of educational institutions have been sufficiently significant to merit serious discussion and were not to be lightly dismissed, as perhaps some of those whose views were otherwise close to mine were inclined to do. The only caveat I would add is the familiar one about the risk of even sincere and justified opposition to communism, that one may be tempted in combating it, to imitate its weapons so closely that the cure will turn out to be quite as bad as the illness. The risk can be taken if one's attachment to liberal values is strong. But if, on the other hand, one cares little for liberal values, then the problem does not arise.

The academic and the political

W. L. WEINSTEIN

There is a very natural starting point for the liberal academic's view of a university's political neutrality and independence. It is his ideal characterisation of academic activity. Such activity, he would insist, is to be understood in terms that are intrinsic to it; its rationale is immanent within the structure of thinking and acting which distinguishes it from other human involvements. The pursuit of knowledge, or its preservation and transmission, must be seen as good or bad, worthwhile or not in principle, not in terms of involvements that *ex hypothesi* lie 'outside' it (eventually relevant as such extra-academic things may become in the theory and practice of a university). For academic activity is to be prized in general and appraised in detail according to standards that are contained in it. As a sphere of human achievement in its own right it is not merely an instrument for achieving human well-being in other respects.

No doubt characterisations of the internal nature of academic activities are diverse, even within the camp of like-minded liberals; and each characterisation may seem less clear as one starts to press its leading concepts, such as 'knowledge' or 'education', or its underlying theses, such as the separation of theorising about practical activities (e.g. politics) from practical involvement in them. Nevertheless, it is by virtue of some internal rationale of the pursuit of knowledge (and allied processes such as training people for it), implying the need for detachment, open-mindedness, impartiality, and objectivity, that the liberal academic typically seeks to justify a certain range of claims that are closely connected tactically and, very probably, conceptually. Academic activity must not, in the first place, be interfered with or otherwise frustrated by the wider community or its agents, such as government. This may go further than the negative demand to be left alone, e.g. not to be subjected to censorship. It may very well lead to positive political action to ensure that the structures of action and opinion in the wider community are favourable to the independence and political neutrality of a university; and even the merely negative demand may issue not in a short, sharp sally into the political arena but a quite durable and systematic involvement. Thus one has to assume, with or without some sense of paradox, that a university, seen as a sponsor of a free, creative activity, cannot remain neutral in the defence of its essential interests, one of which is the preservation of its political neutrality. Or, as another example of deliberate political involvement, when a university uses its political influence to solicit government funds, on this view it must still try to ensure that at least its powers of decision-making in academic matters remain unimpaired. More generally, universities must not allow themselves to become so closely tied to or influenced by the interests of the wider community as to undermine their politically non-aligned position or their independence, both of which are seen as necessary conditions for objective, impartial, open-minded, and detached enquiry and instruction.

Furthermore, even though knowledge and education may be useful or detrimental to individuals or society in non-academic realms, the criteria of excellence and utility that mark the non-academic – not very clearly designated as, for example, 'the political' or 'the economic' – must not supplant academic criteria when academic activity is assessed. As academic activity is conceived as an independent activity by virtue of its intrinsic nature, the institutions meant to embody it are therefore to be judged as debased or corrupted in so far as the internal standards of the activity are compromised and the conditions for attaining them, such as political neutrality and independence, are undermined. The agents or sources of corruption may be specifiable persons or impersonal social forces, and identified in or outside universities. But there is nothing to be understood as corrupted unless there is some conception of what is ideally the internal nature and value of academic involvements.

Of course this whole rationale presupposes a distinct vocational enterprise which can be hived off, though not totally, from the processes of understanding or of serious reflection and criticism in agents actively engaged in other social activities. However, even from the perspective outlined thus far the identity of universities is only understood *by extension* from some pure, abstract characterisation of the pursuit and transmission of knowledge to more or less formal organisations.[1] Moreover, universities have an 'external' identity: they are, obviously enough, institutions operating in real social contexts. *Qua* institutions they have characteristics and interests, such as their size, personnel, procedures, and finance, which normally fall outside the scope of an abstractly conceived internal essence or rationale, but which in various complex ways are judged

---

[1] Although such a characterisation does not strictly entail a historically specific institution (any more than religion, at any rate on some views, entails a specific, or any Church, or love, the institution of marriage), it is of course true that men's understanding of such characterisations of their involvements is typically acquired and developed in their experience, however unhappy, of actual institutions.

in terms of that rationale. So too with the day-to-day professional involvements of the individual academic. From the point of view of the rationale it may seem that '*all* political pressures on the academic intellectual are equally bad; that all deserve to be rejected'.[2] But the external realities may suggest a much more complex if not an altogether different assessment. Again, a university has an external identity as, for example, part of a society's job-market or an agency providing services for outside enterprises (which in certain circumstances can and do become inside ones); and such tie-ups may or may not be held to conflict with its ideal, internal identity. A university, then, necessarily has, but has not only, this external reality: its relations with the wider community, upon which it has and from which it receives various influences, as well as its own concrete institutional form. The effective possibilities of a university's living up to its internal rationale are partly determined by factors in the wider context, e.g. the beliefs and patterns of activity, interest, and power that may or may not be favourable; and partly by the beliefs, dispositions, and practices of its members.

From the tensions between ideal, internal identity and identity in the real world, the precise nature and boundary between each of which are open to conflicting accounts, spring many of the important issues confronting liberal academics. A university is probably always an impure or defective realisation of the values immanent in the activities it is meant ideally to embody; its objectives may often seem or actually be unrealistic pretensions; but what is a sensible compromise with reality for one man may be a decline into corruption for another. How tenable, then, is the commonly made distinction between academic and political considerations? Or at least why is awareness of the problematic nature of the distinction submerged in some situations but very much on the surface in others? When does commitment to political neutrality by a university or its members become self-defeating?

I shall not be able to contend with these questions exhaustively or in very general terms. Obviously there can be real deficiencies in any account in which neither the concept of 'the academic' nor of 'the political' is analysed in anything like the depth each requires. But I shall discuss a few concrete cases which will perhaps point in certain directions. It will be helpful to indicate in advance characteristic types of problem, especially as each case will tend unavoidably to raise several issues at once.

(i) Where the very terms in which academic and political considerations or criteria are distinguished may be questioned (intro-

---

[2] Barrington Moore Jr, 'On Rational Inquiry in Universities Today', *New York Review of Books*, 23 April 1970, where this view is cited for the sake of criticising it.

duced in section 1 with reference to the assessment of candidates for admission; taken further in section 2 with reference to academic appointments, but in the special context of politics as an academic subject; and finally touched on early in section 4 in connection with arguments about what is most worth learning when studying politics);

(ii) How can one strive to live up to liberal academic standards in the teaching of politics in the special context of political conflict over the wider social role of a university? Should this be represented as part of a political and not merely an academic defence of a university's internal values? (discussed in section 4);

(iii) When defence of liberal academic values, including political neutrality, calls for extraordinary measures (political tests for admissions or appointments) which count on the one hand as the injection of political considerations into what were hitherto areas of action and attitude governed by academic considerations, and on the other hand as the legitimate defence of academic values which are conceived in unusually broad terms precisely because the normal conditions for the application of the academic/political distinction have broken down (introduced at the end of section 1 and returned to in section 3a);

(iv) When, although the distinction between academic and political considerations remains reasonably clear and stable, the real world is such that actions taken for the sake of defending academic values, including the independence of a university, have also political effects, some or all of them going beyond the conscious intentions of the agents involved but which none the less suggest important restrictions on the possibility of politically neutral action (discussed mainly in section 3b with reference to overseas students' fees, but other examples are cited in other sections).

Consideration of each case will also presuppose several general points worth making at the outset. The first of these is that academics themselves, and not merely contemporary 'agitators' in or outside a university, may do things which diminish the independence or the political neutrality of their university or their position as academics. A second, closely related point is that liberal academics may suffer from illusions about some situations in which they find themselves; though what is illusion and what is not may well be disputable, for example, when actions represented as 'academic' are also arguably 'political' in some sense. Thirdly, and as an extension of the previous point, illusions may develop when inordinate weight is placed on an agent's intentions. His intention may be described quite naturally in terms provided by the inner rationale of academic activity, but the assessment of the political neutrality of his actions may be distorted by failing to take sufficiently into account the external or, as one might say, the objective features of the situation (but what is sufficient in any given case is often disputable). Reference to the constraints and consequences, which supplement or challenge intention-loaded characterisations of action, suggests that actions cannot be definitely classified as 'academic' on some unvarying basis. Contrast the remark, 'I choose students for admission on grounds of their comparative academic merit alone', with 'You choose as it happens students coming from the most privileged backgrounds, and in so doing confer fresh privileges upon them'. The university teacher claiming to act impartially but also in a politically neutral way (because without political intentions) may on another view be seen as acting impartially yet as *de facto* (and in spite of himself) taking sides on issues of equality of opportunity.[3]

Such complexities notwithstanding, I shall assume that so long as there is allegiance to the internal values and criteria of assessment of academic activity, there will be motives for distinguishing between the academic and the political, even if particular ways of drawing the distinction remain controversial. But balanced against this must be the readiness to consider the possibility, at any rate in some cases, that a university or an academic *qua* academic cannot or is unlikely to be politically neutral. However, it is one thing to be prepared to spot the points of tension between believing that a university and a teacher *qua* teacher should in general strive for political neutrality and recognising when no option of that type is effectively available, or if available is not worth taking; but quite another to assert that universities and academics can never occupy politically neutral positions, and that to strive to occupy them, on the assumption that such an objective is worthwhile, is a typical liberal illusion. The latter view is not one I am prepared to defend, though in this paper I shall not directly attack it.[4]

1 *The academic/political distinction: conventional applications*

I have never been personally involved in a violent or highly dramatic confrontation in a university. Nevertheless there is a small

[3] However the phrase 'as it happens' underlines the importance of the agent's intention; reference to consequences that formed no part of this intention (on some view of the grounds for the proper description of an intention), will not of itself settle the argument as to whether the agent's actions were politically non-neutral.

[4] Nor will it be assumed that (a) the mere fact that an action has political consequences automatically undermines the claim to have acted politically neutrally, which may be made by academics or universities, or (b) that actions that are not politically neutral automatically undermine academic values.

stock of experience of recent, milder controversies in Oxford on which I shall draw for the sake of explaining how in that context issues have arisen about the distinction between academic and political considerations; the responsibilities the liberal academic sees himself as having because of his practical concerns with his institution and his commitments to certain ideals and standards; and about the possibilities and limits of his or his university's political neutrality. As one would expect from virtually any examples taken from the post-1967 period, these issues, as they have appeared in Oxford, have been related to and often derived from ways of thinking and acting at many other universities, in Britain and overseas, where usually in sharper form than in Oxford there have been conflicts over the general validity of our ways of applying the concepts and distinctions constituting the framework in which the liberal academic sees his situation.

I shall focus mainly on issues arising from three examples. One is about 'political files', another the fees of overseas students, and the third the teaching of politics; though certain points about them are naturally similar, they do not cover exactly the same range of issues. All are marked by the fact that the vast majority of people involved, though often in sharp disagreement, appealed to liberal standards. But at the same time circumstances and attitudes were slightly affected by a very small minority's urge to bring about a radical change in the university and society, and to call into question many fundamental liberal beliefs about the ideal, internal nature of a university, supposing such beliefs to be inextricably connected with a self-styled liberal society which they considered unjust and repressive and to be landed with insoluble contradictions between its ideals and practices.

The political files controversy. The first case, political files on students and faculty members, is of very recent origin. In the actual context it was not only a focus of conflict in its own right but was also seen by some people on different sides of the conflict as part of a campaign, begun in 1968, to resist the claims of the authorities (i.e. the faculty) in Oxford to impose on students rules against disruption of the university;[5] it was therefore related to a wide range of issues (not to be discussed here) about the power of students in the university's government, theoretically central to which were conflicting views as to which type of academic considerations, as distinct from others, ought to determine the form of government and

---

[5] Formerly there had been a prohibition upon students behaving in a manner likely to bring the name of the university into disrepute. The Hart Report (1969) recommended abolition of that rule and retention only of a rule against disruption and related offences. So even the notion of 'imposition' in this context is questionable.

in what way. In the files case itself I had the usual tutor's interest because of personal and academic relations with my students, but also a special interest by virtue of my part-time role as the officer responsible for the administration of admissions to my college.

In February 1970 students at the University of Warwick raided the administrative offices, removing papers which were alleged to expose a noxious tie between capitalists and senior officials of the university,[6] and the administration's desire to keep a watch over (and possibly later to control) politically active students and faculty members. One plain implication was that the university's independence and devotion to intellectual values were weakened because its Vice-Chancellor and officials were 'intimately enmeshed with the upper reaches of consumer capitalist society'.[7] Another was that politically active students and faculty might be persecuted by university officials or their outside 'Establishment' allies and patrons (some of whom sat in the university's highest governing body); or that such information might be passed to a government anti-subversion agency or to students' prospective employers, to the detriment of the individual's liberty to engage in political activity and express political opinions in or outside the university. Much publicity was given to a letter from a headmaster about a candidate for admission from his school who had joined a radical group of older school children and been reported in newspapers as having called for militant action and not discussion. The Vice-Chancellor or someone in his administration had reportedly written at the foot of the letter 'Reject this man' and sent a note of thanks to the headmaster. The natural if not water-tight inference was that the decision was a direct consequence of the letter, although the headmaster later denied any intention to prejudice the student's chances, claiming only that such background information could be useful to the tutors if he were admitted. A campaign launched at Warwick proclaimed the right of a student to inspect files containing hitherto confidential information about himself and to delete political references or others he thought were unjust or irrelevant; and demanding that political files, as they were called, not be kept in any form.[8]

---

[6] See E. P. Thompson, 'The Business University', *New Society*, 19 February 1970; and the book he subsequently edited, *Warwick University Ltd., Industry, Management and the Universities*, (London, 1970).

[7] Thompson in *New Society, loc. cit.*

[8] The university agreed to an enquiry by their Chancellor, an eminent judge, who concluded that the charges of improper behaviour were unjustified, *Report of the Rt. Hon. Viscount Radcliffe, GBE, as to Procedures followed in the University with regard to Receiving and Retaining of Information about Political Activities of the Staff and Students*, University of Warwick, 1970; and *The Times*, 15 April 1970; also E. P. Thompson, 'A Report on Lord Radcliffe', *New Society*, 30 April 1970. It is perhaps worth mentioning that the schoolboy in ques-

Agitation, often accompanied by seizure and sit-in, spread rapidly to other universities and reached Oxford, where the raiding party failed to find anything incriminating. Whatever the truth about political files in Oxford (which seemed to be that none existed), the Warwick disclosures had, it seemed to some students, undermined the hitherto little questioned assumption that tutors' confidential reports and testimonials, and not merely those provided by schools, were unprejudiced and objective in respect of academic and character assessments, and non-political in particular. But even among those, the great majority, who retained confidence in their tutors, fears arose as to how the recipients interpreted testimonials; for example, if a tutor cited a man's political interests to suggest liveliness of mind, a prospective employer might take this as evidence of a potential for trouble-making or subversion on or off the job. A few students and perhaps teachers, regarding the university as already aligned with forces upholding the *status quo* in what was to become an all-out struggle between the established order and its enemies, were prepared to take the existence of political files as further evidence of the university's anti-radical position and therefore of the hollowness of its claims to political neutrality; for them the existence of such files was not necessary to support their convictions but would help to win allies from among those who had hitherto regarded the university as still fundamentally unpoliticised.

Less extremely, however, the students in my college, like most at other British universities, drew a distinction between receiving and retaining information about students which is relevant to academic purposes (which are legitimate) and that which falls outside their scope. They recognised the old-fashioned liberal distinction between academic and political considerations, and required, as any usual liberal would, that the latter be taken as irrelevant to the ways in which students *qua* students are to be treated. Agreeing with this line, but with the further purpose of rejecting the demand to open the files to students, college tutors explained the practical objections to opening them in terms that presupposed a separate sphere of functions that came under the heading 'academic', which covered teaching, study, research or creative work generally, but also supporting administrative functions and the selection of candidates for admission. It is interesting how little this argument was questioned, even though there remained finer-textured pros and cons to be argued about the practice of confidentiality itself;[9] the general argu-

---

tion was in fact admitted to another British university, which stood higher in his list of preferences than did Warwick.

[9] And one supporting function, finance, has also provoked political interest in so far as stu-

ment is worth looking at more closely as a full-blooded example of theory-controlled practice in a university.

A student's college file in Oxford begins with his application for admission, which contains a confidential report on his work and character from his school, usually written by the headmaster. The convention is that he tells us anything about the boy and his background circumstances that, in his view, would be academically relevant; and college tutors recognise this convention when interpreting the report, though no doubt at the edges the notion of what is relevant to future academic performance is hazy.[10] In fact each tutor has wide discretion in interpreting the background information that may be given, e.g. about a boy's family (usually to say that it is unexceptionally respectable; or, if in difficulties, because of conflict, divorce, parent's death, or hostility to academic achievement, to explain why allowances ought to be made); his relations with his peers and teachers; and those attitudes and interests which may be relevant indirectly to his academic future if they throw light on his capacity to thrive in the college and tutorial system of Oxford. Assuming such information should be given frankly and fully, to be balanced against equally frank and full assessments of centrally relevant evidence of a candidate's academic promise, anyone accepting the category of legitimate academic purposes and evaluative criteria would see the point of preserving confidentiality in school reports.

However, what if a headmaster, like the one who wrote to Warwick, mentions the political opinions and activities of a candidate, either with the intention of providing a fully impartial and objective report, letting the reader draw his own conclusions (impartially or not) or knowing that they will be drawn in a particular way, or with an unfavourable or favourable innuendo? What sort of notice, if any, is or should be taken of such reports? The standard answer begins to indicate the assumptions, underlying practice and little questioned, on which the distinction between academic and political considerations has depended in such cases.

It has not been all that uncommon for reports to contain some in-

---

dents have sought to interpret college and university investments in South African firms as condonation of apartheid, irrespective of the conscious intentions of the investors.

[10] Its haziness is not always appreciated because an item which might arguably not be strictly academically relevant may be conveniently covered by another convention which is especially strong in the collegiate system of Oxford, namely, that certain aspects of a candidate may be relevant to how well he would fit into the special environment of a college and contribute to its life or spirit. But, Oxford colleges apart, it is not difficult to see that a person's capacity for fitting into a certain institutional setting may be relevant to his academic performance. On the other hand, such a justification may create opening for the conscious or unconscious exercise of the selector's preference for students who are culturally and socially, perhaps morally, most acceptable to him.

formation about a boy's political views or membership of a school or non-school club or society with a political identity. This has usually been set in a matter of fact way alongside other types of interest and membership, all treated as of rather marginal significance compared with academic ability as such. In virtually every case in my experience this information was meant to be, and was, taken as evidence in the boy's favour, irrespective of his particular political views, implying that he was a person with a range of normal interests. The predominant tendency has been for schools to treat an interest in politics simply as evidence of liveliness of mind and diversity of interests – virtually on a par with photography or chess, with a scientist's special interest in literature, a literature student's in science, or with sports and games. Tutors have tended to share this view, and obviously their views and those of school teachers have been mutually re-enforcing. In sucn circumstances, not to report on a boy's real interest in politics if he has one would actually be unfair to him, though perhaps very marginally given the greater emphasis in selection on academic qualities, in so far as these are distinct from extra-curricular interests. And until now at any rate, when there might have been a very exceptional report on the extremity of a boy's political views, even if associated as a cause or correlative feature of his indiscipline at school, headmasters have been inclined, perhaps with condescension or surreptitious political bias, to attribute this to immaturity, treating it mildly and often sympathetically on the assumption that it might well be a passing phase in personal development out of which a normal boy would grow in time; or to take it as one amongst several items, though possibly the major one, evidencing some generally colourful or volatile temperament. Even if not all methods of presenting or interpreting these facts have been absolutely innocent of political bias, it is plain that on both sides there has been a traditional understanding (or assumption of such an understanding) of what political neutrality and non-political criteria of assessment look like. Moreover, against the placid background in which British universities and schools have been working for some time, it has not been questioned that the application of non-political criteria of assessment is both possible and imperative. In such circumstances any attempt to introduce a political ingredient would be resisted.

In the light of all this it will be very much worth noticing whether these attitudes begin to change if political agitation (or what may be counted as such, e.g. demands for changes in the curriculum) continues in universities and if the lowering of the age of radical political consciousness injects more unrest (alongside other, not easily distinguishable sources of unrest) into the schools. It may then become more difficult for university and school teachers to treat all political interests among 16–18 year-olds on a par with chess. But the more any such politicisation creeps into educational institutions, the more will many students be anxious to ensure that assessments should be untainted by political considerations: an anxiety difficult to allay if students resort to hostile action when once they notice their elders imperceptibly or deliberately sliding away from traditional liberal principles, or if those principles become an object of attack. Rightly or wrongly it may then become more difficult for teachers to believe such anxiety is as reasonable or deserving of sympathy as they have done up to now. Through such a process of self-re-enforcing and escalating conflict one might envisage the longer-run possibility that (a) limits to political neutrality in this sphere would be openly set and justified, and (b) the setting of them would further polarise the whole situation, so far perhaps as to make the very act of taking a stand as to when the line between political and academic considerations should be drawn an inescapable non-neutral political act. Furthermore, the more an academic saw it as his vocational responsibility to work actively to prevent those possibilities becoming actualities, the more he might be committed to some comprehensive political strategy, operating within and perhaps outside educational institutions; yet this prophylactic activity requires a kind of politicisation of his role which may be in conflict with the very ideal of political non-involvement to which he remains vocationally committed. What perhaps this line of speculation brings out at this point is that the area for political neutrality is the greater when there is no open conflict as to when political considerations are irrelevant to activity styled as essentially academic (and this of course is to assume so far no conflict over *what* distinguishes political and academic considerations). I shall recur to this point in section 3 and try to take it slightly further.

2 *Problems for the academic/political distinction*

Yet even as things stand at present, I am not entirely satisfied with the general view so far presented. I would find this whole account analytically incomplete even if the distinction between the academically relevant and the political were to provide the most expedient basis on which I, my colleagues, and my students could reach amicable understandings on the issue of access to files and on wider issues. The unease I sense is not, however, steeped in doubt as to good intentions, mine or anyone else's, but as to how properly to characterise our actions. For example, when I say that I intend to assess candidates non-politically, do I *know how* properly to disentangle political from academic considerations, or when it may not be possible strictly to do this?

Probably I feel this unease not so much as Tutor for Admissions but more as a tutor in politics, selecting the students I shall be teaching just as my colleagues do theirs in their subjects. For there may be something problematic about the distinction as it operates, not only in assessing school reports (which may or may not contain information about a candidate's politics), but also the candidate's interview performance and his answers to questions on our entrance examination. After all, the student who wants to study politics normally has political reasons, often critical of the *status quo*; he would tend to be more of a political animal than students who want to study other subjects. Many of the entrance examination questions appear to invite expressions of political opinion. I am bound therefore to ask what makes information given me or impressions I form about a candidate's political views or activities 'academically relevant' (if at all) when deciding whether to recommend his admission to my college as a student of *politics*?[11]

The first part of an answer to this is fully obvious: that the sort of political reasons a person has for wishing to study politics is strictly irrelevant to the assessment of his academic suitability. But this is really connected with the second part of an answer, which runs as follows. I try to put on one side, i.e. to achieve detachment from, my own political views (which are liberal-cum-democratic socialist) when assessing a candidate; and to take into account, for example, whether he can state his position coherently, how well he can argue for it, including how aware he is of difficulties or objections and how he meets them (some signs of open-mindedness, objectivity, and possibly impartiality) and how well he can marshall relevant arguments and evidence, how much he has thought about the topic for himself rather than mastered it mechanically, and so forth. Such evidences of academic quality, one supposes when trying to identify them, stand apart from the candidate's and one's own political beliefs; this much is a standard assumption of the liberal academic.

---

[11] Having an interest in politics in the sense of wanting to know how things work or happen is not of course equivalent to having a partisan political position, though such a position is often inarticulately implied in a certain way of explaining how things work. Some candidates avow only such descriptive–explanatory interests. As a further qualification, but of a different order, it should be added that in any case it is not a necessary condition of admission in my subject to have an interest in politics in either respect. For 'my subject' in Oxford is a course combining politics with both philosophy and economics (or only very recently, with either alone). I have not had, therefore, to face squarely the question of what if a candidate avowed no interest in politics. It is usual in such cases as have occurred in the past to expect him to have an interest in at least one of the three branches; an interest in not more than two has been the norm. It hardly needs adding that in this kind of case the academic relevance of an interest in politics is the same as having an interest in any other subject proposed for study: it is an index of motivation, though not the only one.

But to identify the marks of academic ability, I must myself be open-minded, detached, impartial and objective; and a necessary condition of my success is that I should know how to mark off what is political from what counts as evidence of academic ability. Sincerity is not enough in judging whether I succeed as an assessor, even though consciously striving to adhere to these standards is a necessary condition of success. This, surely, must raise questions concerning the subjective and objective conditions in which it is possible to be open-minded, etc. It is conceivable that some questions arise peculiarly from the subject matter of politics itself (and the social sciences in general). For how far are one's criteria of relevance, of coherence, and of critical awareness (if not consciously) connected with a particular political perspective, supporting it or being supported by it? Put very crudely, would a liberal, a Marxist, and a fascist have the same tests of these academic qualities? Would they also have equally strong dispositions to apply them on all occasions?

The assessment of candidates for academic jobs

The point of these questions may be put into sharper focus by following up one aspect of the political files controversy mentioned earlier, namely, testimonials written by tutors on behalf of students to prospective employers, grant-awarding bodies, and the like. Here, as with admissions, teaching, and examining, the separation of academic from political criteria is held to be a vital principle.[12]

[12] In the ensuing account several aspects of the political/academic distinction in connection with testimonials are not discussed, e.g. for many jobs non-academic criteria are often most important; for others, such as party organisation work or the British Race Relations Board, political beliefs and activities are relevant; and in some cases where the post in question is not academic, one may think that providing political information about the applicant is improper because appointment to it should not be affected by political considerations (a restriction, in other words, on what information the employer can justifiably expect or act on when choosing 'whomever he likes'). No doubt radical, including liberal, critics have focused on the danger of individual academics' and universities' complicity in the 'market capitalist society' and an 'authoritarian state apparatus'. There is therefore growing sensitivity to the possibility that tutors will be asked for information about their students' politics. In judging whether political information is reasonably required, or when discussing this with the student before writing, there is a real enough sense in which the referee is responsible himself for taking, or for advising the student whom he can properly ask to take, the decision. The decision as to whether political information is irrelevant for filling a particular job or role in society is itself a moral–political decision, though how far or in what ways it is politically non-neutral will depend on the decision-maker's intention and on whether his decision affects the balance of power between opposing camps. However, this is still to leave open the question of how severe the standards of political neutrality are to be in such cases; for example, is the mere fact that an academic recommends his student for a given post, or addresses himself to the employer's criteria of employability, sufficient to void the claim to be acting in a politically neutral way? On the other hand, can such facts never be relevant to that judgement? Compare recommending a man as (a) manager of a concentration camp and (b) manager of a capitalist firm, etc.

But when writing about men applying for academic posts, I am not always certain as to how to defend the ways in which I distinguish between academic considerations and irrelevant political ones. To start with, it is of course possible impartially and objectively to say that a man's promise as a scholar has not yet been fulfilled because of the time and energy his political involvements have absorbed (qualifying this if one believes that such involvements have usefully fed into his academic work or may feed into it in future). Judging a man in this way is like saying that had he not, for example, been so much involved with rowing, or chess, or girls, he might have achieved more academically. It is the effect of his political involvement on his academic progress, not my political assessment of the involvement itself, which is relevant. Thus far the parallel with school reports on admissions candidates is clear.

However, when the man is a seriously committed Marxist (or anarchist, or syndicalist, or Catholic – that is, none of the things I am), where precisely does my academic judgement end and the political begin? For example, if he is a Marxist is the line between the two affected by what sort of Marxist I judge him to be (which items of belief or analysis he takes most seriously and how he interprets them, e.g. the doctrine of the unity of theory and practice)? And quite apart from guesses about his potential for disrupting a university or threatening the values I understand it to require, how far is the academic judgement about the qualities of his mind and work tied to political judgement?

No doubt for a traditional liberal academic there is a standard way of tackling these questions, as adumbrated earlier in the case of admissions candidates. For example, if he says that the man's arguments in political theory are too often unclear, or irrelevant, he intends this criticism to apply to him not (or not only) *as a Marxist* (given the standard it might be alleged that Marxists as a class peculiarly attain), but as a teacher and creative worker in his subject. After all, one could sensibly judge a liberal to suffer the same defects, and perhaps identify them as conspicuous in his attempts to discuss Marxism. Again, one practical test of capacity for impartiality is to ask whether a man's commitment to Marxism would any the more disable him from presenting full and fair accounts of rival political ideas than, say, a liberal commitment would. Similar rules of thumb might be used to assess achievements of and potentialities for objectivity and open-mindedness, though some may carry the illicit assumption that it is the liberal academic at his best who is the exemplar in terms of which all others are to be assessed.

In arguing that such academic judgements can be severed from political ones, the liberal seems to presuppose that standards of clarity, coherence, relevance, and critical power on the one hand, and those of impartiality, objectivity, and open-mindedness on the other, need not vary with the types of theory under consideration. The fact that such standards (or at least those in the latter group) may not be readily isolated from what is often meant by a liberal position or a liberal society does not make judgements of impartiality etc., political judgements. Furthermore, adherence to these standards in assessing men for academic posts would lead to the kind of diversity of academic and (personal) political involvements in a politics faculty which, it is often argued by liberals, reenforces understanding of them and dispositions to apply them.

In general I start from this view, though I remain unclear as to whether, and if so at what point, its validity is limited because of any possible substantive connection between criteria of academic assessment and particular political perspectives. How, for example, is one to understand fully a liberal's readiness to accept the possibility of ruling out racists, fascists or communists? He would argue, I imagine, that in certain individual cases their honestly held beliefs may stand in the way of achieving the requisite standards in their politics teaching and research; but not that the mere fact of holding such political views, by virtue of their content alone or their hypothetical political implications, is sufficient to justify the claim that racists etc., cannot be sufficiently impartial etc.; still less that they cannot be of sufficiently high overall or specialist intelligence. One would have carefully to consider the evidence in individual cases and actual circumstances. But if one were to press this position further, one might find lurking behind it the tacit assumption that any (or perhaps any non-liberal?) political commitment that is intense and pervasive for the individual creates legitimate doubts as to that person's capacity to come up to the requisite standards. Yet it might be retorted by the liberal academic that it is entirely proper to take into account, whether the cause is political or non-political, a person's deficient *disposition* to strive to come up to these standards; for this would be crucially relevant to his academic suitability. The mere fact that suspicions of deficiency are more likely to attach to holders of certain beliefs rather than others (suspicions which may turn out to be unfounded) does not entail that the relevant standards themselves are differently *conceived* within different political perspectives; to establish that the latter is the case would require other types of argument. Having thus defended the distinction between academic and political criteria in the face of the allegation that it must be very thin if a certain range of political beliefs – at the extreme, all those except liberalism itself – raise *prima facie* issues of academic suitability, the liberal academic may none the less concede a quite different point. He might well be prepared to acknowledge the fact that the political neutrality of his position may at times be quite limited; for example, in a society where there are political conflicts over whether racists etc., ought to acquire any positions of influence and responsibility and therefore opportunities for acting on their beliefs, the thorough-going liberal academic, when deciding on academic grounds whether or not to recommend the appointment of a racist etc., as a teacher of politics, is willy-nilly taking sides in this wider conflict, whichever way he decides.[13]

Of course such arguable instances of political non-neutrality may in fact be connected with a second kind of judgement that a liberal academic may make in the sort of case I have been considering: a person is less eligible to teach in a 'liberal' university, which is bent on upholding standards of rational enquiry and instruction, if his beliefs actually commit him to undermining deliberately the conditions for striving effectively to maintain the standards. However, if this test of fitness were to be wider than (a) outright determination to produce disruption, or even the wider one of (b) likelihood to disrupt, and was therefore something like (c) an injurious effect on academic standards over the long run, then it would be difficult to detect the difference between this ground and the type that has been adduced in the preceding paragraph.

Thus far all this still suggests the liberal academic's readiness to apply, as open-mindedly, impartially, and objectively as possible, the relevant academic tests to candidates holding any shade of political opinion, even though he may on inductive grounds be disposed to think that the holding of certain opinions is more likely than others to affect the candidate's capacity to come up to the requisite minimum. It does not follow that the standards themselves are distinctively determined by or constitutive of a particular political perspective.

However, as my final, but still inconclusive way of probing this position, consider the case where I once had to write to a university about a strongly committed, politically active, radical Marxist who was applying for a post as a politics teacher. On that occasion I found it difficult to separate clearly on the one hand: (i) my academic values and standards as I understood them from (ii) my attitude towards a man whose academic and political position was critical of (i) and my ways of distinguishing between academic and political considerations; and on the other hand: (iii) my view of him

---

[13] A correlative case of political non-neutrality on the part of liberal academics would be that in which they proposed to appoint the best qualified man in the teeth of government policy discriminating against, e.g. blacks or Jews.

as politically dogmatic from (iv) my fear of his being dogmatic, that is, insufficiently open-minded and in consequence insufficiently impartial and objective, as a teacher. Although much that has been argued in the last few pages could help to understand what was involved in (iii) and (iv), much of my genuine uncertainty sprang from the fact that he held views about the impossibility of neutral, detached political theorising which implied that most if not all academic standards of liberal academics in this field were illusory, and inherently or by implication functioned as part of a political ideology which he rejected. On this view, then, there were important internal connections between political and academic considerations. If this was correct, then the validity of the distinction between these considerations could not be as general as I had supposed it was.

In recognising this I was obliged for the sake of impartiality faithfully to report his views, including how they compared with my own, i.e. in a way that he would have done himself. This still left me and the people who had to decide on his application with the responsibility for declaring whether, and if so, how well (and on whose standards) he qualified. Judged by my own conventional standards, much of his work was very creditable, and might well continue to be. But having considered his theoretical views of academic and political criteria (which were also central to his theoretical work) as objectively as I could, I came to the honestly held though not uncontroversial view that he lacked a certain degree of rigour and conceptual sophistication. It remained unclear, however, whether I wished to suggest either or both (a) that his position could have been formulated more plausibly had he greater ability, or (b) that anyone subscribing to a version of his view just could not be of very high intellectual calibre. Judgements of type (b) are not uncommon in the academic world, especially when there are serious divisions between practising academics in the same field; and there is perhaps a difficulty in distinguishing in one's intellectual adversaries between their taking proper account of serious objections (thus evidencing their open-mindedness) and their sticking to positions in spite of what one believes any open-minded person would have abandoned or very substantially modified in the face of such objections.

If one proceeds on the assumption that perfect objectivity is impossible to achieve, the most open-minded making of allowances for legitimate differences would incline one to put more weight on judgements of type (a). Yet it is just this sort of open-minded recognition of the more cogently argued divergences between intellectual and political perspectives that may well lead to acceptance of the fact (if that is what it is) that at least some, perhaps crucially important, criteria of academic assessment in political teaching and creative work may be connected distinctively with political positions. For example, if there are in political and social analysis both (i) disputes over criteria of relevance as to the facts that would confirm or disconfirm a theory (e.g. the reality of class differences or class struggles), and (ii) close connections between such disputes and political positions adopted, then the judgement of one adversary by another in academic terms, e.g. whether he has a good sense of what is relevant, must take into account the dual possibility that criteria of relevance are theory-bound and that such theories are either constitutive of or have implications for political positions.[14]

Furthermore, what perhaps was also at issue in the writing of the testimonial was the liberal belief that it is possible to sever political activity from academic activity because there is no logically binding relation between theory and action; e.g. theoretical liberals can in their theories provide all sorts of bases for radical criticism of existing society, but that does not strictly entail their commitment to political action. On another analysis this belief could be challenged as based on fundamental misconceptions, and the sincere challenger may well be committed to taking actions that would appear from the liberal academic's perspective to conflate or at least not to distinguish sharply enough academic and political criteria and therefore to diverge from standards of correct professional conduct. One wonders in all seriousness, therefore, whether a thorough-going Marxist teacher writing testimonials on behalf of an anti-Marxist student would see the disjunction of such criteria as I do, or see it as problematic in roughly the same way. If we were to find common ground, I should like to imagine how our argument would proceed towards that point.[15]

3 The distinction undermined

At any rate it seems to be important theoretically and (very closely connected with this) necessary in practice, when attempting to negotiate with students who are anxious that political con-

---

[14] Such an issue is discussed in Charles Taylor, 'Neutrality in Political Science', and Isaiah Berlin, 'Does Political Theory Still Exist?', *Philosophy, Politics and Society*, Third and Second Series respectively, eds. P. Laslett and W. G. Runciman (Blackwell); and S. I. Benn, 'Political Philosophy', *Encyclopedia of Philosophy*, ed. P. Edwards (Macmillan, 1967).

[15] I have not, of course, focused on the question of whether in the context of the case under consideration, where the candidate saw himself, and was seen by many others, as advancing a political cause allied with theoretical position, my assessment of him, according to academic standards as best as I could interpret them, could sensibly be seen as a politically non-neutral act. For was I not, in recommending him (which is what I did in fact), taking sides in some sort of political conflict? Certainly the political sensations which surrounded the man not long after he had been teaching would make this a real enough question.

siderations should not influence admissions, teaching, examining, and recommending and appointing for teaching posts,[16] that one's position be known on such issues as may arise from the academic/political distinction. In a university, if nowhere else, it is essential that, questions of personal sincerity apart, there should be discussion of the range of variability in the distinction and the factors that make for such variability.

To do at least this much may in future be a necessary if not a sufficient condition of maintaining the trust of one's students in one's ability to operate with the distinction. To say only this, however, is to assume, with no guarantee of being right, that my students will continue to support or criticise me in my academic role and the university in ways that presuppose the validity of the distinction, broadly conceived as I shall probably continue to conceive of it. I mean that if a deeply critical situation were to develop, in which my college or the university was threatened by disruption or by gradual poisoning of the atmosphere conducive to serious, disinterested, and open-minded study and enquiry, academics may see it as their cardinal vocational responsibility to defend liberal academic values. The situation would be the more painful if such threats were (i) thought (rightly or wrongly) to be brought about by the actions of people who themselves sincerely avowed liberal beliefs, and (ii) occasioned or aggravated by failures (alleged or real) of the university or individual academics to live up to liberal pretensions. Nevertheless the defence may require extraordinary precautions, e.g. checking the political dispositions of candidates for admission and academic posts.[17] No doubt such action, though much against the liberal grain, could be represented as 'academically relevant' – not in the normal terms of assessing a candidate's ability and promise as a student or teacher, but in those of the essential conditions for the realisation of academic purposes. These conditions constitute the normal background, which when unchallenged makes possible fairly unproblematic applications of the narrow distinction between academic and political criteria of assessment. When conditions are 'abnormal', that is, when the normally presupposed purposes and values are themselves embroiled in a struggle, then the standard lib-

[16] Such concern is, it is worth noticing, often related to liberal political beliefs applied to the wider society (e.g. the career open to the relevant talents, justice conceived in terms of relevant characteristics for given social roles or occupations), which suggest that through the network of concepts and principles that apply to both academic activity and other activities the behaviour of individual academics and universities can easily acquire wide political significance.

[17] Leaving aside, however, important empirical issues bearing on the just administration of any such policy, e.g. on what evidence about a schoolboy, as well as forecasts of the future situation in a university, can one safely predict his political involvement in his next three or four years? *Mutatis mutandis* such questions would be relevant to academic appointments.

eral conceptions of the possibilities of applying non-political criteria and of political neutrality may be doubted by committed liberals themselves, even though their defensive moves may still be labelled 'academically relevant'.

If one takes the extraordinary precaution, supposing for a moment that it would be an effective strategy and justly administered, of assessing political attitudes and activities of candidates for admission and academic posts as 'academically relevant' in the *extended* sense just explained, one can hardly claim in any straightforward way that one is upholding liberal academic values. For in such a case – or in another, which might be envisaged, of liberal academics justifying political files in a no-holds-barred atmosphere – the political has been consciously extended into an area that would hitherto have been understood in liberal terms to be distinguishable and immune from it, namely, the academic.

Perhaps, then, the application of the liberal academic's distinction is easiest, most fully consistent, or a real possibility only when political conditions inside and outside a university do not require him openly to act politically in upholding the distinction itself. But its active defence may well involve, if only (and optimistically) temporarily, assuming part if not the whole of the responsibility for shifting or effacing the previously existing line between academic and political considerations – though how much responsibility would depend on how much one ascribed (no doubt disputably) to agitators the responsibility for 'bringing politics into' a situation which had been seen as essentially non-political at some earlier stage. In the sharply polarised circumstances I have imagined (which have not been all that imaginary in some universities), the liberal academic and his university thus run the risk of either an outright defeat or a Pyrrhic victory of their own values.

The case of overseas students' fees. However, some of the language I have just used to describe the conditions in which the liberal academic may be obliged to redraw the distinction between academic and political considerations and to withdraw his self-denying ordinance against political non-neutrality, especially when the essential presuppositions of his activity as an academic are at stake, depended upon some normal understanding of the distinction between academic and political considerations. For example, 'extraordinary precautions' and acting politically in an 'open' way were mentioned. The latter, at any rate, may have depended upon the controversial suggestion that nothing an academic does in his official or vocational capacity is political unless it is 'open' (whatever that means); or else that there are already things in some 'normal' conditions that are really political but not usually singled out specially as such because they do not diverge from norms included in stable, if unclear, understandings among the agents involved.[18]

These points may be clarified by considering a recent case in Oxford, although it had no element of conflict between students and the University. In this case the agents first accepted placidly a norm for the distinction between academic and political considerations, even though academic policies, as they were styled, in fact harboured a political ingredient. The situation then changed in two ways at the same time: (a) the political ingredient became rather more prominent, and (b) there developed a political conflict in a wholly conventional sense which was both internal and between the university and the government, and where the scope (though perhaps not the desire) for remaining politically neutral markedly diminished. The case is interesting because these two features were so closely related.

Let us take the 'initial' position. It is obvious from what has been said about admissions policies that educational standards must be applied impartially; thus a candidate's social class, religion, colour, country, etc., must be disregarded.[19] Now of course such a policy may actually work to the advantage of certain groups over others; but this fact would not of itself be sufficient to sustain the charge that the university or individual academics *qua* academics were acting politically non-neutrally. On the contrary, they would be much more likely to be exposed to the charge if they sought, at the sacrifice of impartial application of academic criteria, to revise the

[18] The first suggestion may be understood by distinguishing between (a) 'non-open', i.e. covert, political involvements in the sense of the tacit or indirect support academics may be held to be lending to conditions in the wider community, e.g. those which happen to be favourable to the maintenance of academic standards and the achievement of academic goals, such as university autonomy; and (b) deliberate, i.e. overt, attempts to create or maintain such conditions. Since what counts as lending support tacitly or indirectly can be controversial, obviously this distinction cannot be applied straightforwardly in all contexts. However, the second suggestion is even more complex. It does not depend on the idea of (i) covert, in the sense of deliberately concealed and devious political involvement on the part of agents who know very well what they are doing; nor in the idea, often but not necessarily linked with (a), of (ii) agents being unaware of the *de facto* political element in or implications of their position which others may claim to identify. Both (i) and (ii) can be contrasted with 'acting politically in an *open* way'. But the idea needed here is that of (iii) agents being aware of a political element in their position but not, as they see it, obliged to attack or defend that element. It is not a focus of controversy; awareness that it is political may therefore become very dim, though not extinct – or very intense in a situation of conflict, when it then becomes 'open' (or 'more open'). Thus the concept of 'open' or 'covert' political involvement can function in contrast with several different ideas of what is not open, including others not explained here which depend on distinctions between public activity (e.g. taking a public stand such as writing to the press) and private activity (e.g. confining one's comments to university committees). Examples of (ii) and (iii) are given in the ensuing text; those of (a) and (b) in section 4.

[19] Except in so far as any such factors come legitimately into the academic assessment of present achievements and likely performance in the future.

conditions of competition between candidates by deliberately favouring one group over another, e.g. working class over middle class, or blacks over whites. At the same time, individual academics, in their non-academic capacity, could work politically for changes in the balance of educational and other opportunities between groups. The scope for political neutrality of a university or academics *qua* academics would, however, begin to shrink if admissions policies and standards became either very closely tied up with other conflicts or direct objects of political conflict (e.g. because seen from a non-academic point of view as one amongst several obstacles to greater social equality and harmony). Such, then, is the minimum background required to understand the case to be considered: the raising of fees for overseas students in British universities.

But to set the stage more fully let us, as a second step, imagine a university which already has a policy, with perhaps only the occasional marginal wavering from impartiality, of striving for a particular mixture of groups, by class, colour, nationality etc. Is this an academic or a political policy? It is not always easy to say. There are academic arguments, more obvious to those in universities, for mixing people of different backgrounds; but so long as there is no abuse of academic standards to achieve the mixture (more often achieved in any case by accident and given retrospective endorsement than actively pursued by 'open' measures, e.g. soliciting applications) there is hardly a motive for asking whether there is an extra-academic reason for endorsing a certain mixture. So long as there is one good academic reason (as there usually is) and so long as getting the mixture is not incompatible with the maintenance of academic standards, then extra-academic motives for wanting a certain mixture will probably be overlooked, and when not, then accepted as neither here nor there. That is how a minor political ingredient can come, unsurreptitiously yet non-controversially, into the policy, understood overall as essentially academic because the extra-academic feature of it could never of its own accord justify it.

It has long been a policy of British universities to welcome overseas students; Oxford has probably had a higher proportion of them than any of the others; the arguments for having them are regarded as obvious and reinforced in Oxford by the assumption that a university of international reputation would naturally attract and wish to have many overseas students. The admission of such students has not been seen as pushing out well qualified British candidates, or to require any real divergence from impartiality. The partially extra-academic consideration was that it was believed that countries formerly under British rule would be helped economically and politically if their students had part of their education in Britain.

In December 1966 the British government announced that fees for all overseas students in all universities would have to be increased, but not those for British students; and, to force the move, proposed to reduce central government grants to the universities by an amount equal to the income they were expected to gain from the increase in their fees. This produced a storm of protest. To its financial cost Oxford refused until 1970 to fall into line, after every other university except one had done so. The position of Oxford and its academics became politicised in several ways.

In the political context up to December 1966, how foreign students should be treated was not an issue, but after that it certainly became one, against a background of steeply rising demand for higher education from British students and rising costs to be met by the British taxpayer. The argument that what Oxford had been doing was not merely academically justified but also a minor form of foreign aid became more prominent. Furthermore, neutrality on the part of the university and that of individual academics *qua* academics in relation to the government became increasingly difficult to maintain, even if one wanted to maintain it, especially as members of the faculty, who were deeply divided, were asked on several occasions to debate and vote on resolutions to increase the fees. The situation also made more obvious the close dependence of the university on central government financial policy and the general state of the economy; the ability of the government to impose the decision, with hardly any prior consultation and no bargaining, raised to a new level fears for university autonomy (and perhaps involved broadly political attitudes towards a Labour government in as much as many of its opponents also attacked this decision, though of course in the name of university autonomy). For if it was a conscious policy on the part of the university to maintain something like the existing proportion of foreign students (about 12% in Oxford), then the government's decision, interpreted as a deterrent to such students, was an interference with the internal concerns of the university.

Furthermore, complaints about discrimination against a particular group of students were heard; but this was perhaps the most politically complex issue of all. On the one hand, not to raise the fees of all students uniformly was the central government's way of not disturbing a delicate political balance between its own and local governments' financial support for the universities. The vast majority of British students have their fees paid by local government grants; increasing their fees would not impose a personal or family burden on more than a small minority, but a further burden on local governments and therefore payers of local taxes, who would naturally wish to thrust it upon the central government. A university's taking a stand for or against an increase in overseas students' fees was therefore bound to have a non-neutral impact on a conflict between local and central government. On the other hand, all students' fees now represent merely a notional contribution to the full cost of running British universities (only 11% of all university income in 1963 and probably much less now); to increase the fees of overseas students (many of whose grant-conferring bodies at home or in Britain would in any case meet the increase) would only be to introduce a marginal difference in the degree to which both categories of student were subsidised by university endowments and even more so by the central government and therefore British taxpayers. But once these implications were understood it became more obvious that, whichever side an individual academic or the university took, he or it would also be taking sides (effectively if unwillingly) on the political issue of how much and in what form British taxpayers should support non-British students, and possibly on the further issues of the scale and type of government aid to overseas, especially Commonwealth, nations and the impact the decision would have on the relations between the governments concerned.

Thus the pre-December 1966 possibilities of political neutrality for academics *qua* academics and Oxford University diminished with startling rapidity as each defined their stands and acted in accordance with what they understood to be essentially academic considerations. In so far as such agents were unaware of or disclaimed the *de facto* political non-neutrality of their action, their political position may be said to have remained only partly 'open' or 'overt'. But as this example also shows, the initial subsidiary element in the university's policy was not 'openly' political when it functioned against some supposed normal background of 'non-open' (or 'less open') involvement, one in which a lively sense of its political nature was dampened by prolonged absence of controversy. Once the conflict broke out such consciousness quickly sharpened; the foreign aid ingredient became more 'openly' political, especially because its advocates believed that by exposing it their cause would be helped, though it continued to be very secondary to the academic arguments that were used, e.g. those against interference with a university's internal policies.

4 *The teaching of politics*

At this rather abrupt stopping point I should like to turn to my final examples, drawn from events in Oxford of May–June 1968.

Amongst the several targets picked out by students at a high point of agitation was the course in Philosophy, Politics and Economics. It was intensively criticised – as insufficiently 'relevant' to contemporary social issues (a claim to such relevance having first been made some fifty years ago in the university's legislation creating the course); as excessively narrow in its coverage of rival doctrines in all three subjects (and therefore not impartial in so far as not all relevant views on contemporary issues were included); and as effectively, if not in intention, politically non-neutral in its orientation to the *status quo*.[20]

Although many arguments put forward in this period of active criticism seemed to reflect little awareness of their conceptual and empirical difficulties, there seemed to me to be a range of intelligent and responsibly made points against the design of the syllabus in politics and the approach of many politics tutors, myself included, in their teaching. The politics syllabus in Oxford has given very little scope to characteristic American concerns with behaviouralism, scientific methodology, general theory construction, and the conversion of political studies into a 'value-free' science; and normative political philosophy has never been pushed out to the point of extinction. Nevertheless, the range of subject matter has until very recently tended overwhelmingly to reflect, no doubt without conscious political intentions, typical modern liberal–democratic concerns with certain types of empirical analysis and with the stability of Western democracies, the Soviet Union being added for contrast. Over the years there have been gentlemanly tugs of war in my faculty, and occasionally between some faculty members and some students, over what is centrally important in the learning of politics: usually in the mundane form of what topics should be studied, what material used, and so on. It has been harder to accuse Oxford tutors of systematic political bias in their actual teaching because that has tended to emphasise a critical attitude towards virtually any standard empirical generalisations in political science, without attempting to replace this with a coherent overall framework of analysis.[21]

[20] It is necessary here to issue the warning that there were many issues contested in Oxford at this time, and that these disputes stood in many varied relations to one another. Each one and its complex relations with others would therefore require its own very extended analysis, which cannot be made here, in order to identify the possibilities of and limitations upon taking a neutral position. However, it is worth emphasising that the neutrality at stake in each dispute or facet of a dispute was not necessarily political; I shall therefore try to mark some of the points at which this was or was not the case, though it is not always possible to state this without qualification.

[21] As might be found in the works of, for example, Easton, Almond, Deutsch, or Lasswell. Having said this, it is still worth asking whether the critical attitudes inculcated by Oxford tutors nevertheless presuppose certain canons of criticism, which constitute potentially a systematic orientation to the study of politics and which may carry certain implicit political evaluations.

However, as I saw it, many positions taken in discussions of what is most worth learning about politics had certain political implications (in relation to some live political issues) or reflected political positions. It seemed to me that in my own and other tutors' attempts to define the centrally relevant body of knowledge and controversy in political studies, though a genuine academic exercise in a conventional sense (as practised, for example, in traditional political philosophy), it was very difficult to find a neat way of separating academic from political positions or to produce a conclusive argument as to whether one recipe or another was more or less or wholly ﾟolitically neutral. Indeed if the politics course had to be relevant to contemporary issues, the likelihood of its teachers being able consistently to maintain political neutrality in respect of all political contests, even those in Britain alone, seemed rather remote. None the less discussions until 1968 tended to proceed on the assumption – wonderfully satisfying to the academic conscience, but not totally devoid of illusion – that such questions could be settled without reference to the problems of political neutrality. After all, it was widely assumed, real political conflicts could be studied objectively, impartially, and with detachment; to study them in these ways is not *ipso facto* to take sides in them; and indeed it is not.

Given my views, however, I did not see my students' heightening of interest in what a politics course should contain and how it should be taught as introducing fundamentally illegitimate, still less unprecedented, political considerations – though their introduction was of course explicit, and some versions of it were objectionable from an academic point of view (e.g. to teach only radicalism). I agreed with them, for example, though not for all their reasons and not as far as some arguments went, that Marxism and other important radical theories were not given sufficient scope, and that this represented a defect of *academic* balance, operating as a discouragement to open-mindedness and impartiality in teachers and students.[22] At the same time I welcomed the students' discussions and representations because of another controversy of long standing: the added weight of student opinion marginally helped to put through the politics faculty an important change in the syllabus, a new and wide-ranging paper (i.e. course) in political theory, which included anarchism and various shades of socialist and revolutionary theory, and which would have to be studied by almost all

---

[22] In 1969 a new paper (i.e. course) in Marxism was introduced as an optional subject in politics. No counter-balancing paper in conservatism was asked for or introduced; but one must believe in this instance that not politics but academic judgements of intellectual content had much to do with this.

students of politics. I had, because of my views as to what is centrally relevant, for years been urging this very step without success. For some time, then, I had hardly taken anything like a neutral position in the Oxford faculty on this controversial issue (though the absence of any explicit relation between that issue and recognisable political conflicts in or just outside the Oxford context meant that my position was not *politically* non-neutral:[23] that my views and those of others in the faculty were based on acceptable academic considerations had not been questioned).

I and my politics colleague in the college, Steven Lukes, attempted in another way to respond to what we thought was a reasonable concern. Indeed our known attitudes before May 1968 probably created in that month the reasonable expectation that we would take an active part in sponsoring changes or responding to criticism. As there would be an unavoidable delay before the official introduction of studies for the new political theory paper and in any case men then in their final year would miss it completely, we thought we should discuss with any of our students who were sufficiently interested the ways in which political ideas could be studied immediately on an informal basis. Though certainly agitated, the overall situation in Oxford was not so highly charged, and the taking of sides on the revision of the politics syllabus was not so closely related to other positions being contested at that stage,[24] that Lukes and I could not sensibly take up a position that was somewhere between that of many of the most radical students (whose apparent indifference to academic achievement we openly criticised) and that of a great many of our politics faculty colleagues round the rest of the university. The situation was not so polarised that our response to students' criticism of the syllabus was likely to be sensibly interpreted by those tutors in the faculty who disagreed with us as support for radical students' attacks on the authority of the university or their analysis of the university as a repressive agency of capitalism.[25]

Although some students intermingled criticism of society with criticism of the politics syllabus (for example, by taking instances of

---

[23] A verdict which is qualified towards the end of this account.

[24] For example, the form that student involvement should take in the government of the university; and connected with this, the right of the university's disciplinary officers to restrict the political activities of students, an issue that led to a non-violent demonstration in May.

[25] Reference here and below to 'radical' and 'militant' critics must be understood in the special context of Oxford, where I have never encountered anyone like the more extreme campus revolutionaries of the U.S.A. or the Continent. However, I suspect there were some general ideological similarities between them.

deficient impartiality in the latter as evidence of the university's illicit support for an unfree society[26]), it was not difficult for Lukes and me to suggest that our intentions were educational and not political. Our intention in proposing the extra measure of an informal class was to help students achieve more quickly a better grasp of ideas which seemed to us and them to inform various shades of contemporary radical attitude and action; and this help was intended equally for non-radical students. We saw an educational value in choosing to have an influence as teachers that was at least in some respects very arguably neutral so far as many wider issues then being contended in Oxford were concerned (e.g. student representation), and some issues of wider import to which these were connected (e.g. the capacity of existing institutions to create stronger forms of democratic control). Furthermore, in the prevailing atmosphere we judged too many of our students to have too low a level grasp of ideas which seemed to come from Marx, Lenin, Sorel, Sartre, Fanon, Marcuse etc. There was something embarrassing, or perhaps damaging to our *amour propre* as teachers, about students who espoused or rejected ideas that had little or no official place in the politics syllabus as it was then constituted. Though we thought the students should have taken more initiative themselves to raise the level of discourse, we felt some responsibility *qua* academics for the level they reached unaided.[27]

Our proposal, thus based on thoroughly liberal presuppositions and intentions, naturally implied a responsibility not to influence the students in any particular political direction, but only to assert by our own example standards of informed, rational discourse. This would include, we hoped, impartial accounts of rival doctrines, exposure of difficulties as open-mindedly and objectively as possible in both radical and anti-radical views, and as a fundamental issue for discussion, whether political beliefs could be analysed in some 'value-neutral' way, and what such a concept meant. In all this we assumed that our students still adhered to academic standards and were prepared to give and take criticism in such terms. A necessary condition of success, then, was that neither we nor our students would see such discussion itself as politically non-neutral, that is, as

[26] Though a few critics were far from hoping for greater impartiality as a consequence of their criticism: they wished the university to withdraw what they saw as support for one side and to transfer it to another, the radical or revolutionary.

[27] A very recognisable stamp of academic orthodoxy was imprinted on the enterprise by distributing lists of topics and reading, and asking for volunteers to read papers. It should be explained that this informal class involved work for tutors and students over and above their usual academic responsibilities, a fact which is relevant to a point in the next paragraph.

a time-wasting (or valuable) divergence from militant action or turning into a committee of action guided by a politically determined vanguard. For the vast majority, though conscious of the warmer political climate in Oxford, there was readiness to accept our proposal as essentially academic and non-political, notwithstanding their clear appreciation of the fact that it was much less likely to have been put forward without the changes that had occurred in that climate.

Having said all this, however, it may still be asked, *what* were Lukes and I doing? For example, were there any elements of false consciousness in our position[28] – that is, was the account of our intentions, depending on the cardinal distinction between academic and political considerations and supposing possibilities of politically neutral action, misleading? And if so, would it make more sense to see us as personally responsible for this (because capable of abandoning falsity in favour of truth), or as passive victims of 'the system'?

As stated already, I very much doubt that we had the *intention* of influencing the balance of political power in May–June by, say, diverting students into serious academic study when some of them might otherwise have used that time to plot fresh challenges to the college or the University. As for *effects*, we certainly could not see how, as a result of anything we or others would be likely to say about the ideas we proposed to discuss, the political attitudes or dispositions to action of our more militant students would be altered in any way. And it was understood that attendance was voluntary; no one who preferred to do something else, political or non-political, need have been deflected from his alternative. In fact the students' freedom was such that the informal class collapsed after a very brief trial because the initial support it seemed to have quickly diminished. Even if, as some sort of effect of such academic discussions as we planned, some militant student had in fact moderated his political opinions and actions, this I think, given the methods of argument we and our students would have been likely to continue using, could hardly have been held to be a sufficiently direct causal consequence.

Nevertheless, it is worth recalling my earlier remark that part of my conscious response to the criticism of the syllabus as politically non-neutral because of its imbalanced coverage of controversial ideas was to react in liberal academic style – that is, by striving to restore the impartial treatment that would lend credibility to the

---

[28] Seen, however, only through my eyes; this account is wholly mine, and Lukes shares no responsibility for any part of it. Furthermore, it is necessarily an imperfect reconstruction of events seen in retrospect after two years.

separation of academic and political considerations. I now see more clearly in retrospect that on this account it may not be absurd to suggest that I was acting politically in defence of academic values.[29] For the partiality or bias that some students thought to be sinister was a ground for *political* criticism of the university's overall position in society; though, as mentioned above, I was mainly conscious of the need to meet well-founded criticism based on *academic* standards, the criticisms of the syllabus were sometimes connected with wider issues about the position of the university. I saw such criticism sustained over a longer period as a source of disaffection from the general pretensions of the university to sponsor detached, open-minded, objective, and impartial study. At the same time a few militant students were demanding that the university should be transformed into a spearhead of radical change in the wider community, and condemning the existing university, as it is constituted internally and by virtue of its external connections with society, as a bulwark of a repressive socio-economic system. On their view any tutor who acted on the presupposition that he could by his teaching and general example contribute to the university's or his college's commitment to academic ideals was *eo ipso* an unwitting agent of the governing classes and a victim of false consciousness – a person who, that is, intends to realise values that the overall situation in effect deflects into the realisation of others. Against such a representation of the university and my position *qua* academic I could not remain neutral, however much I sought to consider it openmindedly.

But the reality I saw myself acting in and upon was not nearly as much politicised by what I or other academics had done or had omitted to do as by the doctrines and activities of a militant minority (out of the larger critical minority) who were out of sympathy with liberal academic values. Nevertheless reality was much more politicised than it had been, or seemed to be, before 1968. In these circumstances to work against the development of conditions in which there could develop serious hostility towards the internal values of academic activity, which would place in danger the future possibilities of realising such values in practice, seemed to me a responsibility flowing from my vocational commitment to preserving an academic and independent way of thinking, for myself and others. The defence of a university's academic values may therefore require vigorous efforts to remove grounds of criticism of academic practice, in so far at any rate as the liberal academic could accept

---

[29] The case may also be an example to support Barrington Moore's claim that not all political pressures on liberal academics are necessarily hostile to the improvement of academic standards.

them as valid. In Oxford, as I saw it, this affected the practice of educating students of politics. In that context the efforts made may sensibly be seen as having had a political significance, just as in other contexts the defence of these values may call for political resistance to external control, or for politically important withdrawals from certain entanglements in the interests and institutions of the wider community, or even for political action on a broad front when serious threats to the possibilities of realising academic values stem from widespread conditions in the wider community.

PART III

The nature of Part III is that of an extended postscript rather than of a conclusion. It makes no pretence of 'completing' the preceding discussions or of drawing them to a close by a few judicious generalisations; they will on the contrary be left unsystematically open. In it I return to some of the points raised in Part I and which need most clearly to be expanded, modified or retracted in the light of the papers by my fellow contributors and of other critical discussions in which we have had the opportunity of taking part severally or together. There are, it goes without saying, many other points which call for discussion and to which we may, hopefully, be able to return on some future occasion.

1 Kolakowski

In his paper on 'Neutrality and Academic Values' Leszek Kolakowski explicitly disagrees with my approach, in Part I, to a definition of 'neutrality' and implicitly with my account of impartiality. Inevitably, both disagreements turn at least in part on questions of terminology; but they are central to the issues at stake and it is important to try to sort them out.

The point at which the first disagreement becomes explicit can be located precisely enough in the last sentence of Kolakowski's second paragraph.

Neutrality presupposes a conflict and presupposes too that the neutral person is not a party to the conflict. Neutrality cannot be conceived, therefore, as a character trait or as an aspect of personal disposition. I can be neutral only in relation to a particular situation of conflict. *I am neutral in relation to a conflict when I purposely behave in such a way so as not to influence its outcome.*

This paragraph provides the material for a varied pattern of agreement and disagreement between us. Again, it is worth quoting Kolakowski's own statement of our main disagreement fairly fully.

The reason why I am not altogether satisfied with the definition proposed by Montefiore – he defines 'neutrality' as an attitude of helping or hindering to an equal degree all the parties to a conflict; to avoid giving any help or hindrance at all would be the limiting case of this attitude – is because it seems to allow of using the same term for a variety of attitudes which may not only be different, but which may be opposed to each other *both in content and in motivations* in face of one and the same conflict . . . In particular if my neutrality was limited to those cases where I was trying to create an equilibrium of force among the parties to a conflict, it would mean that I was neutral only when giving unilateral help to the weaker side. Either concept of neutrality – that of helping or hindering both sides equally or that of aiming at an equilibrium of the forces in conflict – may hardly be reconciled with the current meaning of the word.

We may put aside for the moment the problems involved in the apparently evident incompatibility of the two concepts of neutrality mentioned in the last sentence of this passage.[1] This apart, the main source of our disagreement appears to lie in an important ambiguity in our common starting point, namely that neutrality presupposes always a conflict and that to be neutral in relation to a conflict is to stand away from or to keep out of it. There is a difference, however,

---

[1] In fact, in Part I, I did not so much define a concept of neutrality in terms of aiming at an equilibrium of conflicting forces as arrive at this notion as at a first approach to a problem; but the theme is one on which Louis Marin lays much stress and we shall have to return to it in the course of reflecting on his paper.

between trying to do nothing to influence the outcome of a conflict to the advantage of one of the parties rather than to that of another and trying to have nothing to do with the conflict in any way whatsoever. The clearest examples of this may be furnished by conflicts whose rules or conditions of dispute are highly determinate, but which may be modified by some third party. Whether any given modification is likely to alter the existing balance of advantage between the conflicting parties is clearly an empirical question, open inevitably to varying degrees of conflicting interpretation, but not to be decided on exclusively *a priori* conceptual grounds. The distinction is masked by Kolakowski's phrase 'so as not to influence its outcome', for again there can be no sharp line to be drawn between the style and 'incidental impacts' of a conflict and its outcome proper; it is not always equally obvious exactly what conflicts are about. It is clear enough, however, that where I was working with the idea that neutrality lies in keeping out of the struggle *between* the conflicting parties, Kolakowski has taken it to lie in acting so as to have no modifying impact on the conflict whatsoever; for in his view even 'to try to soften a conflict' is to abandon one's neutrality.

How far is this disagreement discounted as no more than tiresomely terminological? Since the distinction is a real one, there can be little point in arguing that either one way or the other of using the word 'neutrality' is somehow impossible. Indeed, so far as current English idiom goes, the distinction is probably pretty well reflected by that between such expressions as 'being neutral *towards* a situation of conflict' and 'being neutral *in* a situation of conflict'; another pair of similarly contrasting expressions would be 'non-involvement' and 'non-alignment'. In any case, however one decides the question of terminology, both concepts are evidently important. It makes, for example, a substantial difference to discussions of the political neutrality of the university that one should take 'neutrality' in the one way or the other. If it has been central to traditional liberal demand that the university should do nothing calculated to advance any one permissible political cause at the expense of any other, it has surely *not* been any part of this demand that it should do nothing to modify, hopefully in more rational and humane directions, the general tone or level of political debate and struggle in the community in which it exists.

If both ways of taking the term 'neutral' can find support in current idiom, both of them can be pushed to give rise to idiomatic difficulty. It would, for instance, seem odd to have to argue that any neutral country or international body which was able by virtue of its very neutrality to mediate in a conflict or to help in damping it down by providing a peace-making force, should as soon as it sought so to act thereby lose its qualifications as a neutral. Nor need this have to do with questions of motivation. Different parties may decide to remain neutral in relation to one and the same situation of conflict from a wide variety of motives, some admirable and others wholly the reverse. This seems to follow straightforwardly from the fact, on which Kolakowski and I agree, that neutrality is intentional; the concepts of motive and intention are so related that it must always be possible to intend the same act with different motivations, the question of a man's motives for acting in a given way being necessarily left open by mere knowledge of his intention to do so.

Kolakowski says that 'to sell arms to both sides at war with each other is to be actively involved in the conflict – regardless of the reasons for one's involvement and regardless of whether the help given is equal in absolute terms or proportional to the relative strength of the conflicting parties and aimed at securing a balance of force'. This is certainly true. On the other hand, according to Oppenheim in his treatise on *International Law*,[2] 'A neutral Power is not bound to prevent the export or transit, for one or other of the belligerents, of arms, munitions of war, or, in general, of anything which can be of use to an army or fleet.' For him, the supplier is acting in the role of a merchant rather than that of a soldier and for this reason may still be regarded as a neutral. No one could deny that the distinction between these two roles can become very fuzzy at the margins; one notorious way of exploiting this fuzziness is for the supplier to supply also technical assistance in the mastery and effective utilisation of the merchandise that he sells – and sells perhaps on implausibly generous terms. Nevertheless, however politically controversial the example of the arms trade may be and however further controversial the distinction that may be alleged between the political and the legal, Oppenheim's position also reflects an important point. Independently of the motivations or the interests at stake, not all involvements in situations of conflict need be interpreted as either intended to favour or in fact favouring any of the parties at odds.[3]

A father may confiscate his sons' flick-knives and supply them with boxing gloves instead without thereby departing from neutrality in the conflict *between* them, intending simply to render it less dangerous – unless, of course, he knows that one of them is very much better with knives and the other very much better at boxing. But at this point we find ourselves back with the problems of assessment of responsibility that were raised in Part I.

[2] 7th edn, Vol. 2, p. 739.

[3] Conversely, in cases where it is possible to determine close criteria for legal neutrality, it may also be possible to find practical ways of favouring the cause of some one party without thereby departing from strict legal neutrality.

In fact, both Kolakowski's and my own way of construing neutrality run into very much the same and this time substantial difficulties at analogously crucial points. For if, as we agree, neutrality is intentional, then it must always be presumed to be open to the would-be neutral to act after all in a non-neutral manner; one cannot sensibly be said to intend something that one knows very well is inevitable. This means that the intending neutral must believe, as I argued on p. 6, 'that there must be some sort of causal or otherwise practical relationship existing between him and at least some of the parties to the conflict in question'. All this makes it as difficult to argue that there is *any* way in which he could opt to have strictly no influence on the outcome of the conflict as that there is *any* way in which he could opt to give strictly no differential help to any of the parties in conflict. Similar difficulties raise similar issues and have to be met with similar considerations; I shall return to this point shortly. But first something may be said about two other prominent and associated differences between the lines that Kolakowski and I have taken.

The first of these concerns his claim that 'neutrality, whether justifiable or unjustifiable, always results from weakness, though', he immediately adds, 'that weakness may not always be blameworthy nor always attributable to the person involved, but sometimes attributable to certain peculiarities of our culture'. In fact he does not advance a general argument in support of this position; nor does he appear himself to stick to it with unvarying consistency.[4] Nor, more importantly, does it seem that his conception of neutrality actually requires him to maintain the existence of such a universal link between it and weakness. A strong power might, for instance, decide to remain neutral, in Kolakowski's sense, towards a conflict between two much weaker powers, not because the state of conflict was somehow to its advantage, but as a matter of principle. Such principled action may be unlikely; it is not therefore impossible. Nevertheless, the thesis that neutrality always results somehow from weakness does have a closer natural affinity with Kolakowski's way of explicating the concept than it does with mine.

The basis for this affinity may be shown as follows. If (i) 'I am neutral in relation to a conflict when I purposely behave in such a way so as not to influence its outcome', (ii) everything must prop-

---

[4] It is not easy to be sure of this, as the important notion of a weakness or imperfection that is to be attributed not to the individual involved but to his perhaps extremely general situation, leaves open a wide margin for interpretation. However, when Kolakowski says, very justly, that 'if I considered myself in duty bound to intervene in any and every personal conflict involving other people, I should be an importunate meddler. . . .', it is hard to think of any plausibly relevant weakness from which the neutrality he here clearly favours may be said to result.

erly be counted as belonging to the total outcome of a conflict that may be produced among its consequences and (iii) 'I can be neutral', as Kolakowski says that his main definition implies, 'only if the conflict somehow falls within the field of my interest', then it may well seem that there can be no question of my opting *not* to influence the conflict, unless I am relatively weak or unless there is some relative weakness or flaw in the context in which I have to act. For to say that something falls within my field of interest is to say that I have a natural motive for acting so as to ensure that it continues in or changes to a state appropriate to my interest. But if I have a natural motive for acting in a certain way, then if I am strong enough and in a situation which permits me to exercise my strength without suffering disproportionate penalties, it is to be presumed that this is the way in which I shall in fact act; for not so to do would require some other overriding motive. This could be furnished only by some feature of my total situation which obliged me so to count the alternative costs of acting in one way rather than another that the best available option could be no better than the least imperfect of a set of imperfect alternatives. Any source of such imperfections might not unnaturally be set down as a 'weakness' in myself or in my situation.

The main reason why this argument attaches itself more naturally to Kolakowski's way of interpreting neutrality as an avoidance of all involvement is that the fact that a conflict 'somehow falls within the field of my interest' does not necessarily give me an interest in supporting one side against the other. Indeed, I may have a positive interest in not so intervening, an interest that may be not only compatible but even closely associated with that which I have in the situation of conflict in general.[5] It is doubtless true that it is also often from a position of weakness that one may be led to seek refuge in a neutrality of mere non-intervention (one may, for example, need to placate both sides in equal degree). At other times, however, such non-intervention may only be possible from a position of strength; Ten Chien Liew's paper, with its description of the situation as it used to be in the University of Singapore, illustrates this point.

[5] A different kind of involvement in or of non-neutrality *towards* a conflict may be associated with an interest in seeing that neither side gains a decisive advantage over the other; but this would naturally lead to a series of non-neutral *interventions* in favour of whichever one judged to be the weaker side at any moment of apparently critical disequilibrium. Here I should tend to join with Kolakowski in rejecting any argument to the effect that a series of non-neutral interventions on alternate sides could be held to balance out to a position of neutrality over a long period of time. But this does not mean that there would be no point to such an argument; after all, the intervener is not 'basically' in favour of one side or the other to the extent of being prepared to help it to prevail. It means only that there is probably stronger point in rejecting it; after all, the intervener does deliberately intervene *between* the contending parties.

This argument probably does establish some sort of presumptive connection between weakness and neutrality as Kolakowski conceives it. Even so the connection is still not a necessary one and could only be made so by stretching the notion of weakness to a confusing extent. It is not a personal weakness in any ordinary sense to succeed in binding oneself by one's own self-imposed principles of non-intervention; nor need it be regarded as a *weakness* in either one's particular or one's general cultural situation that respect for such principles may carry risks of concomitant distress or harm for oneself. No doubt there is something unsatisfactory about such a state of affairs; there is a lot that is unsatisfactory about the human condition. Perhaps, but only perhaps, the very existence of any sort of conflict whatever *may* be regarded as an imperfection or a weakness in the culture or society in which the conflict arises. But granted the existence of conflict, it is an exaggeration to suggest that any reason for remaining neutral must indicate weakness located in one place or another, even if one supposes with Kolakowski that to remain neutral towards a conflict is deliberately to abstain from influencing its outcome in any way whatsoever. As for the neutrality that consists merely in deliberately abstaining from intervention in support of one side or another, we have noted that this may on occasion have to be associated with a position of comparative strength. The point may be summed up by saying that one may need a certain kind of strength to be able to influence a conflict through a refusal to be drawn *into* it.

The other immediately notable difference between Kolakowski's paper and what I wrote in Part I concerns his assertion that 'neutrality and impartiality are incompatible with regard to the same situation'. Kolakowski's account of impartiality is that 'I am (or I try to be) impartial if I evaluate the conflict and the rights and wrongs of both sides by assessing the situation in terms of more general rules that I accept *independently of this particular case* . . . I am not neutral, however, since "to be impartial" in a conflict implies intervening in it to try to influence its outcome.' And certainly if to be impartial in a conflict is to be construed as constituting a kind of intervention in it, and if neutrality is to be taken in the sense in which Kolakowski takes it, then the two *are* incompatible.[6]

---

[6] According to John Stuart Mill, 'Impartiality as an obligation of justice may be said to mean being exclusively influenced by considerations which it is supposed ought to influence the particular case in hand, and resisting the solicitations of any motives which prompt to conduct different from what these considerations would dictate.' On the face of it this might appear to run directly counter to Kolakowski's formulation. The appearance is, however, misleading. Considerations which *ought* to influence the particular case in hand ought also by clear implication to influence any other case like it in whatever may be the relevant respects; the motives which are to be resisted are those which would prompt to conduct inappropriately peculiar to the particular case in question.

There are, however, two ways in which this seems to be partly un-satisfactory even on Kolakowski's own general view of the matter. In the first place, it is not clear that simply assessing a situation must of itself be counted as an intervention in it with a view to influencing its outcome. It is the practical business that may be involved in the assessment, or the actions that may be consequent upon it, that constitute the intervention rather than the assessment itself. For example, those who have to assess candidates in competitive examinations, for appointments to jobs or for limited university places, are clearly engaged in determining the outcome of situations of conflict; yet the same assessments could be carried out simply in the interests of research, or out of pure curiosity, and be both intended to and in fact remain wholly without influence on the particular situation that is being assessed. There is perhaps some temptation to reply that it is misleading to characterise these sorts of non-intervening assessments as either partial or impartial; but this does not seem satisfactory either – even pure research may be biased without its bias being aimed at or in fact having any impact on the situation studied.

Secondly, there is a rather familiar sort of objection that may be brought against Kolakowski's general formula for impartiality to suggest that it would need some tightening amendment. A judge may act in accordance with a general rule of accepting the evidence of witnesses coming from one social background whenever it clashes with that of witnesses coming from another. In his application of this general rule to particular cases he may no doubt be said to be acting either partially or impartially; but any reference to him as an impartial judge would seem to carry a certain irony. Surely the fact that the partial application of a partial rule amounts to a double partiality cannot mean that its impartial application removes all taint of partiality whatsoever?

Could one clear up this matter by simply extending Kolakowski's formula? 'I am . . . impartial if I evaluate the conflict and the rights and wrongs of both sides by assessing the situation in terms of more general rules that I accept *independently of this particular case* and if these rules are themselves impartial.' This suggestion leads into a variation of an old and well-known entanglement. Justice, it is said, consists in treating like cases alike; but are not some ways of picking out relevant likenesses more or less just than others? Impartiality consists in assessing particular situations in terms of independently accepted more general rules; but are not some general rules more or less impartial than others? On the one hand, one may wonder whether it even makes clear and proper sense to talk of the impartiality of a rule (as compared with its application). On the other hand, the implication is uncomfortable that I may show myself to be impartial no matter what the content of the rules that I may be applying. It would be surprising, moreover, if Kolakowski were entirely content with this implication; for surely it too leads to using 'the same term for a variety of attitudes . . . in face of one and the same conflict'.

It is in fact clear that there is no briefly definitive way of settling all these issues. It is, however, worth noting that one may speak 'naturally' enough of a man as acting impartially in 'impartial' application of some grossly discriminatory rule so long as he himself has no responsibility for its content or for the fact that it has application to the cases to which he has to apply it. If the fact that he finds himself responsible for applying the rule in a particular case is to be explained simply in terms of the role that he has to play in some total complex situation for which he is in no way responsible, then this situation provides the material framework within which he may or may not act with formal impartiality. Of course, there is, as always, all sorts of room for differing judgements as to the degree and kinds of responsibility that may be in question. Nevertheless, there may be reason not to hold him responsible in the relevant way, even if he happens to have a personal interest in the impartial application of the unjust or discriminatory rule; so long as he is judged to have had no share in its creation or in its maintenance, there is no need to insist that its partiality rubs off onto him.

But how now does this line of argument fit with the apparently equally 'natural' feeling that a certain irony must lie in the description as an impartial judge of one who is (merely?) impartial in his observance of such a rule as that instanced three paragraphs ago? One way of seeking room for both these *prima facie* incompatible reactions is to elaborate in appropriate manner the distinction between a role and the man who is holder of it. The role of a judge, one may say, only exists in relation to the legal system of which judges are officers; hence any bias in the network of laws by which their judgements are governed may be held to affect their impartiality as judges. The question of the partiality or impartiality of the men who fill these roles and of their performance of them is to be seen quite differently. There may well be two views as to whether a man should agree to play what may be seen as a biased role and on whether, if he does so, he should carry it out impartially or not. But any possible disapproval of the impartiality with which a man may fulfil an unacceptably partial role evidently depends on the conceptual possibility of recognising such fulfilment as impartial.

There is no doubt a great deal to be said for this line of analysis.

Moreover, it enables one to accept very neatly the further contention that in so far as a man who holds the position of a judge has
been and remains unable to influence the nature or structure of the
judicial role, no question of his partiality or impartiality can arise
other than concerning his performance of the role as it is given to
him. In refusing to recognise him as an impartial *judge* we are denying the impartiality of the role. But this is in itself to say nothing
about the partiality or impartiality of the *man* who is role holder;
nor is it to prejudge the issue of whether he must as a man be held
morally responsible for the partiality of his role in proportion to
even the least extent that he may be in a position to influence its
nature – and if thus morally responsible, so to share in its partiality.

It is true, of course, that an insistence upon this distinction between role and role holder is characteristic of much 'liberal' analysis; and that it has been attacked as providing an unwarrantable
defence for the individual against the need to assume any responsibility for the inadequacies of his society. But while it may be that
not all conceptual–social frameworks admit of this distinction, it by
no means follows that those whose concepts do admit of it can dis-
card it by simple choice. In any case, liberal individualists can
already express an insistence on an individual's total responsibility
for the exercise or non-exercise of any reasonably foreseeable causal influence that he may have. The remaining question, therefore,
is whether one can or must sometimes assume moral responsibility
for matters over which one may have *no* foreseeable causal control;
or, to put it another way, of whether one's moral assessments of
oneself or others can or must be limited to considerations for which
they bear some responsibility; and this in turn must evidently
depend on how one is to construe the notion of 'morality'. It is only
too clearly impossible to rely on an independent understanding of
any one of these terms for a subsequently neutral analysis of all the
others. For the present it is perhaps enough to re-emphasise how
wide is the room for differing judgements over degrees and kinds of
responsibility; and to take further note of the fact that to some it
may go simply and without saying that the partiality of a discriminatory rule must rub off onto its willing impartial adminis-
trator whether he has had any share in its creation or maintenance
or not.

The question remains, however, of what sort of account to give of
the impartiality of rules; and with it, the further question, of more
restricted but particular relevance to the context of these discussions, of the relationship between Kolakowski's account of impartiality and that which I gave in Part I. From a theoretical
standpoint the most unsatisfactory feature of my earlier account

was that it was based exclusively on consideration of the nature of impartial exposition without providing any explicit line of transition to a more general treatment of the concept such as Kolakowski's. An obvious first suggestion, therefore, is to see whether my account can plausibly be interpreted as an application to a particular context of that offered by him.

The first approximation of an account that I gave in Part I ran as follows: 'A "liberal" professor would presumably do his best to be impartial (let us say) in the sense of trying to set out every relevant view . . . fully and fairly by using their own terms of reference and trying to expound them as they would be expounded by their own partisans.' Compare this with Kolakowski's 'I am (or I try to be) impartial if I evaluate the conflict and the rights and wrongs of both sides by assessing the situation in terms of more general rules that I accept *independently of this particular case*.' In one way Kolakowski's account is in fact more specific than mine in that it includes a reference to evaluation.[7] If this reference is omitted, we are left with something like 'I am . . . impartial if I deal with the situation in terms of more general rules that I accept *independently of this particular case*'; (where *one* way 'of dealing with' a situation could be by assessing it in terms of 'more general rules' of evaluation); this omission seems reasonable enough, since questions of partial or impartial treatment can arise in purely practical terms and in contexts where evaluative rating is not an issue. What happens if we try to apply this now very general principle to the special case of the exposition of competing views on the nature of, say, some controversial political situation?

In fact, its direct application in this form is not yet enough to give us the kind of impartiality of exposition that I was trying to delineate. It is, for example, possible to formulate general rules of distortion whereby all views, including that of the expositor himself, may be presented in systematically caricatural form. Such a rule may be applied with perfect impartiality, yet its application would produce the very reverse of a full and fair exposition in the same terms as might have been employed before a similar audience by adherents of the theories being expounded. Unless, perhaps, they too may be thought likely to have preferred to give a distorted representation of their own positions? But in that case either *no one* is giving a full and fair exposition; or a full and fair exposition would, to be full, have to include a self-frustratingly straightforward account of its own otherwise distorted nature. To put the matter another way: one can well suppose that the partisans of certain positions might choose

---

[7] In my Part I discussion I tended towards dealing with such references under the heading of objectivity.

not to expound their views in any way that might make them intelligible to certain types of audience; indeed this choice might be directly connected with the views in question. In such a case it is clear that there can be no question of the would-be liberal expositor expounding these views just as they might have been expounded before the same or a similar audience by their own partisans. So either one has to suppose that one can include in one's exposition an account of why anyone holding the views that one is expounding would not himself have expounded them in just such a situation, and yet that this particular feature is so contingently connected to the rest that no essential distortion is anywhere involved; or one has to conclude that of such views no full and fair exposition is possible. And this means – to return to the main point of this paragraph – that, however impartial one's application of a general rule of distortion and even though the holders of all views under consideration may have adopted the same rule themselves, there will remain a crucial gap between this kind of impartiality and that of a full and fair exposition.

The moral of this may appear now to be essentially simple: namely, that a full and fair exposition is one that involves no distortion as it is communicated to its audience. The simplicity is, however, still only apparent. For one thing the notion of distortion is itself far from straightforward; for another there are many contexts in which the terms 'undistorted' and 'impartial' are simply not interchangeable. For example: a photographer may openly produce deliberately distorted pictures of, say, certain still life objects for the sake of producing certain aesthetic effects; yet no questions of partiality or impartiality need here arise. That this is so has more than idiomatic significance. For Kolakowski is surely right to link the notion of impartiality to that of a conflict – or, it should be added, competition. Yet another reformulation of his principle might be, 'I am (or I try to be) impartial if I deal with all sides in a situation of actual or potential conflict or competition in terms of more general rules that I accept *independently of this particular case*.' Distortion involves lack of impartiality when (i) it risks deflecting one's own or someone else's judgement or attitude from what they would have been had an undistorted account been given; and (ii) this deflection of judgement or attitude has a potential bearing on some actual or potential conflict. Thus it would be in place to talk of an impartial photograph of purely material objects, only if the representation given of them had a potential bearing on some conflict in views as to their 'real' nature. So the question becomes one of whether my account of the impartiality of a full and fair exposition may be shown as a special case of some version of Kolakowski's principle by modifying our earlier additional reference to impartial rules to make the whole now read: 'I am (or I try to be) impartial if I deal with all sides in a situation of actual or potential conflict or competition in terms of more general rules that *I accept independently of this particular case*; and if *either* the application of the rules involves no potentially misleading or otherwise inappropriate distortion *or* I have no share of responsibility for such distortion as may be involved in the rules which it is my overriding duty to apply.'

This is undeniably not only a clumsy but also an odd-sounding formulation, which may look as if it had been concocted merely in order to provide an overall cover for my special account of what constitutes impartial exposition, while conjuring a general account of the impartiality of rules out of the peculiarities of the special case. For what, after all, may be meant by talking quite generally of rules whose application may involve potentially misleading distortion? No doubt a general rule of accepting the evidence of witnesses coming from one social class whenever it clashes with that of those coming from another may in fact tend to distortions of the truth. But there is no necessity in such an outcome and it seems unsatisfactory to suggest that the partiality of a rule might lie in the purely contingent consequences of applying it. And quite apart from this, it seems very forced to introduce a reference to distortion in characterising a rule such, for example, as one that may stipulate that members of certain social groups must obtain higher marks than those of others before qualifying for admission to a university institution. The case is a real one and the rule may be thought highly partial; but what exactly would such partiality *distort*?

To take first the rule of selective acceptance of evidence: one *would* doubtless still consider it as partial even if verdicts arrived at through its application regularly just happened to coincide with the actual truth. But what if there were some overwhelmingly powerful reason to believe that this was likely to be the case? Then one would have grounds for saying that there was after all nothing biased about the rule; for it would simply embody a recognition of the reality that witnesses of one class *were* more reliable than those of another. On the contrary, to follow any other rule in the light of such knowledge would be highly distorting or biased. Here, too, the bias would lie not in the contingently resulting distortions of most consequent verdicts, but in the deliberate adoption of a rule that was likely to have such a result. If it is the rule of selective acceptance of evidence that is in fact most likely to be considered a partial one, it will be because most people believe that there is no *a priori* reason to suppose that members of one class tend to be more truthful than those of another; in which case, to follow such a rule *would* be likely to involve a lack of fidelity to or a distortion of the relevant realities. It is logically possible, of course, that this general belief may not be correct.

The conflict involved in the case just considered is a conflict of evidence; the distortions likely to follow as a result of dealing with such conflicts in terms of partial rules are distortions, first, in one's understanding of the reality that the evidence is about and, secondly, in one's treatment of the conflicting parties in the light of that understanding. In the case of university entrance, the conflict may take either of two forms. If the total number of places is limited, the conflict will be one of direct opposition; the place that A gains is *ipso facto* no longer available to B. If, on the contrary, places are available in unlimited number to all who reach certain standards, 'conflict' is perhaps no longer the right word; but one can still talk of (quasi)-competitive effort in a situation where success and failure lead to different and, if not conflicting, at any rate sharply contrasting outcomes. In either case, application of a rule of differential attainment in the entrance examinations can be seen as resulting in an interference with or a distortion of the 'natural' order of successful candidates. And since such a distortion would serve as basis for a consequently distorted distribution of positions of sought after advantage and disadvantage, it would be appropriate to speak of it as involving partiality or bias.[8]

Of course, the notion of an absolutely undisturbed original order of nature or of reality is here, as elsewhere, a fiction. It is, however, a strength rather than a weakness of this analysis that it should show how just as behind any assessment of distortion must lie some, usually implicit, view of the 'real' or 'proper' order of nature, so behind any assessment of rules as partial or impartial must lie some view of the 'real' or 'proper' or 'natural' order of human affairs. For notoriously there are possible many different views of the proper order of human nature, including the view that there is no such order. It is thus understandable that there should be possible many different views on the partiality or impartiality of different sets of rules, including the view that there is no sense in making such assessments, apart perhaps from formal considerations concerning the relation of subsidiary to more general rules. It is important to understand how, for instance, the application of a rule of differential attainment may from some points of view actually be seen as a means for the impartial restoration of a 'natural' or 'proper' order; and, more generally, why it would be naïve to expect everyone to be bound to accept the same view of the impartiality of rules as oneself.

[8] The issues involved in this example are, however, extremely complex. For some further discussion of them, in terms this time of neutrality, see pp. 263–8.

If it is true that there may be many different views on what constitutes the impartiality of rules, is it going to make sense to attempt an impartial exposition of them? My own starting assumption was that an impartial exposition was one that set out to expound all points of view 'fully and fairly by using their own terms of reference and trying to expound them as they would be expounded by their own partisans'. We seem now to have arrived at the position that an absolutely impartial exposition is one that aims not to distort any of the rival views – in so far, of course, as they permit of undistorted exposition. But do these two requirements necessarily come to the same thing?

Here once again the notion of an undistorted reality gives rise to a characteristic and essentially controversial difficulty. It goes beyond that posed by the views of those who in fact rather than in principle could hardly have known how to express themselves in order to succeed in communicating with a given audience; or who would have chosen either not to express themselves at all to certain audiences or to have done so in deliberately misleading terms; or who would have insisted that an accurate exposition of their views could only be given in certain contexts of practical endeavour. It is the further special difficulty of deciding whether those whom one is expounding are necessarily the best authorities on what their own views 'really' amount to; or whether the very terms in which they would themselves naturally expound them may not embody important and unsuspected elements of distortion. Certainly, everyone must agree that there is a sense in which people's conscious views are necessarily what they consciously take them to be. But, quite apart from the multiple ambiguities of which they may be aware and which may leave them consciously uncertain of the nature of their own positions, may there not be dimensions of meaning to their views as they choose to express them of which they have no clear awareness at all? To this question there is no uncontroversial answer but, notoriously, a variety of highly contro-versial ones. But clearly anyone who believed that he did have the key to these concealed dimensions of meaning might think that he would be giving a distorted and hence less than impartial account, if he left all mention of them out.

This, then, is yet another reason why there are bound to be different views as to how and where, if anywhere, the impartiality of rules may lie. Moreover, rules enjoining impartial treatment do not determine their own criteria of non-distorting application. Thus, we may agree on a rule which lays it down that all candidates for university admission should be treated in impartial fashion, but still disagree over what in practice that fashion may be; we may agree on the need for strictly impartial exposition, but disagree as to that in which it may consist. And, in particular, we may disagree over whether the demand of full and fair exposition in terms which would be acceptable to those whose views are being expounded and that of an account which involves no distortion may not in the given context conflict.

What does all this show about the possibility of analysing the impartiality not of rule application but of the rules themselves in terms of conflict and of non-distortion? For one thing, that these references are neither rigorous nor precise. Not only are we left with some rather wide margin of disputable interpretation of the terms 'conflict' and 'distortion', but also with some rather wide variations in the exact ways in which, in different cases, the various factors (rules, conflict and distortion) may be related to each other. However, perhaps this too can be made into a strength rather than a weakness of the analysis. All the concepts of our present concern are to be understood as emerging from a certain sort of conceptual background, a background of shifting light and shadow, whose terrain may be mapped and re-mapped in an indefinite number of criss-crossing ways. It is anyhow not easy to talk of the impartiality of rules; certain pressures lead towards doing so, others run in the opposite direction. If one does accept the need for so talking, then the concept is to be located in this general area of non-distortion and actual or potential conflict. Of course, it would always be possible to stipulate very precise defining relations between the terms in question; but it is perhaps better to settle for just that degree of precision which, while making for clear distinctions, will allow us to understand how naturally their clarity may be re-called into question.

It is also to be noted that this account of the impartiality of rules is not a purely formal one. Even if one attends only to the impartial treatment of situations 'in terms of more general rules that one accepts independently of the particular case', the apparent formality of one's resulting account is in an important sense misleading; for the interpretation that is necessary in order to bring particular cases under the descriptions that occur in these 'more general rules' may clearly be no mere formality. But if once one accepts the however awkward inescapability of having to find some sense for the impartiality of rules, all hope of a purely procedural characterisation of impartiality has to be abandoned – as indeed of the other concepts here in question. Indeed, even a denial of any sense to talk of the impartiality of rules reflects back on the formality of the more restricted account; the restrictions of a would-be purely procedural analysis have their own material significance.

The most important point to be stressed, however, is that any account of the impartiality of rules in terms of non-distortion must serve to bring out the links between this concept and those of objectivity and neutrality. Roughly speaking, the more closely the rules are concerned with matters of judgement or exposition, the more closely the conditions for their impartiality will approach those for their objectivity; while the closer their practical concern with situations of actual or potential conflict, the closer the connection between the conditions for their impartiality and those for their neutrality. However, this first rough characterisation of the situation does need some rather more careful examination.

'Objectivity', as we have already noted in Part I, is a term that has a multiple history of partly overlapping, partly incompatible analyses; but as with 'impartiality', my own way of introducing it was through a limited reference to the context of exposition. For someone to strive for objectivity was for him to seek to 'check all these different versions of the situation against the background of such facts as were available to him – which could not, of course, be facts as they were "in themselves", but only and necessarily facts such as he understood them to be in the light of the available evidence and of what he took to be the most accurate principles of interpretation rather than in that of his own personal preferences and interests'. There are many different ways in which the form of this checking may be understood; by reference to interpersonal agreement, to sensory observation, to general internal coherence, by conformity to certain favoured models or whatever. But whichever way such debates may go, the point of such checking is to ensure that the theory or report being checked is as faithful as possible to the reality that the theory or report is about – which is to say that the theory or report should embody as little distortion as possible.

To aim at objectivity and to aim at overall impartiality is in both cases, then, to aim at avoiding distortion. Wherein does their difference lie? Impartiality is concerned with equal dealing in a situation of conflict – not only with treating all sides alike, but with treating them alike in terms of rules whose general application tends not to deflect or to distort the development of such conflicts from their 'natural' course. Objectivity bears no necessary reference to conflict; as such, its concern is only with truthfulness to the facts of a given situation.[9] Thus there are contexts where one may speak appropriately of impartiality, but hardly so of objectivity; and vice versa. This is obvious in so far as the impartial and non-distorting

---

[9] This means neither that true accounts can only be arrived at by objective checking nor that all objectively checked accounts are true. The most checkable and best checked theory may still be false; subjective prejudice and chance may combine to give one a theory which, hardly checkable as it stands, may nevertheless be true.

application of general rules is concerned; similarly, in contexts where one is concerned with particular judgements but where there is no suggestion of conflict, it would be pointless to speak of impartiality – for example, one may speak of an objective but not normally of an impartial diagnosis of cancer. But the same is true of certain kinds of general rules – at least in certain kinds of contexts. It would be natural enough to speak of impartial rules for the regulation of conflicts between black and white, but far from clear what might be meant by calling them objective, except perhaps by transference from the objectivity of any factual theories on which such rules might be based. They might, however, have no such objective basis, but derive from a simple subjective preference for impartial. rules in these contexts, without their being any the less impartial for that. In fact, it does not seem normally appropriate to speak of the objectivity of rules for the guidance of behaviour at all, except for rules designed to guide one's checking of the truth of judgements, theories or reports. But while one might indeed characterise as objective a rule for the triple re-checking by different investigators of all important experiments, there would seem little normal point in speaking of it as impartial.

However, if there are contexts of distinction between impartiality and objectivity, there are also contexts of overlap, most notably contexts of report, exposition or assessment. For the sake of schematic simplicity we may distinguish three main cases.

First, there is the case where one's concern is to report a situation of disputed fact and where the facts do not themselves consist, either in part or in whole, of theories about other facts. For example, one may have to determine what actually took place on the streets during the transformation of a procession into a riot. On this there may clearly be different and incompatible opinions. In checking the objectivity of one's own report, one needs to take into account all these rival views and the light that they may shed on each other; and to do this one has to obtain of them as accurate and as impartial an understanding as possible. Here impartiality belongs to the procedures of objectivity; the objectivity of one's study and presentation of the facts depends, among other things, on taking impartial account of all relevantly conflicting theories about them. To claim that an account is objective is to imply that it has been checked from all possibly relevant points of view, which must include those of rival theories; to claim that it is impartial is to add, as one must if one is to sustain the claim to full objectivity, that in making use of these rival theories one has in no way distorted them or the bearings they have on each other; and this in turn is only possible if one has an objective understanding of what they are.

The second case is that where one is concerned simply with exposition of the rival theories and not with the assessment of their adequacy or inadequacy. Here the objectivity of one's account of each particular theory is a necessary part of the overall impartiality of one's exposition of their conflict. It is possible to be incompletely objective, that is, to be objective about some but not all of the views in conflict; but in such a case, one's total exposition is simply not impartial at all, since the nature of the conflict is presented in distorted fashion. There may no doubt be a certain formal impartiality in an equally biased or non-objective treatment of each of the theories under consideration; but there can be no fully impartial treatment without full objectivity all round.

Finally, there is the case where one is concerned both with exposition and with assessment of the rival theories expounded as regards their adequacy or inadequacy to the facts. This can be understood as being in effect a combination of the first two cases; and the mutual interdependence of objectivity and impartiality over the relevant area is here correspondingly tighter, more complex and more complete.

The contexts of closest overlap between objectivity and impartiality – and hence of easiest idiomatic interchangeability between their respective vocabularies – are, then, contexts of exposition or assessment. In so far as the application of rules for the assessment or exposition of conflicts constitutes no intervention or, on Kolakowski's severer requirement, no causal influence on them, no questions of neutrality or non-neutrality arise. On the other hand, we have already seen that when it comes to dealing in practical terms with particular situations of conflict, the application of general rules of impartiality may affect them in very non-neutral ways, depending on what the particular conflicts are about or on how they may be pursued. The same is true for general rules of neutrality; this point was already illustrated in Part I in reference to the neutrality of the role of a referee.[10] General rules secure their application to particular cases, however, by reference only to some subset of the characteristics which in their totality constitute any particular case. Thus a rule of neutral conduct can only forbid the giving of differential help or hindrance to any of the parties engaged in conflicts in so far as they, the conflicts, the parties and the types of help or hindrance in question, are identified under the relevant general headings. A rule of impartiality will prescribe even-handed treatment of all parties engaged in actual or potential conflict in ways which will neither 'distort' the nature of the conflict nor deflect

[10] Kolakowski's definition would need a lot of stretching to enable him to speak of a neutral referee at all.

its 'intrinsic' course of development – in so far, once again, as the conflicts, parties involved and forms of treatment in question are identified in the relevant general terms. But now it seems natural to suppose that any form of unequal intervention in a conflict must be bound to divert it from its own 'intrinsic' course of development. In which case it would seem to follow that whenever a rule of impartiality is designed to have practical application to conflicts of some given general type, it must, out of its very impartiality, enjoin conduct that is strictly neutral; and that, vice versa, a rule of neutrality forbidding differential intervention must *ipso facto* enjoin impartiality.

In fact, although this argument does hold under certain import-. ant conditions, it need not be seen as holding under all. One may regard the cases in which it may not hold as falling into two broad categories. First, there will be those in which conflicts are seen as taking place within a framework of already established distortion. Here impartiality may be seen as demanding non-neutral intervention in order to restore a 'normal' or 'undistorted' balance; that is to say, for example, that the framework of established order may be seen as providing the baselines for what is to be counted as intervention at the same time as it is seen as itself constituting a standing condition of distortion. Secondly, there may be cases in which an impartial respect for the 'morally natural' order of events may be seen as demanding intervention in conflicts whose development would otherwise lead regularly to the triumph of 'bad' over 'good'; in conditions in which, for example, bullies are normally able to dominate their victims, impartiality may be seen as demanding a non-neutral holding in check of the greater strength of the former. Others might say, of course, that even under such conditions overall neutrality and impartiality would still come to the same thing, though neither might be morally justified. The point is simply that *which* one says and *how* one sees it will depend on one's understanding of what constitutes the 'natural' or 'normal' order or orders; and this, as we have seen, is an essentially disputable question.

When neither of these two classes of cases is in question, however, the conditions for the impartiality and neutrality of rules will indeed overlap. The overlap is nevertheless different from that of impartiality and objectivity and does not normally give rise to a triple coincidence. Impartiality overlaps with objectivity where the risk of bias is the risk of a distortion of truth; it overlaps with neutrality where the risk of bias is that of a distortion of some 'natural' or otherwise given state or development of affairs.

A triple coincidence may in a sense occur in the following special case. Some people believe – or are conceptually committed to be-lieve – that, in certain contexts at least, to hold certain factual beliefs is to be committed to undertake or to refrain from certain forms of action;[11] that is, the practical commitment is taken to be a criterion of the reality of the factual belief. More specifically they may believe that where the undistorted factual assessment of a given state of conflict discloses a 'distortion' in the terms of struggle, it carries with it a practical commitment to non-neutral intervention; and that where the reverse is shown, there is a commitment to a neutral abstention from intervening, since to do so would be to distort the existing 'natural' or 'normal' balance. In this latter case, the accept-ance of the impartial and objective assessment may be seen as tanta-mount to an acceptance of a commitment to impartial and neutral behaviour. We may still say that it is the impartiality of the relevant behaviour that coincides with an attitude of neutrality in so far as one is concerned with action, while the impartiality of the assess-ment coincides with objectivity in so far as one is concerned with judgement. But in saying so we must remember not only that in this case even more than elsewhere the line between judgement and action is to be seen as one of blurred emphasis rather than of clear-cut division, but also that the very terms in which the distinction of emphasis is to be made, have to be understood as mutually impli-cated in each other – i.e. judgement as involving action and action as involving judgement.

It may be objected to the whole of this analysis of impartiality, and more especially of the impartiality of rules themselves, that it leaves out a central feature of the concept, namely the sense in which impartiality demands a setting aside of all personal preference or in-terest. The objection is to be taken seriously. For there is no denying that impartiality *is* often understood to consist simply in the setting aside of one's own partialities.

A main reason why this is so, however, seems to lie in a half-misinterpreted recognition that personal preferences or interests are a particularly powerful source of distortion. This need not neces-sarily be the case; one may try to take one's own preferences into im-partial consideration along with those of other people, or one may simply have a strong preference for or interest in the adoption of im-partial rules. The preferences and interests which are to be set aside are those that are likely to distort. But not only does the meaning of 'distortion' vary from one context to another, so too may the precise sense of 'set aside'. Thus, as we have already noted, objectivity also demands the setting aside of preferences – the setting aside from all influence on one's judgements of any preferences that may get in the

[11] See, for example, R. G. Braithwaite, *Moral Principles and Inductive Policies.*

way of checking for the truth. Neutrality in its turn demands a disconnection from action or a neutralisation of personal preferences wherever they would lead to intervention in favour of one party to the conflict against another. That impartiality overlaps at different points on its spectrum with both objectivity and neutrality makes it natural that it should be understood as having a more especial connection with the setting aside of preference. There is scope here for the suggestive tracing in and out of a variety of linguistic patterns: personal preference is of the subject and hence incompatible with objectivity; partiality being only partial is naturally distorting of any whole. There is ample excuse, even justification, for the uncertain variability of idiom in this conceptual area. But even if the setting aside of preference were a necessary condition, it still would not be a sufficient condition of impartiality or objectivity; there are too many other sources of distortion – lack of imagination, blindness and ignorance standing high on the list.

This same objection also arises in relation to a certain line of thought in moral philosophy concerning the concept of an impartial, sympathetic observer. In this version it starts from the observation that opposing moral views may be held by those who agree on the objective or factual nature of the circumstances to which their views apply. Does this mean, one has then to ask, that conflicting moral principles may both be equally impartial? And even if they may, is it not also 'possible to have a systematically distorted moral perspective which is not based upon factual distortion? One claim that has seemed plausible to some is that a selfish perspective is "distorted"'.[12] The impartial, sympathetic observer is, according to this account, simply one whose understanding and judgement are not 'distorted' by his own selfish interests or preferences.

The answers are still essentially the same: First, on a strictly autonomist or positivist view, there is in logic no reason why a given set of facts should not support quite different but equally non-distorting or impartial moral perspectives. Secondly, there are, as we know, other views of the relations between fact and (moral) value, according to which certain forms of goal-directiveness so enter into the facts that a failure to appreciate how to evaluate them amounts to an at least partial failure to appreciate the nature of the facts themselves. Thus, thirdly, it is possible to see 'a systematically selfish perspective' as involving distortion either on the basis of an appropriate non-autonomist view of the relation between value and fact such that selfishness appears as necessary evidence of some fail-

---

[12] I owe this objection to Leslie Francis, to whom I am most grateful for much valuable criticism and discussion.

ure of factual perception or judgement; or on the basis of a belief that, as it contingently happens, rational observers and agents will always agree on an unselfish assessment and evaluation of facts once they have an undistorted view of them. Fourthly, we must not forget that some would be doubtful of there being any sense to talk of the impartiality of rules or perspectives over and above that of the manner of their application; if one wishes to insist on it, the partiality of a radically selfish perspective may be seen as simply the way in which it involves differential application to oneself of rules which in themselves might or might not be considered impartial. But fifthly, in the light of all these and previous similar considerations, it is neither to be denied nor regarded as surprising that impartiality *is* sometimes just taken to lie in an absence of selfishness. Which – once again – is surely mistaken; it seems clearly possible to be quite unselfishly biased.

There is another rather different type of consideration to be taken into account. It is not only individuals, but also institutions that may be capable of partial or impartial action, of exercising a neutral or partisan influence or even of coming to objective or biased judgement. There is no doubt good sense in talking of institutional interests, even perhaps institutional preferences; and it may be that institutional partiality, non-neutrality and bias may always be seen as doing at least relative service to some interests rather than others. But it would be a very restricting – and unlikely – assumption to suppose that all such cases have to be worked out in terms of such interests or preferences as might serve as direct motivation. It is on the contrary arguable that certain forms of institutional bias so distort social relationships that they work out against the long-term interests of all concerned, including those who may appear to gain the comparative short-term advantage, but who might also themselves consciously prefer radically to modify the situation – without perhaps having any idea of how to set about it.

Such institutions may be seen as providing the framework for conflicts and hence for both neutrality and non-neutrality; they may also be seen as caught up in the fabric of conflict itself. The point is one that has been made already and to which it will be necessary to return. First, however, it is time to pick up another and not unrelated point that has been left hanging for too long. It arises from the problem, common in different ways to both Kolakowski's and my own analysis of neutrality, that 'there must be some sort of causal or otherwise practical relationship existing between [the would-be neutral] and at least some of the parties to the conflict in question. And given that the intending neutral must at least believe this to be the case, this makes it as difficult to argue that there could be *any* decision open to him that would have strictly no influence on the outcome of the conflict as to argue that there is *any* way in which he could act so as to give strictly no differential help to any of the parties in conflict.'

'Neutrality consists in non-intervention in other people's conflicts.' To say this is easy enough; the problem remains of knowing what, if anything, may safely be counted as non-intervention. In practice, too obsessive an insistence on this difficulty may become either irrelevantly pedantic or else constitute a particular form of actual intervention; under 'normal' circumstances there tends to be a fairly wide measure of agreement as to the approximate point at which intervention may be said to begin. This point can, however, have no absolute status in total independence of all the perspectives from which one set of persons or another may view it or, indeed, deny its very existence. Schematically, the position may be set out as follows: One man, A, may see himself as being in a position of choice whether or not to intervene in a conflict between two others, B and C. The conflict, as he sees it, is not his conflict; either it was already engaged before he came contingently upon the scene or it would have started anyhow, taking just the form that it has taken, irrespective of his appearance. B, maybe, sees the situation in the same way. He may wish that A would abandon his neutrality in his, B's favour; but he recognises that in fact he is not at present intervening. For C, on the other hand, A may be already, and whether he likes it or not, part of the situation of conflict. His particular attitude of 'non-intervention' is actually already a way of intervening in favour of B; it is perhaps also a way of protecting his own interests. Indeed, even C's view of what the conflict is 'really' about is not quite the same as those of A or B. D, meanwhile, a non-involved observer who is out of all causal reach of the conflict, 'sees' not only that the particular form of A's would-be non-intervention in the conflict constitutes a more or less disguised intervention in it, but that 'in fact' the situation is one in which 'genuine' non-intervention was never 'really' open to him as an option under any form whatever. And so on and so on; with all sorts of further possible permutations and combinations.[13]

There are at this stage two main comments to be made about this situation. First, although there is no position of apparent neutrality or framework of rules, legal or otherwise, in terms of which neutrality may be defined, which may not be contested as effectively non-neutral from *some* other point of view, it is hard, if not actually im-

---

[13] One must add, of course, that to talk in terms of the views of individuals rather than in those of social perspectives or ideologies makes possible a spectacular over-simplification of the problem.

possible, to conceive of a perspective from which no option of neutrality would ever appear to be available with respect to any conflict whatsoever. The reason for this is not that neutrality bears some sort of universal moral value. It is rather that there is a radical difficulty in the supposition that everyone must somehow or other belong to the situational context of every conflict upon which, by whatever quirk of fate, he might find himself in a position to exercise some causal influence. Disagreements there may always be as to what should be counted as a normal on-going situation, in whose structure and genesis those who may be counted as outsiders need play no essential part, and as to what, on the other hand, should be counted as a situation of inescapable intervention or involvement. But the very notion of intervention would lose most, if not all, of its force, if *every* attempted refusal to exercise potential causal influence on a conflict had already to be counted as an intervention.

Secondly, it is natural that options of neutrality should become more ambiguous, uncertain and controversial during periods of thoroughgoing social or personal change than during periods of relative stability. A framework of stability allows of settled expectations as to the sorts of circumstances in which conflicts might 'naturally' arise and take their course independently of one's own contingent appearance on the scene. The baselines from which interventions would have to start are given, so to speak, from within the framework of normality. In periods of structural change baselines of this sort are among the once settled landmarks that are called into question. It is natural, too, that in such periods of change there should be deep divergence and incomprehension between members of older and younger generations. For the former the old frameworks retain much of their meaning; to the latter no firm lines are given and unavoidable and unpredictable commitments may be lurking behind every corner. Positions of agreed neutrality and overall impartiality are only possible in societies where certain states of affairs, certain lines of development and certain norms of behaviour are taken for granted. When there is no longer sufficient relevant agreement on what may be thus taken for granted, one man's neutrality or impartiality may quite understandably appear as the next man's non-neutrality or bias.

2   Taylor

I turn now to a passage to be found near the beginning of Charles Taylor's paper, where he is discussing the example of the football referee:

'In calling a penalty kick against side A in the last moments of the tied game, [the referee] is obviously in one sense helping B. But this does not suffice for us to accuse him of lack of *neutrality*, something we would only do if his call were in some way suspect. For he is applying the rules *impartially*, which means that he is awarding penalty kicks only where fouls are committed.

Now superficially we could argue here that there are two ways of describing what he is doing . . . Under one description his action is identified as quite in keeping with neutrality, under the other it is identified as highly partial . . . Thus we privilege the description 'applying the rule', and judge the referee's performance as *neutral* because it is of the essence of this being a game of football that he apply these rules. But this doesn't mean that his being *neutral* is just a matter of stipulation; rather it is that we are operating here against the background of an overriding common interest in the game which is presumed of all who engage in it . . .' [The italics throughout are mine.]

This passage provides a good example of a context within which the terms 'neutral' and 'impartial' are used as apparently easy synonyms for each other. What lies behind this appearance? Would it have been better to say that the referee achieves neutrality through the impartial application of the rules? Or that he achieves impartiality through the preservation of the neutrality of his role? Or are these no more than idle philosophers' questions? It is worth returning to pick up the threads of the discussion on the overlap between neutrality and impartiality that were left hanging a little too loosely a few pages ago.

There is only one class of conflicts in which the referee can intervene *qua* referee, namely the class of game-conflicts, the very possibility of which is created by and dependent on the constitutive rules of the game. Not all the roles which are defined by these rules are neutral. The role of the goal-keeper, for instance, is to prevent, in certain specified ways, the kicking or heading of the ball into his own side's net. He might, of course, fail to fulfil his role impartially; for the sake of bribes or whatever other reason, he may deliberately fail to prevent certain other sides from scoring. But in this case he would be acting against his own side; he may be partial or impartial in the fulfilment of his role, but neither way does he have the option of neutrality, since he is by his role already a party to the conflict. The role of the referee, on the other hand, is defined not as a participant in, but as a regulator of the relevant conflicts. It is a neutral one in that its duties are so defined that any influence that the referee may exercise on any footballing conflict is to be determined solely by factors for which provision is made within the rules of the institution and which could, in principle, count for or against *any* conflicting party. The neutral referee may intend to disadvantage the offending side when he calls a penalty against it, but he does not therefore intend to disadvantage side A as such, despite his evident knowledge that on this occasion the two coincide. To preserve the neutrality of his role he must treat each incident in each conflict alike in terms of the general rules of the game – which is simply to say that he must be impartial in the fulfilment of his role.

The role of the referee is a neutral one and a neutral referee is one who respects the neutrality of his role; in order to do so he must fulfil its obligations with complete impartiality. Should we also characterise the role itself as impartial? 'A rule of impartiality', we suggested a few paragraphs ago, 'will prescribe even-handed treatment of all parties engaged in actual or potential conflict in ways which will neither "distort" the nature of the conflict nor deflect its "intrinsic" course of development'. The formula is no doubt a clumsy one; nevertheless it can at least be used to point up the difference between the role of a player and that of a referee. There is no question of a player having to deal in even-handed manner with 'all parties engaged in . . . conflict', for his own role is precisely to be one of the parties; the contrast with the position of the referee is straightforward enough. But since football conflicts can have no existence outside the framework of the rules of football, what sense can be given to any reference to their distortion or deflection by any of the rules through which they are constituted?

An answer to this question may be sought in seeking the answer to another: could a role such as that of a referee, whose business it is to deal with all parties engaged in conflicts as determined by the rules, be anything *other* than impartial? Consider the possibility that the referee be enjoined by the rules not only to use a wide margin of discretion in his application and interpretation of them, but in doing so actually to take differential account of the class origins of the opposing teams. So defined, his role would lead him to intervene not only on the basis of those constitutive terms on which alone teams can enter into footballing conflict with each other, but also on a basis of essentially extrinsic considerations, having nothing to do with the terms of conflict as such; for the class origins of the different teams can form no part of the game as such. In so far as the referee's interventions were determined by such factors they would appear as impinging upon a conflict from the outside rather than as springing from any features of its own internal development. They would constitute interferences as well as interventions; as such, they may very well be seen as distorting or deflecting the development of a conflict according to its own rationale within the terms of its constitutive rules as they are recognisably observable by all competing parties.

A role so defined may be said to be neither neutral nor, as a role, impartial. Anyone who *observed* it impartially in the sense of giving his own preferences equally free rein in each particular case would thereby be acting non-neutrally; individual referees could only achieve neutrality in so far as they imposed their own personal restrictions upon their role as determined within the general framework of the rules. For while class origins may or may not be of justified political relevance, they do not belong to the constitutive terms of a game such as football. Of course, the holder of a class-biased role of referee may be as committed to ignoring his own personal preferences and interests as the holder of the most impartial one; but to temper his discretion according to the class origins of the competing teams is still to 'distort' the 'natural' run of the play.

Interventions based on such 'extrinsic' factors may, then, be seen as 'distorting' or 'deflecting'. But it may be wrong to assume that distortion can arise only from 'external' sources. Here games may no longer provide the best analogy; but some situations may quite plausibly be seen as bearing within themselves their own springs of unfolding distortion. Whether such interpretations can in the end be worked out in coherent and convincing detail is not the immediate question. But one must certainly not overlook the long and complex tradition of dialectical analysis which sees it as a standard pattern of personal and social histories that they should produce their own characteristic factors of, as it were, quasi-external interference in the course of their own internal development.

Secondly, some may think that this example of possible bias in the very role of a referee is a somewhat odd one. If so, it should be remembered that a not infrequent objection to industrial arbitration has been that the very role of the arbitrator has acquired a built-in bias; or that in an increasing number of cases those who stand accused before judges of the criminal courts object to the whole proceedings on the ground that there is an ineradicable bias to the very framework of law and that theirs are in fact not criminal but political trials. This is not the place to assess the truth of such accusations; their possibility, however, is an entirely serious one and has been the object not only of polemic but also of recent serious study.

The third point is this: One might be inclined to object that while such a role as that of the goal-keeper makes no pretence of impartiality, the goal-keeper is not to be seen as by his normal interventions distorting the 'natural' run of the play, of which on the contrary they constitute a 'natural' part. This is true. But then it would be a mistake to suggest that absence of impartiality must always involve distortion or, indeed, some sort of failure. 'Impartiality is concerned with equal dealing in a situation of conflict – not only with treating all sides alike, but with treating them alike in terms of rules whose general application tends not to deflect or to distort the development of such conflicts from their "natural" course.' A rule governing the behaviour of *partisans* to a conflict does not distort, precisely because it does not fail of an impartiality at which it never aimed. Or, to put it another way: the partisan aspects of the role of a goal-keeper are properly internal to the game of football; the rules associated with this type of role are explicitly not concerned with equal dealing or with treating all sides alike. Goal-keepers are not impartial, but neither are they biased; they are simply partisan. Not only does the absence of impartiality not always involve distortion or failure; it does not always involve partiality or bias.

To return, however, to the passage from Taylor's paper. It is true enough that his movements backwards and forwards between the terms of neutrality and impartiality are somewhat easy going. But it can now be seen how this should be so without such lack of strictness obscuring the main contention of this part of his argument.

This contention is expressed in the last sentence of the passage: 'We are operating here against the background of an overriding common interest in the game which is presumed of all who engage in it . . .' Certainly, I agree with Taylor when he says that neutrality reposes 'on commitment and hence is always relative'. But 'commitment' and 'common interest' may not be exactly the notions that are required. There may be a defining presumption that the role-holders within an institution, in so far as they are identified under their role descriptions alone, have a common overriding interest in the preservation and furtherance of the institution. But this is not to say that the individuals who happen to hold these roles must have each the same overriding interest in doing so; nor that only those individuals who are personally committed to the values of an institution are capable of impartial or neutral performance of its roles. For these purposes, all that has to be presumed of those who engage in the game of football is an *acceptance* of the institutional framework that it provides.

This point has much clearer and greater importance when one refers to the intricately ramifying institutions of society in general; but it can be made even with respect to a game like football. At first glance, one might suppose that no one who was not in some sense committed to the game need ever take part in footballing activity. As soon as one stops to think, however, one knows that this is not true. How many schoolboys, for example, must have taken full and active parts in football or in other games without having any overriding interest in or commitment to them, but just because participation was as much a passively accepted as an actively enforced feature of their school society? But even this is not yet quite the point. Someone who actually rejects the institution of football in that he wishes to see the game abolished, may still have no difficulty either in recognising impartial or neutral refereeing, or in actually acting as an impartial and neutral referee himself, so long as he accepts a recognisably clear distinction between footballing and other types of conflict and interests. It is when this distinction is rejected that the baselines of non-intervention become blurred and perhaps finally lost – as when, for instance, and as Weinstein shows, the distinction between what is of academic and what is of outside political concern loses its common acceptability and becomes itself a matter of dispute. But – to repeat – the opposite of rejection is acceptance. Acceptance of a distinction need not imply any particular interest in or commitment to it; nor need the acceptance of a framework of 'normal' reference within which neutrality and partiality may be commonly assessed.

Within the terms of reference of the institution of football, then, the role of the referee is a neutral one – just as, so one may say, the role of a judge within the terms of reference of the British legal system. In particular instances, however, an unneutral referee is not so much an embodied contradiction in terms as someone who is, as it were, cheating with the very framework which makes his kind of cheating possible. If such cheating is sufficiently blatant, persistent and widespread, it may, whether intentionally or not, come to undermine the framework itself. But much cheating can take place before this point is reached; many referees, as indeed many judges, may indulge in partisan behaviour without actually destroying the acceptability of the institutions within which alone such behaviour is possible. Meanwhile, and as things stand, they owe the possibility of their own particular non-neutralities to the official, if contestable, neutrality of their roles.

There are two further points which Taylor makes quite explicitly, to which it is here worth returning. The first concerns the relations between neutrality, autonomy and interests. In Part I, I suggested that there was something to be said for taking 'independence' to refer to the absence of any constraining or partly constraining factor and 'autonomy' to the *failure* of such factors to achieve any effective results. In fact the distinction would be better formulated as one between those situations in which there are no actually or potentially constraining or partly constraining factors and those in which the presence of such factors is *unaccompanied* by any effective results; 'failure' is too limiting a term – there is no failure involved in the self-denying restraint that a powerful potential constrainer may impose upon himself. At any rate Taylor's use of 'autonomy' would seem to fit within this general frame. Here are some of his most immediately relevant sentences:

'. . . It is the possibility of disinterested research which is being defended here, and the ideal sought is the old one of autonomy of the university. If this is the standpoint from which the criticism is levelled, then it is obviously firmly based in the value of neutrality, and its aim is to realize this neutrality more fully, to defend it against encroachments. For the ideal of autonomy is grounded in the same background of value as neutrality, that the options made in the pursuit of truth should be maximally free from restrictions and limitations. But . . . since the university always has been and will have to be paid for by society, it will always have to . . . come to some kind of *modus vivendi* whereby it fulfils some of society's goals as well as those defined by the research goals of its members. The crucial questions concern the degree of this autonomy and the scope of disinterested research which society will support.'

Is it true, in the first place, that to defend the possibility of disinterested research is *ipso facto* to seek the ideal of the autonomy of the university? In practice Taylor may be right in thinking that the two tend to go together; but in theory at any rate there seems to be no universally necessary connection between them. We have already seen in Part I that the notion of 'interests' is one that contains many shifting uncertainties. When someone talks of disinterested research, he means presumably research that is carried out 'for its own sake', out of no other motive than an interest in the results that the research may bring. Obviously enough the autonomy of the research can provide no guarantee that his research will be disinterested in this sense; the most that could be argued is that disinterested research depends on autonomy as a necessary condition. But does it? Certainly it does not depend on total independence. A man may depend on his patron for all material purposes and yet, for so long as he is allowed or even encouraged to do so, he may pursue his research for the pure interest of discovering where it may lead. Nor need the fact that his patron may have some 'ulterior' motive for supporting his work mean that the researcher himself can no longer be regarded as disinterested; as to whether the research itself is to be seen as disinterested in such a case – *this* is a question that is hardly worth pushing further.[14]

---

[14] Or rather it is worth pushing further only in a context in which one is pushed to decide whether the work of research is to be seen primarily in its social or in its individual setting. Even so, what will really be at stake will be the disinterestedness (or otherwise) of whoever or

It may be replied that a patron who allows his protégé to pursue his research with no other end in view than the pursuit itself is precisely the patron who allows his protégé to retain full autonomy. But this would be to ignore the possibility of a patron making use of his constraining power to oblige the researcher to abandon all interests which his research might have served other than the attainment of knowledge itself, while yet leaving him free simply to give up his research if its intrinsic interest is insufficient motivation for him. Such disinterestedness would be by no means autonomous. 'Obligatory disinterestedness' of this sort may seem unlikely to feature in the normal relations between universities and their supporting societies; yet it may not be too far-fetched to see an approach to such a situation in the circumstances in which centres of 'disinterested' research were established in some of the universities of what used to be colonial territories.

If this argument is correct, it shows that the possibility of disinterested research does not necessarily depend on the autonomy of the university.[15] But what of Taylor's assertion that 'the ideal of autonomy is grounded in the same background of value as neutrality'? It is again evident that autonomy is not a sufficient condition of neutrality. The question, as in the case of disinterested research, is whether it is one of its necessary conditions.

By way of approach to an answer consider the following two arguments.

(A) If, when faced with a conflict in which I am not immediately involved, I am to retain the option of effective neutrality, then *either* I must possess such strength of my own as to enable me to resist any attempt to enlist me on one side or another *or* whoever might have the constraining power to embroil me in the conflict must by his forbearance allow me such autonomy as is necessary for my choice to be a real one. There may be cases where the space for my autonomy and the possibility of my neutrality is created by the counterbalancing powers of the conflicting parties each of whom could destroy me if the others would let him do so.[16] But where power is brought to bear on me so that I have no choice but to take sides or be crushed, then the limits of my brief neutrality are to be measured by the time

whatever institution is to be judged in the relevant context as relevantly responsible for what is being done.

[15] We have already noted that it is by no means the case that disinterested activity must necessarily be neutral. If neutrality is a partly intentional concept, disinterestedness is primarily a matter of motivation; and while intention and motivation are themselves both partly interpretive concepts with, furthermore, important links with each other, they are never simply interchangeable.

[16] For a very different treatment of such cases see Louis Marin's paper and the later discussion on pp. 261–70.

that it may take to crush me, a time that is likewise the measure of my vanishing autonomy; and even within this time my resistance to the pressure to take sides may be seen as a forced abandonment of neutrality as I am led to push back in the opposite direction.

(B) Faced with a conflict between X and Y, I may wish to intervene in favour of X. X himself, however, may prefer to succeed or to fail unaided. If, then, he is more powerful than I am, he may be in a position to threaten me with destruction should I actually make any move to bring differential help either to him or to Y. Or, more commonly perhaps, it will be not X but some further party, Z, who himself chooses to remain neutral in the conflict and is powerful enough to constrain me to do so too – if, once again, I do not choose to be immediately crushed. This argument may be challenged on the grounds that such causal power of intervention as I may have is cancelled out by whatever greater power is able to prevent my intervening; and hence that my non-intervention cannot properly be described as neutrality. Up to a point this may be regarded as a matter for marginal stipulative definition. Nevertheless, there is a 'real' and not merely a verbal difference between having *no* causally effective relationship to a situation of conflict and, on the other hand, being in a position where (a) one *would* be able to intervene with impact were some other inhibiting factor removed and (b) one has in any case already the power to provoke inhibiting counter-action in effective favour of whichever party one moved to intervene against.

Argument (A) seems, then, to imply that autonomy *is* a necessary condition of neutrality, Argument (B) that it is not. In effect Argument (A) relies on simply recalling that some, however vanishing, degree of autonomy is a necessary condition of any voluntary action whatsoever. It achieves its grip on the concept of neutrality through the intentional dimension of the concept. Argument (B) seeks to show that one may after all be constrained to neutrality by the circumstances of one's situation. It achieves *its* grip through the situational dimension of the concept. Both arguments may appear to be, as in a way they are, vulnerable to the pressures of the other. In fact they have to be taken together as expressing between them a counterbalancing truth (the precise point of whose balance is, needless to say, essentially unstable and contestable). Thus there is point in saying that some residual autonomy at least is to be seen as a necessary condition of any effective neutrality. But it is also to the point that just as there may be circumstances in which I may be effectively 'compelled' to abandon neutrality, so there may be others in which I may be 'compelled' unwillingly to preserve it. (It must be remembered, of course, that neutrality is not the same thing as indifference.) Taylor is doubtless right as to the normal practicalities of the situations of contemporary universities; where autonomy is squeezed out it is typically in the interests of compelling rather than of preventing alignment. Moreover, to fight for the option of neutrality is *ipso facto* to fight (non-neutrally) for the relevant autonomy. (One cannot fight for that to which one is compelled, but only for the right to make the same choice freely.) But certain potentially important distinctions are blurred if one says *simply* that 'the ideal of autonomy is grounded in the same background of value as neutrality'.

To these considerations it is worth adding the following. It is clear that the degree of, say, a university's autonomy will be a function both of its own strength and of that of the government and other social institutions and forces; and also of the government's, or of society's, willingness to refrain from using their strength to override or to thwart the university's decisions. In practice it may often be impossible to make any very clear distinction between these various factors; and sometimes even in principle. It is also worth noting that lack of autonomy may often be due more to positive weakness than to constraint exercised by others. Idiomatically it is hardly appropriate to speak of constraint in cases where one party has no desire that the other should be dependent upon him and it may be unwelcome to you that I should be, or put myself, within your power – perhaps to the point at which if you do not support me, I collapse altogether; but this does not mean that you do not have constraining power over me. The possession of power need by no means always be welcome to the possessor; and the weakness of a dependent can be a source of reciprocal power over him on whom he depends.

The other main point of Taylor's that should be mentioned here is expressed in his remark that it is 'the university's vocation' to provide the neutral *context* within which opposing views may be brought into confrontation with each other – the famous 'marketplace of ideas'. This view of the university as providing an institutional framework within which conflicts may take place according to prescribed rules and without any interference from the framework, bears analogy on the one hand with the liberal pluralist view of the democratic state and on the other with our familiar example of the game of football. The analogies are evidently imperfect. In particular, the institution of football provides the constitutive context for the types of conflict which can only take place within its framework and which are the only ones to do so;[17] in con-

---

[17] Though there are, of course, as many informal adaptations of 'football' which still go by

trast, neither the university, nor the state as conceived by liberal democratic theory, stands in such a constitutive relationship to most of the conflicts for which they may provide the primary contexts. Partisans of rival theories of physics, biology or philosophy, for example, may pursue their disputes outside as well as inside the university; arguments about the proper nature of an academic discipline lead directly into arguments about the structure of the syllabus, which in turn spill over into questions of organisation, staffing and allocation of funds; academic disputes in economic or social theory may not only resemble, but interlock with practical economic or social disputes in society at large. As for the state, it is today only too clear that many of the disputes that take place within it between one social group and another are continuous with disputes about what its very structure should be. The neutrality of these framework institutions is in the nature of things more uncertain and precarious than that provided by the rules of football.

Nevertheless, if the analogies are imperfect, their imperfections should not be exaggerated. Is it really true, for example, that the actual games are the only conflicts that take place 'within the framework of the institutions of football'? This depends, no doubt, on how one construes the reference to 'within the framework of the institutions of football'. Not all the rules that are associated with the playing of a game are necessarily to be counted as rules *of* the game – for example, that it should not be played on Sunday mornings; but there is room for much varying argument as to where and why this line is to be drawn. Moreover, even among those rules which *are* to be seen as being *of* the game there may be important differences of type. Some will specify its objects and modalities, others again the terms on which players may enter into 'licensed' competition with each other. Is there to be a system of initial assessment and handicapping? What sorts of equipment are to be permitted and what forbidden? Are substitutes to be allowed? Are drugs and stimulants to be forbidden? Are individuals of every religious, national, class or racial origin to be allowed to compete with and against each other?

It may at once be objected that there is something misleading about the way in which this last question has been slipped in. The issues referred to are, of course, overtly and notoriously political; but do they not concern the question of who is to be allowed to play the game at all, or under what conditions, rather than that of the constitutive terms on which it is to take place? And is not the former an essentially external question? The institution of football provides a neutral context within which football contests may take place; it is

---

the same name as there are 'proper' or 'official' games of football without inverted commas but with a referee, eleven players a side, etc.

the business of those who are responsible for the game to preserve this framework of neutrality for all who may find themselves able to take part in matches played within it – it is not their business to take part in disputes over who these latter may be. Conflicts about apartheid in sport are not footballing conflicts. If football administrators as such seek to remain neutral in conflicts of such a political nature, it is precisely in order to preserve the proper neutrality of football as a framework within which games of football can take place undisturbed.

What is of immediate importance is not to try to determine the rights and wrongs of this familiar argument, but to understand why different circumstances or assumptions may tend to make it appear so obviously the one or the other. In order to do this, however, it is best to look first at a rule which, unlike one of apartheid or nonapartheid, may seem at first sight to belong clearly to the internal concerns of the game.

Consider the question whether the rules of football are to lay down any conditions as to what type of boots may or must be worn. Football is a game that involves kicking a particular type of ball; but when the game is instituted, and for a long time afterwards, it may occur to no one that there is any need for a rule about what kind of footwear may be permissible, even perhaps for a rule excluding footwear that might be dangerous. Suppose now that it is discovered that a particular type of boot gives notable advantage to the teams that wear it, but that it is in short supply and very expensive. The question arises, are the legislators of the game to forbid the use of this type of equipment in order to avoid allowing 'unfair' advantage to the richer teams; or are they to refrain from tampering with what has always been recognised as the purely sporting constitution of the game? At the point of decision there is a sense in which there can be no neutral resolution of this question. The richer teams are either going to be helped or they are going to be frustrated; to change the existing framework by the introduction of an equipment rule or to leave it as it has always been is, either way, to affect the balance of advantage between one lot of teams and another. But in another sense the question remains unanswered whether the necessarily non-neutral decision to change the framework of rules or to leave it as it is may or must have as effect the introduction of an element of non-neutrality into the framework itself.

Here of course, as in earlier contexts, all depends on what is taken for granted as being in the natural order of things. Implicitly or explicitly, the rules must either allow or disallow the use of any particular item of equipment. But there is the usual room for variation in the degree to which an equipment rule may be seen as either central or ancillary to the constitution of the game itself; much will depend on how far general social and political conditions are such as to sensitise people to the different consequences of notable inequalities of wealth. On the one hand it may be generally accepted that freedom to develop and use expensive new kinds of boots is the normal and natural right of all who take part in football and that if this freedom happens to offer greater chances of success to the rich, then this is a social accident and nothing to do with the game as such. On the other hand it may be objected that the basic point and skills of the game will be distorted if differences in equipment are allowed to play 'too great' a part in determining the outcome; so that if the framework of rules 'gratuitously' allows the advantage of expensive equipment to the minority who can afford it, then it cannot be considered to be neutral with respect to the terms on which football is actually played. Thus, while from one point of view the (perhaps impartial, but) necessary non-neutrality of any decision to come down on one side or the other in a conflict over what the rules of the game are to be may be quite compatible with the neutrality of its resulting framework in whatever version it is decided upon, from an opposite viewpoint the non-neutrality of the decision may be seen as necessarily seeping over to affect the particular framework to which the decision gives rise.

Conflicts between such points of view are, we have just seen, connected with discrepant understanding of which rules are directly constitutive of the game as a game and which merely govern the manner and occasion of its playing. A reference to the same sort of discrepancy was already involved in my earlier suggestion that the role of a referee would be a partial one if it were so defined as to permit or to enjoin referees to adjust their control of games in the light of such considerations as the class origins of the competing teams. The grounds for this suggestion were that interventions based on such 'extrinsic' factors may be seen as 'distorting' or 'deflecting'. It may be that I was here taking it too easily for granted that while references to the class origins of competing teams or to the personal preferences of the referee might perhaps find a place in the rules specifying his role and spelling out the range of his discretion, they could scarcely count as contributing to the constitution of the game itself – that is, they would not feature in the rules of *play*. But however this may be, it is some such (irremediably contestable) distinction between rules directly constitutive of the game, in that they specify what the players must try to do and how 'essentially' they must try to do it, and rules laying down present versions of the variable detail of the manner of their trying or the terms on which the referee shall see to the observation of the first-order rules, that makes room *within* the overall framework of the institution for the characterisation of certain rule-sanctioned actions as 'extrinsic'. There is hardly any sense in which the *centrally* constitutive rules of a game could be said to be neutral or partisan, biased or impartial. But in the situations here imagined the unneutrality of the institutional framework of play would be determined by the presence within it of elements regarded as arbitrary or contingent with respect to the aims of the players *qua* players. Arbitrary though these elements might seem to be, however, they may tend to produce distorting effects in favour of one party or another to contests the very meaning and possibility of which are constituted by the central defining rules.

Ancillary rules enjoining the referee to exercise his interpretive discretion along lines of class origin would tend to make for partisan distortion of play. They would tend also to fill in the gaps of continuity between factors clearly internal to the game and wholly external factors of general social and political significance and thus to blur, and ultimately to erase, that element of subsidiary self-enclosure which is a necessary condition of a game's being a game. *A fortiori*, if such references to social class (or to the personal preferences of the referee) were to be read as making a central contribution to the constitution of whatever institutionalised activity was in question, such a directly intolerable strain would be placed on the concept of a game that games of this sort would collapse into immediate continuity with political or social life in general. To avoid such consequences, it may seem more plausible to take such references as neither directly nor even indirectly constitutive of (the point of) the game itself, but rather of the going conditions of entry to its competitions and of the handicaps under which different categories of competitors might be allowed or encouraged to play.

Handicaps in fact provide an interesting case study of their own. The 'normal' rationale of introducing a system of handicaps is not so much one of interfering with the 'natural' run of play as of protecting or of sharpening its point. This point may be lost if there is too great a disparity between the strength or skill of the various competitors. To take one example: at certain schools it is the custom for the fathers of boys of thirteen or so to play their sons at a yearly match of cricket, and at many of these schools the fathers have on this special occasion to use a cut-down cricket bat known as a broomstick. This device is introduced in order to redress the otherwise inevitable balance of inequality between the children and the adults. To see its introduction as partial or unneutral would be to misunderstand the situation, since without it the game would hardly be likely to be meaningful to any of those taking part. On the contrary, it has become an accepted convention of the game as played on these institutionalised occasions between teams of adults on the one hand and of small boys on the other that they would bat with different equipment as specified in the special additional rules pertaining to this sub-set of games. Indeed, this point can be generalised; for it would in general be fair to say that handicap games or tournaments (golf, tennis, rowing, polo etc.) are devised in order to make the games better, that is, to enable the opponents to compete on terms more interesting and satisfying to them all within the framework of the game or sport as they conceive it.

From this point of view, then, systems of sporting handicapping are to be seen not as neutral or unneutral, biased or impartial, but rather as additional rules, the adoption of which may be freely agreed on particular occasions in order to preserve the point of the game as embodied in its centrally constitutive set of rules. But while the basic rationale of such systems may be given in this way, they may of course be misapplied or put to other purposes. To take an example of no present-day seriousness, one can imagine the governing bodies of a given sport laying it down that royalty should be allowed to compete in public tournaments under especially generous handicaps. In such an extreme case, even if such conditions were written into the official rules of the game, they would fairly clearly appear as 'extrinsic' or 'distorting'; they would have nothing to do with the point of the game as such or as one open to anyone interested to play. It would be easy to imagine, perhaps even to cite, other ways in which systems of handicaps might be used or devised to further essentially 'extrinsic' purposes, many of which might fairly be regarded as political. But the point is already clear enough. It is in as much as a system or a particular use of handicaps may be seen as fulfilling functions 'extrinsic' to the game itself that it may after all appear appropriate to assess it in terms of (political) neutrality and impartiality. And since it may not only be contestable whether the system is being used in support of one function or the other, but it may also sometimes contribute to fulfilling both at once, its introduction may serve either to blur the line between games and other social activities or to strengthen the analogy between them – whichever way one likes to look at it.

This brings us back to the question of football boots. 'Implicitly or explicitly, the rules must either allow or disallow the use of any particular item of equipment.' Is it not equally obvious that the rules must either allow or disallow people of different coloured skin to play with or against each other? What indeed makes it obvious in the case of equipment? In the case of a game of chess, for example, one might think it obvious that the kind of chessmen used can make no difference to the game played with them and that it would be entirely superfluous to deal with such matters in the rules. But perhaps even this is less obvious than it seemed in the days before Bobby Fischer. And since football is directly concerned with kicking a ball, should it not rather be obvious that the rules *must* specify what is to count as (permissible) kicking? Well . . . obvious only in so far as it is obvious that kicking may turn out to be a contestable concept; but this may not become obvious to anyone until, precisely, the invention of the superior, expensive boots – and even then only to those who want to contest it. Others, on the contrary, may continue to ask why the rules need say anything about what is to count as kicking; for is it not this that is obvious and that to kick with left foot or right, with cheap, expensive or with no boots at all, is still simply to kick?

Of course, kicking and boots, whatever view one may take of them, are closer to the heart of football than is the colour of the players' skin. If the 'natural' presumption is that anyone may try to play football if he so wishes, why *should* the rules of the game say anything about the conditions under which one particular class of people or another may be allowed to play? But perhaps this presumption is not so 'natural' after all. *Is* it obvious or 'natural' that the rules should silently permit of women playing with or against men? Either way, of course, the rest of the rules might be the same; but so they might be in the case of the expensive boots – or, if it comes to that, in the case of the rule which allows the goal-keeper to handle the ball, but only within his own goal area. Perhaps it is for a long time simply taken for granted that women do not play with men; and for so long as this is so, then, 'naturally', there will be no mention of the subject in the rules. Then one day a woman appears on some field as a player in an otherwise all male team; or a team of women challenges a team of men to a game. There is at once a scandalised outcry and in response to popular feeling, which anyhow they share, the legislators of the game move to impose a rule of sexual apartheid in football 'in order to preserve the traditions of the game'. Is this an arbitrary imposition? Should one say that if mixed teams played unauthorised matches, they would still be playing football even though the results might be in some sense 'unrecognised'? As usual there is no one privileged answer to this question. Some games are formally institutionalised and their institutionalisation makes some difference to what is normally counted as the game even when played in the most informal and casual contexts; others have no such formal, governing institutions. Even where they do exist, opinions may differ as to their power to modify or otherwise determine the general nature of the game itself; and here the social strength of an opinion may be a major factor in making it true or false. Quite apart from these very general considerations, there will be the particular disagreements of those who maintain that it will no longer be the same game, if men find themselves playing against women; and those who reply that whatever one may feel about such mixing, the constitutive rules of a game can be concerned only with what the players must do and not with the question of who may or may not be allowed to play. But this question of whether a game consists simply in the rule-governed attempt to achieve certain objectives or whether it is also in part constituted by the spirit and style in which it is traditionally played, is evidently not one that admits of a purely factual answer.

Is a dispute over whether the sex of the competing players should come within the scope of its rules one that is internal to a game; or are the issues that it raises already continuous with the overtly political issue of women's place in society as a whole? We have seen why this may be regarded as an essentially contestable question. From sexual to racial apartheid there is no doubt a further step; in particular it is harder to produce even the semblance of a rational argument to establish any connection between the observable biological differences and the characteristics and capacities relevant to the activities involved in playing football. Nevertheless, here too there will be men of total subjective sincerity to adduce arguments about the spirit, style and traditions of the game and about the incompatible attitudes and approaches that competitors from different cultures may be expected to have – or, indeed, to evoke in players from the native culture when playing alongside or against them. They may argue, furthermore, that if the mixing of races in sport seems almost bound to arouse such passions and attitudes as to distort its 'true' nature, this will be due to the conditions prevailing in society as a whole; so that, however regrettable the overall state of affairs, the preservation of apartheid in sport may actually be seen as necessary for the preservation of its political neutrality. But the same point may be put in an opposite way: that in certain circumstances the preservation of the internal political neutrality of a sport may become so caught up in the prevailing politics of the time that there is left no way of taking part without, by so doing, becoming politically partisan. What happens then is not so much that the referee may not retain his neutrality *vis-à-vis* whatever teams actually oppose each other in matches; it is rather that the total framework of rules within which such matches take place has come to contain a political bias such that anyone who takes part in the game is *ipso facto* led to range himself on one side or another in a political conflict that would itself be extrinsic to the game, *if* it could still be regarded as a game and nothing more. In the last resort, after all, football, as any other game, is only conceivable as such within the framework of a society that is possessed of the concept of sport as an at least semi-autonomous activity, the point of which is contained in itself. But this is a concept the grounds of which may be undermined by changes in the structures of the society in which sport has hitherto been played. Sport is no doubt a form of life; but forms of life are historical products and subject to historical pressure and change.

There are, of course, other ways in which contests of an apparently footballing nature might be given direct and not merely adventitious political significance. To take just one (presumably far-fetched) example, one could imagine a society in which 'football' matches were ritualised as taking place only on special occasions between teams drawn from members of rival political parties or groups and in which, perhaps, all goals scored counted towards the weighting of votes on issues of national importance. 'Football' would then resemble one of those institutions in the framework of which warring tribes may decide their combats through the ritual jousts of their chosen champions. Of course, children, or anyone else who felt so inclined, might always practise or 'play' at 'football' or at 'jousts' in the sense that they were only preparing for or pretending to the political significance which such contests would normally bear, much as some people play 'war games' and more or less, perhaps, as others play at Monopoly. But in neither case would they really be playing football or war; for war is not a game to be played nor, in the case imagined, would 'football' be so.

It emerges, then, that while the central point-giving or constitutive rules of a game can only with difficulty be assessed as either neutral or non-neutral, there is no absolute or sharp line to be drawn between them and subsidiary rules governing the methods and conditions of play; and about the neutrality of these latter there can indeed be meaningful dispute. Further, in the case of these ancillary rules neutrality may be held to consist in their being successfully designed to preserve or give effect to the central point of the game in contexts in which the actual circumstances or conditions of competitors might otherwise lead to a loss of its point. Conversely, they may be considered as unneutral to the extent that they may be seen as favouring the chances of one group of competitors rather than another over and above any point-preserving function that they may have. This is only one of the ways in which the defining break in continuity between the concerns and objectives of a game and those of the rest of life may become filled in. In the last resort a game which is so heavily or directly politicised as to lose its discontinuities altogether, is no longer 'really' a game.

'A game which is too heavily or directly politicised is no longer "really" a game.' It may likewise be said that an academic debate which is too directly a continuation of some political dispute is no longer strictly or 'properly' academic; or that a university whose educational practices and programmes of research are too directly geared to given political objectives is no longer functioning as a 'true' university. Those who take such views are in effect following the (typically 'liberal')[18] analogy of a game in their conception of universities as institutions which can and should be largely sealed off from the functioning and concerns of the societies in which they are situated and on which they depend for their material support. But the questions remain, first, how secure or how limiting are the presuppositions and conditions necessary for even games to be held apart as politically neutral; and secondly, how far anyway can such an analogy be pushed?

One major limitation on pushing it any great distance is, it was noted a few pages back, that while 'the institution of football provides the constitutive context for the types of conflict which can only take place within its framework and which are the only ones to do so . . . neither the university, nor the state as conceived by liberal democratic theory, stands in such a constitutive relationship to most of the conflicts for which they may provide the primary contexts'. But if the constitutive rules of a game may be not all equally constitutive, the claim that the university does not stand in constitutive relationship to the disputes which take place within its framework also needs some guarded qualification. Theories which are developed and expounded against each other within the university market-place of ideas may, certainly, be advocated by those who do not belong to universities at all. Nevertheless, the forms taken by some academic disputes may be determined in what is counted as their adequate detailed presentation by their setting within particular university institutions. If a subject such as philosophy may be seen as essentially dialectical in its nature as well as in its practice, then the sub-institutions of lectures, seminars and learned societies may in their varying forms impose a particular shape on its dialectic; and in principle the line between content on the one hand and shape, form or presentation on the other is neither sharp nor uncontroversial. Another more complex qualification lies in the familiar consideration that if teaching, research, intellectual debate and the general transmission of culture stand at the heart of

---

[18]   It is, of course, 'no accident' that I have allowed (or been led to allow) consideration of this example to loom so large in these discussions.

university activity, much else must take place in their support by way of administration, economic planning, discipline, etc. What actually goes on in direct pursuit of these central activities obviously depends in many different ways on decisions taken in other parts of the university framework than within the classrooms and the studies; and there is a sense in which many of these decisions are only constituted as such by the institutional forms within which they take place. In most of the English-speaking world, for example, it is normally only within the framework of a university, by act of one of its duly constituted committees, that nominations can be made to university chairs or other appointments in teaching or research, or that candidates can compete and be selected for admission as students. Appointment committees can thus have a direct and obvious influence on what is studied and taught, and how, within the university. Since it is only such people as are thus properly appointed that, acting together in further properly appointed committee, can take decisions on such matters as syllabus and examination reform, library acquisition policy, acceptance of topics for graduate research and so on, these appointment committees also exercise a widely ramifying indirect influence within the university – which includes, of course, control over the pool from which their own subsequent membership will be drawn.

Nevertheless, these qualifications serve mainly to make more precise the central disanalogy. For in so far as university rules or institutions can reasonably be seen as in part or indirectly constitutive of the studies and conflicts in and over teaching and research that take place within their framework, it must be in general constitutive of their status rather than of their theoretical point. No doubt the intellectual rationale of any given piece of research may in fact be secondary to a variety of purposes, both personal and institutional, which could not exist outside the constitutive framework of the university. But just as the defining point of a game is to be distinguished from the motivations of those who take part in it, so that of theoretical activity is normally to be distinguished from the actual motivations of teachers, researchers and students. Moreover, even if it is true, as certain 'liberal' theorists have argued, that education and research are activities whose rationale is internal to them, it does not follow that the rationale of university education and research is internal to the *institution* within which these activities happen to be carried on. To put the point another way: if it is 'the vocation' of the university to provide a neutral framework for a certain type of education and research, this is not because education and research can *only* be carried on within the university, but because their most satisfactory pursuit is understood to demand what is thought to be a neutral framework of this kind. In so far as there is any working analogy, therefore, it is rather with those sub-sets of rules which concern such matters as handicaps and equip-ment, that is to say, rules specifying the manner in which the main point of the relevant activities is to be secured, and which may, as we have seen, be assessed as neutral or partisan.

It is, then, for the same sorts of reasons that the framework pro-vided by the university for teaching and research may also be effec-tively unneutral – sometimes, or from some points of view, inevitably or necessarily so. It is, for example, part of a university's standards and procedures that only those with certain kinds of qualification should be admitted to it as students or appointed to its staff. But the 'equipment' needed in order to obtain the appropriate qualifications may not be easily available to those who do not come from the culturally or materially richer classes of society. If so, it may be correspondingly likely that the best qualified candidates should be interested in certain lines of study rather than in others and in their studies tend towards certain points of view rather than towards others. Under such circumstances the procedures of uni-versity selection or appointment will naturally work in favour of certain theories and the market of ideas will in practice be not quite so free as all that. Nor is it only that certain kinds of theory and cer-tain lines of investigation are likely to be given more effective devel-opment and support simply because they are those of the ablest members of the university; for by the same token, the decisions that such people make on questions of syllabus and research will deter-mine what is to be authoritatively received as worthy of serious study and what on the contrary is to be cast out as beyond the limits of the intellectually respectable.[19]

Even so, and with these and other similar and by now well-known qualifications, it is still relatively easy for the university to provide a neutral framework for the conflicting interplay of theories, in what-ever domain of study, as long as they do not call this very neutrality into question, either because they have little direct bearing on mat-ters of social structure or because they take for granted as accept-able the university's present relation to society and to the studies that take place within it, including the ways in which the nature of these studies is determined. There remains, however, another cru-cial consideration, another crucial dissimilarity between the univer-sity and an institutionalised game. We have seen that it is of the nature of games to be relatively self-enclosed, for their activities to be relatively discontinuous with any other outside concerns. But the nature of a university's embedding in the society to which it belongs

[19] Of this point see also Louis Marin's paper in Part II of this book.

is not only essentially contestable, it is itself a proper and natural subject of university study. There is, therefore, bound to be some degree of contestable non-neutrality in the university's attitudes and procedures with respect to theoretical conflicts over the nature and range of issues on which the university can or should be neutral. This arises from the familiar fact that there are those who do and those who do not believe in the existence of some sharp dividing line to be drawn between theoretical opinion and practical action. If one believes that there is in principle such a line to be drawn, then it should in corresponding principle be possible to devise an institutional framework within which all available theoretical opinions may be worked out and advocated without the framework itself producing any distorting interference. One has to stress the qualifying 'in principle', since in practice mundane considerations of timetabling, provision of rooms and lecture halls, of research material and so on may always make it necessary to favour some lines of research or teaching at the expense of others in any given university at any given time. Indeed, the fact that such considerations can never be totally ignored is not itself a purely contingent one. However, and providing still that one believes in this separability of theory and action, it may seem possible in ideal or limiting principle to devise a neutral or impartial institutional framework for the expression of all competing views on all possible academic subjects through reference to a set of procedures that might be agreed upon by all 'rational' potential parties to such academic conflicts, consulting together in advance and behind some Rawlsian 'veil of ignorance'.

It may at once be objected that the acceptability of any such claim must be severely limited by the impossibility of establishing any definitively neutral criterion of what is to be counted as academic or rational. Even more fundamentally, however, the matter must appear quite differently to those who would insist on the impossibility of drawing any such line between theory and practice, between opinion and action, a belief in the existence of which has been so characteristic of classical liberal thought and a standing presupposition of so much classical liberal practice. Indeed, such practice is strictly inconceivable except on the basis of such a presupposition. If rival opinions on matters of political concern can be formed, expressed and taught in the absence of any corresponding carry-through into action, then the institutional framework within which they are so expressed need in principle neither impede nor be threatened by their expression. On the other hand, if the expression and, *a fortiori*, the teaching of political views is necessarily left incomplete or even distorted unless carried through in the forms of action appropriate to them, then the detailed and even general nature of the framework of university institutions may naturally be drawn into an at once theoretical and practical conflict and hence impinge non-neutrally on the various parties involved.

It must always be possible, then, to see certain continuities between issues concerning the ways in which universities are or should be embedded in their surrounding society and more general political issues dividing that society itself. To take one further example. There exists a general dispute over the ways in which a greater equality in the distribution of wealth and power in society may depend on a more equal distribution of university places among different social classes. Some would argue that this is a topic on which it is impossible completely to dissociate one's views as to the facts from the value judgements that one would make about them; and of these people some would maintain that the holding and expression of value judgements involves appropriate practical action. From this point of view it will appear inevitable that educational and social theorists within the university, who hold different views on the relation between the distribution of wealth in the community and the distribution of university places between different classes of the community, should be led to try to influence admissions procedures in different and opposing ways; and that the actual nature of these procedures at any one moment is bound at that moment to favour one party rather than the other to both the narrower and wider conflicts – even if the precise ways in which such influences may operate may be unobvious and controversial.

There are thus a number of different perspectives from which Taylor's remark about the nature of the vocation of the university may be understood. From within the perspective of a certain tradition it may be taken at its face value as a statement of fact about the role of the university; with a slight shift of focus it may equally be taken as a statement of fact about the nature of the tradition itself. At the same time it may be construed as a value judgement based on and, in a sense, about that tradition. Hence it would also be possible to agree with Taylor that the vocation of the university is to serve as the neutral context in which opposing views may be brought into confrontation with each other, while adding that this vocation has itself its openly partisan aspect. After all, there can be no absolute neutrality in the aim and effort to establish or to maintain the social conditions necessary for a certain sort of neutrality and impartiality in education and research. A similar analysis could no doubt be applied to the framework of the liberal democratic state itself, to such claims as that it is its function to provide a framework for the struggle of competing pressure groups while at the same time ensuring for each of its individual members an area of possible privacy in which they may adopt, if they wish, positions of contemporary political neutrality.

It would, however, be beyond the scope of the present discussion to move any further towards the analysis of such general political issues. For the moment, we may simply note that if the effect, whether in principle or in practice or both, of bringing the discussion of conflicting political'ideas into the neutral market-place of the university is to cut them off from their natural practical prolongations, and even perhaps to sterilise them from 'contamination' by their powerful emotive associations, then the existence of such university traditions and practice can hardly be a neutral factor in struggles in which the social consequences of pursuing such ideas are at stake. It is not for nothing that people like Taylor are sometimes accused of being anti-revolutionary in their efforts to get the would-be revolutionaries to submit their ideas and their aims to institutionalised university discussion. It may be rational, but it is not always neutral to point out that not all revolution is enlightened or that the transformation of physical force into the language of reason may sometimes be the most appropriate means of serving the most 'truly' revolutionary needs. Nor, of course, do we have to suppose that it is *always* the most desirable or rational means; only that it would be irrational to suppose it is not normally so.

3   Marin

A particularly interesting and perplexing challenge to the views expressed in most of the rest of this volume and to the mode of their discussion is presented by the contribution of Louis Marin. This challenge is appropriately and characteristically double and reflexive; the challenge of understanding the nature of the challenge is included as part of that of meeting it. Clearly, the range of questions raised by his paper and by its inclusion in the context of this volume involves not less but rather more than the whole problem of the relations between the so-called Continental and analytic styles of philosophy. All that can be done here, however, is to pick out certain themes of apparently immediate concern and to try and see how they might bear upon those of the discussion so far.

Three of these themes might be presented under the following labelling: (1) the theme of psychoanalytic and related interpretations; (2) the theme of 'le neutre' as both 'an absence' and a form of self-reflexivity; (3) the theme of 'le neutre' in relation to certain kinds of violence and force. But already these brief labels call for a word or two of further explanation.

(1) It is well known that psychoanalysis has exercised a live and pervasive influence on French philosophy in general, both on those who accept and develop and, by way of reaction, on those who reject and resist its categories and its claims; and that this influence has had no parallel in the world of English philosophy. The translation of Marin's paper presented, of course, among many other problems, the major difficulty of the French term 'le neutre', which covers what in English would appear, at first sight at least, to be the fairly distinct concepts of 'the neutral' and 'the neuter'; and in the present context this feature of French must certainly facilitate the integration into Marin's analysis of its important Freudian dimension. The English-speaking philosopher of analytical training has thus to face the immediate question of whether this central feature of Marin's analysis depends on what may turn out to be no more than a punning and conceptually accidental overlap that happens, no doubt for etymologically intelligible reasons, to be built into French; or whether, on the contrary, it rests on a deep conceptual or otherwise 'real' connection, which tends more easily to pass unnoticed in English.

(2) For Marin, to say that 'le neutre' is in some sense or other 'an absence' is to say something rather more complicated than that there is in principle no position of absolute neutrality anywhere to be found – a point which throughout all the discussions of this book has been taken as not plausibly assailable. It means also (and among other things) that neutrality is to be understood as both the foundation and the goal, as the rationale of certain sorts of undertakings, even though it may be in principle impossible for such a foundation actually to be established or such a goal actually to be reached. Neutrality consists, one might say, in the attitude that comes of a proper understanding of its own unattainable necessity; or again that it lies in the positions that one possessed of such an understanding might unceasingly strive to attain. Moreover, the neutrality of such undertakings would characteristically lie in the way in which they continually turned back upon themselves to bring their own status into question either explicit or implicit. It is in this that consists the self-reflexivity of 'le neutre'; the search for neutrality is reflexive in the double related senses of a turning back, as of light bouncing back off a mirror, and of a reflecting in thought upon itself. There would thus be a crucial difference on Marin's analysis between saying that philosophy, for example, has no foundations and that it is founded on an absence; even though, he might no doubt wish to add, this difference is both unstable and strictly speaking unstatable.

To this it should be added that 'le neutre', according to Marin, is an absence whose nature may be manifested in many different ways, but which is not to be identified with any of its manifestations. Or rather, since to speak of 'a nature' may be misleading, it is the in itself empty possibility of a number of related but different manifestations, aspects or figures; or again, since its 'nature', if it can be allowed to have one, is so elusive that it can only be indicated rather than caught in explicit formulation, we may think of it as the possibility of endlessly rapid movement from one of these possible positions to another – the constant possibility of moving to look at the position one has just left from some other position, which includes, as it both must and yet in a way cannot, the possibility of moving · from wherever we may find ourselves at the moment of indicating just these very possibilities.

(3) There is more than one way in which Marin suggests the existence of important relationships between neutrality, force and violence. For example:

(a) The emergence of neutrality as an effective possibility, or even perhaps as a necessity, may depend on the existence or establishment of 'a real zero of opposition', that is to say a state of impasse in which the fact that nothing is happening, or that there is no development in the situation, results not so much from an absence of forces as from the way in which the forces in conflict are so balanced as to cancel each other out.

(b) 'Le neutre' derives its own force from those that thus cancel each other out in their mutually sustained opposition. It then 'turns back' upon these conflicting forces to present them with the threat of a violence, which, while it is in a sense their own, is now taken or borrowed from them precisely in order that it may be reflected back upon those from whom it is derived.

(c) Discussion or debate that aims at a certain neutrality or disengagement, and in particular a rational discursive enterprise such as philosophy, may itself be the means of 'neutralising' some essentially non-discursive enterprise or force. Here Marin's account of what happens to Thrasymachus as he gets caught up into the Socratic dialogue may be compared with his opening analysis of the significance of the 'neutral' position of the university as one among other institutions of liberal democratic society.

In attempting to relate these themes to those that have run through the discussions so far the first question to be faced is, then, that of the relations between the concepts of 'the neuter' and 'the neutral'. As a start we may sketch in the rough outlines of two different kinds or families of accounts, which we may label respectively the conceptual and the genetic.

Conceptual accounts. The root idea of both the neuter and the neutral is given by their common etymology; it is that, much emphasised by Marin, of 'neither the one nor the other'. That which is neuter *is* neither one nor the other; he who is neutral is neither *for* nor *against* either one or the other. In fact, even in English the distinction is not always marked by a rigorously consistent use of the one term or the other, though the first at any rate never seems to be used for the second. But this may be because there is in a sense a relation of one-way implication between the second and the first. If A is neutral in respect to some conflict between B and C, he cannot be (identical with) either B or C; he may, on the other hand, be nonidentical with B and C without being neutral between them. So we may say, if we like, that neutrality presupposes the relevant state of neuterness, but that the converse does not hold. Or that neutrality is in a way a special case of neuterness.

One direct implication of this, for example, is that to compel someone to neutrality is to render him or to restrict him to being neuter in the appropriate respect. It also follows that anyone who chooses to be neutral in a given conflict, chooses thereby to be appropriately neuter, to be neither one nor the other. But such a choice need by no means imply any surrender of one's power subsequently to abandon neutrality, to become partisan, to join or to identify oneself with one side or the other. Thus, on this purely conceptual account there is no generally necessary implication running from neuterness to impotence. *This* implication is built in only to those special cases in which to be neuter is to be of neither sex and therefore of no sex at all – (and into such other cases as may be modelled on this special case). But not only is the associated impotence impotence only in respect of a certain specific power; there is in conceptual principle (and, it would seem, in plenty of historical practice) no reason why the neuter, the castrato or eunuch should not in appropriate senses or situations of conflict, act in favour of one party or the other in an essentially sexual conflict, and hence be very unneutral.

But, it may be objected, this last consideration is blurringly irrelevant to the central point at issue. Of course, the castrato may act in favour of one side or another in a directly sexual conflict; but, if it comes to that, one can be a fully sexed man or woman and yet in many situations of what may be called sexual conflict act in favour of the party who is of the opposite sex to oneself or, *a fortiori*, stand aside from the conflict altogether. The question cannot be whether the fact of being neuter is in itself a guarantee of neutrality. It is rather whether it may not be at least a sufficient condition for never

becoming involved as a leading protagonist in a purely sexual conflict.

This reformulation, however, is still more evocative than rigorous. For what *is* it to be a leading protagonist in a purely sexual conflict? What, for that matter, *is* a purely sexual conflict? Indeed, this
is a context in which the notion of conflict itself will need careful
handling, since even 'normal' sexual attraction and love-making
may be said to contain a conflictual dimension as a necessary element of the unity that is sought through its overcoming. Presumably, if one lays suitable stress on the not very precise notion of
'normal', and if one gives suitable interpretation to that of a direct
protagonist, one can show it to be true by resulting definitions that
to be sexually neuter is a sufficient condition for being unable to
enter directly into this sort of conflict. But while it is obvious that a
castrato cannot enter into normal or full sexual relations with a
woman or vice versa, it is equally obvious that there is a whole range
of sexual relations into which he can enter with members of either
one sex or the other. Even supposing that he does not desire to do
so, he may yet have the welcome or unwelcome power of arousing
such desire in others. Of course, in so far as he is technically impotent, he cannot become a direct protagonist in a conflict in which to
be a protagonist is, by definition, to have the sexual powers which
he lacks. But this point does not establish any peculiar connection
between neuterness or impotence and neutrality, other than that
very general connection which we have already noted and which has
no special relation to the sexual case as such.

According to this argument, then, there is no special conceptual
connection between impotence and neutrality, whatever the
psychological or sociological facts might turn out to be. To put the
point in this way is admittedly to take for granted the existence, in
this context at any rate, of some reasonably clear-cut distinction
between factual and conceptual issues. Nevertheless, there seems
firm enough reason for saying that the only sense of neuterness
which is strictly presupposed by neutrality, is one which carries
with it no particular suggestion of impotence, but involves only the
absence of whatever characteristics would define a participant in
whatever kind of conflict was in question. Indeed, Marin explicitly
agrees with the other contributors to the volume in holding that the
neutral must possess a power of acting upon the parties in conflict
should he choose to do so, and thus belong to the situation of conflict at the same time as he remains outside the conflict itself. He is,
if one likes to put it that way, neuter in respect of the conflicting
powers between whom he is neutral, but over whom he himself
nevertheless exercises a certain power. None of this means that he

does not possess the *kind* of power which they, the conflicting parties, bring to their struggle. Only that his power is neither identical nor aligned with theirs.

Genetic accounts. 1. There are a number of variations on Freudian themes which, when applied to the development of individuals, present the emergence of neutrality, as a possible position and as a power of acting in a certain manner, as deriving from an earlier neutralisation (neuterisation or frustration) of the agent and of his desire. Again the paradigm model of neutralisation is that of castration, of rendering sexless; but, also as usual, what matters is not the real act of castration, but its symbolic and fearful shadow, the genuine eunuch having at best but a marginal part to play in the story. It may be that in certain historically determined situations he became uniquely fitted to serve as go-between and even perhaps as one to whom appeal might be made for certain sorts of sexually disinterested judgement (which is not to say that he was necessarily sexually detached or indifferent). But by far the most important transformation takes place, according to this type of account, through the representation, the fear or the threat of castration which accompanies or accomplishes the frustration through the power of the father of the son's desire for his mother. The son's acknowledgement of this power is said to result in its acceptance as authoritative and in its internalisation as the voice of impartial (or neutral) law. This law presents itself as speaking from inside the subject, but as distinct from, and often even opposed to, his own subjectively recognisable desires – and typically as carrying, moreover, the same general prohibitions and instructions as are to be met with by himself and others in the social world; and hence as objective, independent and disinterested in suitably appropriate senses of these terms. Furthermore, the force of this internalised law is but the reflected/reflexive transformation of the force of the desires that were frustrated in the first place. And so on; with appropriate adjustments to this explanatory myth, no doubt, to deal with the formation of conscience in girls. Strictly speaking, the formation of an apparently neutral point of reference, and of such power as may be attached to it, would thus be based not on any actual rendering neither-the-one-nor-the-other, but on the frustration, the rendering null and void, the rejection of a desire to such an extent that it has not only to be hidden, but even self-denied as desire; so great is the fear of neuterisation that the whole process may be experienced, so it is said, as a symbolic castration. Thus, a neuterisation that is deeply felt, though in fact never takes place, leads to a belief in the existence of an independent, impartial and neutral authority, involving, however, in its turn a partial mystification in so far as, concealing its own dependent origins, it presents itself as an absolute.

2. At the other end of the scale a variety of accounts may be given of the relationship between neutrality and neuterisation in terms of the formation and transformation of institutions and of the development of social forces.

(a) One might hope to show how the emergence of state and legal institutions presenting themselves as impartial, neutral and no respecter of special interests, however socially or economically powerful, was a function of some sort of social or historical adaptation of the different groups and classes in society to the neutralisation or frustration of 'their own aims and interests. Such frustration may most characteristically be seen as deriving not so much from deliberate manipulation as from forces belonging to the social system itself and embroiled in relations of mutual opposition and dependence. A major difficulty with this sort of analysis from our immediate point of view, however, (and quite apart from those of making it stick in actual historical detail), is that it may embody a further extension or slide in the senses of neuterisation and impotence. We start with a fairly specific form of sexual impotence that comes from being made neither-one-nor-the-other sex when castrated. This is then assimilated to sexual impotence in general, which may of course affect many people who have not been castrated at all, but who are *as if* they were neither-one-nor-the-other; and finally we find ourselves moving to speak of impotence in general, whether sexual or not.

Thus we may speak, for example, of the neutralisation by the workings of the economic system of the efforts of the working class to better its condition. But very often, to speak of neutralisation in this way is to mean little more than that the working class is rendered effectively powerless to achieve its aim. This does not mean, however, that it is reduced to working in favour of neither party to the conflict in which it had itself been hitherto engaged; which in turn would mean that it was no longer even a party to the conflict and hence that the conflict itself had been dissolved. A different twist might be given to the analysis by the claim that the working class had been led into a position in which it was, without understanding what it was doing, in fact frustrating its own aims and interests by its acceptance as neutral or impartial of a law and general conditions of conflict that really belonged to the opposing class as its instrument of domination. In any account based on such claims there do certainly re-appear themes of reflexivity and mystification. Nevertheless, the impotence of the working class in such cases is to be seen as derived neither from any real elimination of the conflict nor from some symbolic fear of being reduced to being neither-one-nor-the-other of the parties involved in it. And even though the effective power of the mystification must rest in the illusion that as far as the law is concerned there is no conflict of overall interests to which the working class could be a party as such, this argument would make the apparent neutrality of the law the instrument rather than the outcome of frustration and self-frustration – though it could admittedly also be represented as both.

Other accounts are of course on offer according to which frustration by apparently impersonal forces may be experienced as determination by impartial fate or law – another form of compensatory mystification. But why *should* it be experienced in this way? Fate perhaps, but why neutral or impartial fate? At this point there appears a strong and familiar temptation to retreat to the original sexually mediated relationship between neuterness and neutrality. It is clear, however, that if any serious link is to be made out between that enforced, if symbolic, neuterisation which was supposed to lie at the origin of individual conscience, and that social impotence the internalised acceptance of which is here supposed to lead to the acceptance as neutral of the civic framework of state and law, we require some integrated theory by which the two may be held together in a relation not merely of symbolic representation, but of real genetic (and perhaps reciprocal) connection. Such theories do indeed exist; but again the difficulties in the way of making them stick, certainly in the present state of knowledge and research, are only too obviously formidable.

(b) We have already noted that Marin lays great stress on the emergence of 'le neutre' as a resultant of a confrontation between forces so equally balanced in their reciprocal inhibition of each other that they produce a state of tension in which nothing actually occurs. A historian who took this theme with suitable seriousness might aim at showing how the appearance of powers or institutions held to be or able to function as neutral, always depended in fact on the prior establishment of some dynamic deadlock. The existence of such a deadlock might make possible a position of genuine if restricted neutrality, any pretence to which would have been merely deceptive had the conflict been one-sidedly decidable, its main function then being to enable the would-be neutral to claim (to himself or to others) that his own hands had remained reasonably clean. One might further hope to show how, in certain cases at least, the cost of sustaining such a tension of deadlock was socially so unacceptable as not only to make possible but actually to demand the emergence of some neutral power to whom the contestants, or society, could look for the resolution of a deadlock whose prolongation had become unendurable. Since such a neutral would of necessity be neuter in being not only *for*, but also *of* neither side, one could say:

(i) that the forces in deadlock had effectively neutralised each other (i.e. rendered each other impotent to produce their otherwise to be expected effects);

(ii) that the result of this mutual neutralisation ('neuterisation') was to make necessary the emergence of a neutral, who would at the same time be neuter (but not so much impotent as neither-one-nor-the-other of the parties in conflict);

(iii) that the function of this neutral was to neutralise ('neuterise') the deadlock in the sense of rendering *it* impotent, that is, of defusing it or of taking away from it that which made it a force. Once again the links in the chain from the removal of sting or force, through sexual impotence, back to the root senses of being first sexually neuter and then neuter in general, have to be established either at some level of interpretive symbolic overlay or by some overall theory of reciprocal socio-psycho-genetic relations. Otherwise the argument tends to reduce to a movement of conceptual slide.

(c) At the same time, one might seek to identify the historical factors that caused certain kinds of alleged neutrality to take on such large, if problematic, importance in certain societies or cultures at certain periods. The 'neutrality' of the state as the framework institution of institutions, the political 'neutrality' of the educational system at large and of the university in particular, the 'value neutrality' of philosophy and the social sciences or of teachers and teaching methods – all these one might hope to show as arising as themes or as problems out of a background of various kinds of impotence, whether self- or other-induced. Some historians might equally hope to show how beliefs and behaviour based on the possibility or reality of such neutrality served once again as 'mystifications', as disguises of their own partisan origins and their own continuing partisan force; and how even certain kinds of impotence, or façades of impotence, might in fact constitute or conceal forces of crucial effectiveness. 'It can be no accident', so they tend to say, 'if in our modern age problems of neutrality have started to turn up in so many different theoretical and practical contexts'; and if no accident, then there must be explanations to be sought.

There are two problems of particular immediate importance about the significance of such genetic accounts. The first springs from the fact that in following these accounts it is not always clear whether what one is being offered is an explanation of the nature and genesis of concepts or one of the nature and genesis of the phenomena to which the concepts may apply; the second concerns the bearing of a genetic history of concepts on our present understanding of them. Inevitably, the two problems are to some extent interconnected.

If explanations of the nature and genesis of concepts tend to run into explanations of the nature and genesis of related phenomena, this need not be taken as over-simply damaging or remiss. Concepts as among the possessions or powers of a people, a culture or an individual have their roots in what have become known as forms of life, the ways in which people adapt to the contexts in which they have to live, the purposive activities which they undertake or purposively refrain from undertaking. It would, certainly, be impossible to give an account of the nature of concepts without central reference to language; but it would be equally impossible to make plausible such an account in restricting it to language alone. Certain concepts, indeed, are fully intelligible, or can be fully explicated, only when seen in relation to the forms of life of which they are extensions and on which they in turn play, making them available for 'manipulation' in thought or in practice, modifying or stabilising them, as the case may be. Conversely, there are concepts fully to possess which is to understand the nature of certain types of society. It is thus not surprising that there should be overlaps between descriptions of the genesis of complex patterns of behaviour and those of the introduction into a culture, or into some individual's growing awareness, of some new concept or concepts.

This said, the concept of neutrality is still not the same thing as the conditions which may underlie its emergence, still less the same as those which may make possible the actual taking up of a neutral position, and even less the same as that position itself. It may in some sense be true that in as much as the concept is an intentional one, its availability, if not its actual possession, may be a necessary condition of the taking up of neutral attitudes or positions.[20] Nevertheless, the understanding of the concepts available to us still

---

[20] For the finer purposes of analysis it is important not to blur the distinction between actual and theoretical availability. Theoretically there can in the last resort be no totally unbridgeable discontinuities in human history or in the understanding of one society by another; to suppose otherwise is to suppose that we should have no basis on which to interpret what we observed as being the manifestations of human language or society at all. No doubt many of the features of present-day society could scarcely be given intelligible expression in the languages of the remote past. Nevertheless, what has actually happened as history has built itself up out of its own past *might* have been constructed in advance in the imaginative thought of some unnaturally gifted individual living, say, in the time and society of pre-Roman Britain and speaking one of its languages; as each stage grows out of its preceding ones, so this hypothetical individual must in principle have been able to create in thought the historical development actually needed as underpinning for the inter-related development of

cannot consist in the understanding of their historical genesis alone. At any given stage of development we have the concepts that we do. To think clearly we have to articulate their network; and if this demands an exploration of its history, the clarity of such exploration must depend in part on the first provisional clarity with which we may have succeeded in articulating our network of concepts as we first find it. An understanding of the history of our language, of our discourse, of the concepts available to us as well as of the criss-crossing conceptual/non-conceptual nature of this history may well be necessary to a full awareness of the sense of our own present thought. But to make of such historical reflexivity the only movement of understanding would be to make of it a parody of that 'absence' or 'neutre' of which Marin speaks, a search for a position endlessly removed from that from which one speaks, a search that can never properly even begin. So even if the natural history, whether individual or social, of positions and concepts of both neuterness and neutrality includes some form of relationships between them, even if they often symbolise or take over something of the force each of the other, still genetic accounts such as these would seem to offer appropriately modifying supplements to conceptual analyses such as are to be found in most of the discussions of this book rather than any ground for supplanting or for abandoning them.

There is one other type of account of the relationships between neuterness and neutrality, which could be characterised both as genetic and as conceptual and according to which the full analysis of one concept or of one stage of discourse will show it as 'giving rise to' another standing in opposition to it, yet as its necessary complement. The patterns of such a dialectical logic play a particularly important role in Marin's paper. Once again exegesis and textual commentary are beside the immediate point. But the question is pertinent whether, while recognising the *difference* between neuterness and neutrality, a full analysis of the one may not be found to lead of necessity to an analysis of the other; that is, whether an argument cannot be constructed to show, not indeed that the idea of neuterness must on its own 'give rise to' that of neutrality, but that it does lead in this direction when taken in the special context of a mediating connection with the further idea of a conflict. This, at any rate, seems to be the basis of certain crucial stretches of Marin's argument; and the notions of conflict, and of some real causal relationship to the conflict, are both essential features of our own earlier analyses of neutrality.

concepts, even if each succeeding stage in his creative thought depended on his having already been able to elaborate the (perhaps necessarily) preceding one.

How might such an argument work? To be neuter is to be neither-the-one-nor-the-other.[21] But already the-one-or-the-other in question are conceived as standing in some significant relation to each other; to be neuter is to be neither-the-one-nor-the-other of a meaningful pair, not of just any two randomly associated objects. There are, for example, stamps which are printed in pairs, different designs but of the same issue and denomination; a collector might well want to know whether the single specimen he possessed belonged to such a pair or, whether having perhaps a different watermark or having been issued at a different time, it was neither-one-nor-the-other. As usual, nothing of importance need be made to depend on the niceties of current idiom. Still, it is worth noting that there is a certain air of absurdity in the suggestion that such a stamp would be neuter. Use of this term starts to become more generally appropriate in relation to pairs whose members are seen as capable of acting upon each other. Even so, the point would be lost if one were to apply it to anything whatever that happened to be neither-the-one-nor-the-other member of the pair. If in chemistry a neutral substance is one that is neither base nor acid (this is one of a number of points at which, in its own way, English idiom reflects the common origins of neuterness and neutrality), the mere fact of being neither an acid nor a base is obviously insufficient to mark out an item as chemically neutral; similarly, it is only such items as may be thought of as belonging to the domain of sex that may significantly be characterised as sexually neuter, as standing outside the pair male-and-female.[22] Thus, the concept of neuterness already carries with it the implication that that which is neuter has some special connection with the pair of which it is not a member; it belongs to the same domain.

What happens now if the pair in question is a pair-in-conflict – or, more generally, if the relation of actual or potential reciprocal action existing between members of a pair is one of actual or potential conflict? It is at this stage that neuterness becomes neutrality; whoever has the effective possibility of figuring in the conflict but does not in fact do so, remains or becomes not merely neuter but neutral. Once again the familiar point needs to be borne in mind that at the margins the questions of whether or not a particular type of interaction is to be seen as conflictual or of whether a particular

[21] In ordinary contemporary English the word 'neuter' normally carries, of course, a restricted reference to contexts of sex or gender. The more general (and etymologically primary) sense, however, does or at any rate used occasionally to occur.

[22] This point is complicated, but not invalidated, by the fact that there are both a variety of domains, and a variety of ways of marking out these domains, in which objects may or may not be regarded as candidates for sexual classification, on grounds which may produce different results in different cultures and – at the level of grammar – in different languages.

party really had an effective choice of involving himself in a given conflict, are essentially contestable; as indeed is that of just how broad these margins may be. Still, however such questions may be decided in particular cases, the relation which the neuter/neutral party has to bear to the conflicting pair in order to count as neutral, depends on the effective possibility that it might in principle have belonged to the conflicting pair, that it might itself have been a party to the conflict; which in turn is to say that, in standing apart from the conflict, it is already exercising some causal influence upon it. We are back to the problems which caused so much perplexity at earlier stages of the discussion.

The next notion to be introduced into the argument is that of an equilibrium in the balance of the conflicting forces. The neuter, N, has, as we have seen, to lie within the domain of the pair, P1 and P2, without being drawn in as a participating member. Let us suppose that the natures of P1 and P2 are such that (i) on their own either would normally exercise a dominant attractive force upon N, but (ii) taken together each inhibits the other from so doing. In such a case N would owe the possibility of its existence as neither-the-one-nor-the-other to the inhibitory action that each had upon the other. But to speak of forces P1 and P2 that stand in relations of such reciprocal inhibition as to prevent each other from exercising its otherwise natural powers, is to speak of forces in conflict. It is only as long as the conflict is so evenly balanced that neither P1 nor P2 can gain the ascendancy needed to free itself from the inhibitory pressures of the other, that N can remain at a sufficient distance from both as to ensure its existence as a neuter/neutral; at the same time, it only exists as a neutral in relation to this pair of opponents in as much as it could, in principle, align itself with one or the other. Its general power of acting as one or the other derives from its own nature; but its neutral power of acting as *neither* the one *nor* the other derives from the balance of power that exists between P1 and P2.

The argument of this last paragraph raises, however, a number of points that must not be allowed to pass unrecognised. There is first the background restriction that we are concerned here with a P1 and a P2 which are assumed to have it within their normal power to constrain N to act in ways not of its own nature or of its own choosing, but of that of whichever of the powers is concerned. It by no means follows that there may not be positions of neutrality with respect to conflicts between powers that would not normally have control over the behaviour of the neutral concerned. Next there is the question of whether after all we have as yet built sufficient elements into the situation to generate the notion of neutrality. This is in effect the question of whether one may usefully talk of a conflict between opposing forces if they·are not also to be thought of as goal-pursuing or, if this is found acceptable, of whether one may speak of neutrality with respect to a conflict between non-goal-directive forces. (It has been implicit in our account of neutrality throughout, and from time to time explicit, that any N must have some power of choice whether or not to remain neutral if it is to count as neutral at all.) Happily, however, there is no need to linger over these issues here, for whatever the general pros and cons of settling them in one way or another, the cases with which we are primarily concerned are those of political neutrality in or towards political conflicts and hence we need only consider conflicts in which goal-pursuing parties capable of forming intentions are involved. Thirdly, there is the clearly expressed assumption that for N to be neutral it must have the power of choosing to abandon its neutrality, *either* on behalf of P1 *or* on behalf of P2. But can we not envisage a situation where N might have only the choice of providing differential help to P1 or of providing equal help or hindrance to both P1 and P2, the possibility of providing differential help to P2 being excluded? And would this not still be a choice between helping P1 and remaining neutral?

This last point is worth exploring a little further. Let us take the case in which P1 and P2 are parties at war with each other. N is a further party, not itself at war but possessing stocks of ammunition suitable for use with the weapons with which the forces of P1 are equipped, but unusable with those in service with the forces of P2. We may suppose, in order to simplify matters, that there is no impact which N can have on the conflict other than by supplying, or refusing to supply, the ammunition in its possession. In such a case, N can give direct help only to P1. It is true that he can help P2 indirectly by refusing to help P1; but the basic asymmetry of the situation remains. (This asymmetry must work both ways. If N can give direct help only to P1, he must be unable to help P1 indirectly in the way in which he can help P2, in as much as there is no direct help he can give to P2 and which he can help P1 by withholding.) There is, of course, no point in making a major issue of whether such asymmetries might be taken to justify a refusal to use the vocabulary of neutrality. However described, such situations are not only possible, but even commonplace; and in fact it would surely be very odd to refuse to speak of neutrality in connection with them.

On more substantial matters we may recall earlier considerations concerning what may or may not be taken as lying within the range of natural or normal expectations. Suppose, first, that N is already a 'normal' supplier of ammunition to P1. In this case, a cessation of supplies on the outbreak of war might naturally be accountable as a non-neutral intervention in support of P2; for by ceasing supplies to P1 N would be going out of his 'normal' way to help P2, perhaps even whether he meant to or not (unless, of course, it was already a matter of common expectation or understanding that third party suppliers should cease supplying ammunition on the outbreak of any war). If N was not a 'normal' supplier of P1, then to start providing supplies on the outbreak of war could, conversely, be interpreted as a going out of his 'normal' way, though this is not a necessary interpretation, for the margins for conflicting interpretations are here significantly wide; there will, obviously, be conflicts over what should be counted as a 'normal' response of an arms manufacturer to a 'normal' commercial demand, more fundamental conflicts over what type or system of transactions can or should be counted as 'normally' and neutrally commercial. Suppose, at any rate, that N, not being a 'normal' supplier to P1, does nothing to make his supplies exceptionally or 'abnormally' available; he would then be helping P2 much in the way in which the weather might help one side or another, that is, with no intention at all in the case of the weather and no 'abnormally' intervening intention in the case of the supplier of ammunition. Clearly there would be no direct sense in speaking of the weather as either neutral or non-neutral; so any point there might be in treating as neutral the non-supplier of ammunition that is anyhow not normally supplied, would seem to depend on the assumption that he was so related to one or both of the conflicting parties that it would at least not have been surprising if he had changed, or been prevailed upon to change, his normal patterns of behaviour and supply in this new situation. As for the 'normal' supplier of ammunition who continues his supplies after the outbreak of war, there will be both the temptation to insist that in so doing there was no infringement of neutrality, since after all the outbreak of conflict had brought no change in his established pattern of activity; but also the opposite temptation to treat such a supplier as so closely linked with one of the parties to the conflict as to be effectively identified with it. (But one need not as a rule expect the same people to experience both temptations.)

The four possibilities of this pattern of relationships may be summed up, then, as follows:

1. N is a 'normal' supplier of ammunition to P1 and continues to supply him after the outbreak of conflict.
2. N is a 'normal' supplier, who then, however, ceases to supply.
3. N is not a 'normal' supplier, but commences supplies on the outbreak of conflict.
4. N is not a 'normal' supplier and continues not to supply.

In each of these cases the baselines for differing interpretations of neutrality are set by whatever is taken to be the appropriate framework of normal relations and behaviour in the light of changing circumstances. It is in any case an obviously necessary condition for N's neutrality that neither P1 nor P2 should succeed in attracting or forcing him to their side, (whatever the criteria for such an alignment might be held to be). It may be that neither of them has the power needed to achieve this; or that either or both freely agree to allow N to remain at the distance required for neutrality. But the case which is of special concern to Marin is that in which both P1 and P2 possess the necessary power and would be inclined to use it, but effectively inhibit each other from doing so. Whatever the actual genesis of the concept may be, however, it is unclear, even within the terms of his own account, why Marin should take this latter alternative as conceptually basic or paradigmatic for all kinds of neutrality. It is true that if any of the forces already committed to the conflict seek to involve N on their own side, he can retain his neutrality only if they are somehow 'neutralised'. It is true too that if he is himself led to try and neutralise first one and then the other of them, he may naturally be represented as taking a non-neutral part in the conflict on the side of the party opposed to that which had been trying to drag him in and which he is now engaged in 'neutralising'; unless, indeed, he finds himself having to 'neutralise' them both equally and at once. But even in this case reciprocal 'neutralisation' by the forces in conflict or N's simultaneous and equal 'neutralisation' of them both are not the only ways in which the neutrality of his position may be assured. A further possibility would be the existence of yet another more or less outside party, whose main object it was to intervene impartially against whichever of the conflicting parties might try to implicate would-be neutral outsiders as their unwilling allies. Such an outside party might be decisively more powerful than any of the other parties belonging to the domain of conflict and hence capable of holding the ring and preserving for N his freedom to choose neutrality, if he so wishes.

To hold the ring, to watch over and to insulate a conflict are, however, among the characteristic functions of a referee; and the instances of the so-called neutral referee or judge are, of course, of peculiar importance not only to Marin but to these discussions as a whole. Here it may be argued that a judge or referee can only function as such, or at any rate can only function in a properly neutral manner, if the contestants who have to submit to his judgements place themselves before him as if in a position of equal force. Certainly, to submit one's dispute to judgement is, provisionally at least, to renounce the possibility of settling it in one's own favour by use of force alone. The judge can only constitute himself as judge, or the referee as referee, in relation to parties who place themselves on an equal footing in respect of his rulings. Thus there is a certain sense in which to enter into the domain of a conflict as its judge is only possible to one who has secured a balance of force between the contesting parties. It is, however, important to see just how special is the sense of the balance required. For clearly two contesting parties may agree to accept the ruling of a neutral referee without *actually* divesting themselves of their perhaps very unequally balanced forces; it is rather that they have to agree to behave as equals before the court of arbitration. How this special type of equalisation may be secured for effective recognition must clearly vary from one type of case to another. At this point it may be helpful to look at three schematic examples: one, Marin's discussion of my own earlier example of the father and his two children; two, the familiar example of a game, a game in which handicaps are introduced as part of the terms of play, and three, one of the examples close to the problems of academic life itself with which Weinstein's paper was concerned.

My example of a father and his children was introduced, perhaps over-lightly, simply to illustrate the problem of what room there is for neutrality when two parties to a conflict are obviously unequally matched and the would-be neutral cannot help knowing which of them will win, if he merely leaves them alone. To do nothing is knowingly to allow the stronger to prevail; but if this is likely to appear 'a very odd form of neutrality to the weaker child', would it be any more neutral to intervene on his behalf so as to give him at least equal chances of success? So should one say that neutrality may sometimes lie in an inactivity which one knows will allow P1 to win? Or that it may consist in intervening with carefully limited help for P2? Or that in cases like these no option of neutrality is available?

Let us first return to the example of a game. We have noted that the introduction of some agreed form of handicap under the terms of sporting competition would not normally or 'naturally' appear to interfere with the neutrality of the framework of rules and conditions under which the contest takes place. The handicap may (normally) be seen as belonging to the terms of entry, which anyone is free to accept or not as he wishes. That this is so has to do with the point or rationale of the game and that of introducing a system of handicapping into it. Different games embody different selections of values, but in general the point of taking part in them lies in the attempt to win through some varied balance of skill, effort, natural endowment and luck. If the difference in strength between the participants is known to go beyond a certain point, then there will be insufficient incentive or even opportunity for the stronger to exercise his skills, while, depending on the exact nature of the sport in question, little point may be left to the efforts of the weaker. The point of introducing a handicap, then, will be so to redress the balance of inequality as to give the weaker sufficient chance of winning to restore meaning to his efforts and the stronger sufficient obstacles to overcome to draw out his full efforts and abilities. Thus, while the approximate equalisation of forces or the chances of victory for one side or the other may not be the direct point of the introduction of a handicap, they are linked with it as a necessary means to the end which it is designed to achieve. A game is no longer a game if victory is too automatic and easy; the introduction of a handicap may be the means by which the conditions of contest between otherwise too unequal opponents are restored to those of a game. No doubt, the matter will appear differently when, for example, the game is over-professionalised and victory is seen no longer as an end in itself, but as a means to prizes belonging to the mainstream of life; or when what is 'played as a game' is really the symbolic representation of some political contest. But so far as games *qua* games are concerned, the quasi-equalisation of forces that is achieved through the introduction of handicaps is something to be seen as belonging to the rationale of the game itself.

Games are only possible, then, between players whose relevant forces are not too unequal; if their initial inequality is (known to be) excessive, some form of equalisation may have to be brought about. But this is not a matter of 'no equalisation, no referee', but rather one of 'no equalisation, no game'; from which would no doubt follow 'no referee', but only because there would be no game over which to officiate – and even this is a little misleading, since within the framework of an institutionalised game he might still officiate in accordance with the rules over one of those meaninglessly unequal contests that are appropriately describable as 'not providing a game'. Any temptation must, therefore, be resisted of running together the argument which shows how one of the necessary conditions of a game lies in some sort of equality or equalisation of effective playing forces; and that other argument according to which the position of the referee within the game depends, as another necessary condition of its constitution, on the equal submission of the players to the whole set of its rules – that is, in the end, their equal acceptance of it *as a game* and not as a contest of natural force.

It is here, of course, that rests the point of the analogy with that equal submission to law that makes possible and is in a sense expressed by the position of a judge. The analogy has this striking imperfection, however, that where real social laws are concerned, the necessary equality of acceptance may derive directly from the impasse of an equality of brute force or be imposed from without rather than chosen from within (in so far as the distinction is always a clear one); on the other hand, while some people may be compelled to play games at times, this can hardly be the paradigm case. Moreover, there is, precisely, no analogy to be pursued with that substantial equality or contrived equalisation of playing forces, which is the first necessary condition for the existence of at least certain games *qua* games. It may be, as many socialists have argued, that a certain general equality is a necessary condition of the good or 'truly human' society. But (a) this is notoriously controversial; and (b) it is evidently not a necessary condition for the existence of society *tout court*.

The situation that has sometimes arisen in recent years over the selection of candidates for admission to certain British universities provides a different sort of comparison. During this time there has been continuing controversy over the social composition of the universities in general, but more especially – to make this example specific – of that of the collegiate universities of Oxford and Cambridge. The dispute is a highly complicated one and includes sub-disputes as to the very nature of the facts whose evaluation is at issue; but there is broad agreement at least that Oxford and Cambridge have been attracting a relatively small proportion of their candidates from schools coming under the direct administration of the local education authorities, schools whose pupils come in general from the socially less favoured majority of the population. Why is this so? To this apparently simple question the answer is no more simple than to that of whether this is a desirable, acceptable or undesirable state of affairs. One explanation which is frequently and plausibly offered, however, is that candidates from these 'poorer' schools feel that the Oxbridge selection procedures put them at a competitive disadvantage and hence prefer to aim elsewhere, either because they despair of getting acceptance at Oxbridge or because they feel that they would be out of place there or both. Up to now opinion at Oxford in particular has been widely opposed to abandoning these entrance examinations; but some of those responsible for selection have tended to the view that they should make allowances for the lower standard of achievement in them that may be expected from candidates coming from certain of these 'less favoured' schools, in order to offset their comparative disadvantage in the face of those coming from schools with much richer resources and with a longer tradition of preparing their students for this kind of competition.

Nobody need dispute the fact that the marking of such examinations as are not purely 'factual' is not only in practice but even in principle an inexact and variable matter. But why exactly should anyone think it right to enquire into the social and educational background of the boy or girl whose record of achievement he was assessing and whose entrance examinations he was marking, rather than mark each script as it came and take such marks as the best available index of their competitive merit? Indeed, many who would agree in deploring the situation of social 'imbalance' in the field from which Oxbridge has to select its candidates, would still insist that the only right place to deal with the problem is at its source in the schools. For, they would say, it is both unfair to penalise those who have done well in the competition simply because they may have received better teaching in better conditions, and unwise to discourage such schooling simply because it may be at present unequally financed.

It is of crucial importance to this dispute that one should make oneself as clear as possible as to the purposes of selecting people for a university education. Thus, if one takes the present structure of examinations as given and assumes that the main purpose of selection is to choose those candidates likely to obtain the best results in their final examinations three or four years later, it would be only sensible to look for any evidence to show that the weighting of examination marks according to some empirically discoverable formula would give rise to the most reliable predictions. Within such a framework of assumptions one might well see life as a whole as somehow unfair to seekers after university places coming from one social background rather than another, but there would be no reason to locate the unfairness in the procedures of the university selectors themselves. If the point of weighting the records of the competing candidates is assumed to lie exclusively in the effort to obtain the most reliable predictions of subsequent degree performance, there can be no question of such weighting itself being used to preserve or to modify the social distribution of candidates actually likely to obtain the best final degrees. But the limitations of this framework make it of course very unreal. For most people and for most purposes, university degrees are not ends in themselves but are related to subsequent careers. So too are other features of university life. These subsequent careers carry in turn many different implications both for society and for the individual; in any case, either to go or not to go to university may have great positive and negative significance (or both) for the individuals concerned in other than career terms. Last, but by no means least, there is no good reason for taking the degree structure itself as given – on the contrary, it too may embody many of the same social and cultural weightings as the entrance examinations themselves. To be as clear as possible as to the purposes of selecting people for a university education is to look for clarity in a complex and not fully determinate area.

Against this background it is possible to distinguish two broad areas of primary dispute. One concerns general social and educational aims: questions of what sort of relations the university should bear to society as a whole, which necessarily lead on to wider questions concerning the nature of that society. The other centres on the proper treatment of individuals as they try to work out the next stage of their lives within the given society in which they find themselves: on the basis of what criteria should one select some rather than others for a limited number of places? There is inevitably further dispute on the proper bearing of each of these sets of considerations on each other. And all of these disputes find a focus in debates over how to use the data provided by the actual examination performances of different sets of candidates at the age of 18+.

It is clear that many different lines of argument may find their starting points within this nest of issues. For the sake of this example, however, we may concentrate on the position of those who do feel that allowance should be made to offset factors of 'relative cultural deprivation' that tend to set certain classes of candidates at competitive disadvantage in relation to others. On the one hand they may recommend this policy as a contribution towards so changing the overall social and cultural context that in succeeding generations an increasing number of candidates may come forward from local government schools and that, as a complex causal concomitant, this increasing number may be increasingly well prepared. On the other hand, or indeed at the same time, they may argue that it is unfair to the individuals concerned not to try to offset the competitive disadvantages which, through no fault of their own, have been built into their upbringing so far. As always there are several ways of representing this situation. Some selectors, for example, will claim that there is no point at which any question of neutrality arises. Within the present state of society any system of selection will necessarily favour one set of contenders against others. If they as selectors were to administer it with total impartiality, they would, since they themselves are part of it, be acting unneutrally against those candidates who are at present at a disadvantage. If they chose rather to manipulate it in the interests of this set of candidates, their choice would be an equally unneutral one in favour of one section of society rather than another. Whether and from what point of view it might make sense to suppose that there could ever be a state of society in which an essentially neutral or non-distorted system of university selection might be devised, raises questions that are by now sufficiently familiar. It is at any rate most characteristically thinkers of the Marxist or so-called radical left who, according primary importance to frameworks of conditions which they wish to call into question, refuse accordingly to treat them as providing baselines for individual options of any sort of neutrality. Left-wing liberals are likely to lay more stress on the contributory and intrinsic value of individual initiative and hence to see the existing framework, whether itself assessable as neutral or not, as providing baselines from which these individual initiatives at any rate may be assessed in terms of their neutrality or non-neutrality. Thus, they may characterise their policy as one of *a deliberate departure* from the immediate neutrality of impartial assessment based on the marks as first given for the sake of achieving more important ends. And they may see the situation this way whether their primary aims are the bringing about of general shifts in society and its educational institutions or those of simple fairness to particular individuals; though it is also possible that they should see what they regard as their restoration of the natural balance of competitive chances as a personally neutral elimination of the partisan distortion secreted by the system which they have, as things stand, to administer.

Let us now set aside the positions of those who believe that there is in principle no sense in seeking any kind of neutrality in this area, in order to follow the thread of argument of those who seek to restore or to create a balance between competitors who, the balance once having been created or restored, may *then* be judged in an impartial and neutral manner by a university which is neutral in relation to conflicts in which the interests of one social group may be opposed to those of another. The details of their arguments will vary depending on how they see their action. They may see it as taking place in a context in which no option of neutrality is immediately open and, therefore, either as unavoidably unneutral or as lying outside the domain of neutrality and partisanship altogether; they may take it as a deliberate departure from a kind of neutrality that they find in the circumstances indefensible, that is to say, the restricted and individual neutrality that is the only such option open to a judge called upon to administer biased and partisan laws; or they may regard their attempt to eliminate distortion as essentially neutral in its own individual rationale. But, whichever of these views they take, the value of their action – and *a fortiori*, in the third alternative, its meaning as an action that is essentially neutral – lies in its being performed for the sake of an institutional neutrality that, as Marin puts it, is to come, a neutrality on which the university as an institution ought to be founded and out of which it ought to be able to act, but which has yet to be created. Thus, whether or not their attempt to redress the balance of inequalities in favour of a new equal balance of forces is to be regarded as already neutral in itself, its justification is to be found in their conception of a position of impartiality and neutrality which they, acting in the name of the university, should at all times aim to establish.

The overall neutrality of the university as an institution among other institutions is something that can only be fashioned over time. In terms of the immediate selection of individual candidates, however, university tutors may see themselves as proceeding from a position of purely subjective to more effective neutrality once the overall allowances for offsetting the overall inequalities have been made. That is to say, to put it very roughly, that once the appropriate 10% or whatever has been added to the marks of candidates from the 'poorer' schools, they may proceed to measure them against their initially more favoured rivals as if they had now given themselves working baselines for unequivocally neutral selection. But how is this likely to appear to those candidates whose initially individual superiority has in this way been 'neutralised'? It is at least possible that their initial reaction will be one of resentment of what they take to be unfair and partisan discrimination. But, however this may be, one of the assumptions of the position out of which the tutors concerned are acting must be that the successful education of those students whom they do admit to the university must in due course bring them at least to appreciate, if not actually to accept, the rational nature of the principles underlying both their selection and the teaching which they have received.

There is perhaps little reason to suppose that individual candidates who do not survive the discrimination against them and so never arrive at the university, are similarly likely to arrive at such eventual insights. The analogy does hold more closely again, however, as soon as one looks to the long-term and overall institutional neutrality of the university in relation to the rest of society. For here the main point of contriving such a shift at the margins in the social composition of the student body would be (i) to help bring about changes in general expectations and attitudes so that the Oxbridge image ceased to be one of offering peculiarly favourable opportunities first of admission and subsequently of social advancement to the children of the richer or upper and middle classes; while ensuring (ii), through continued close contacts with the old established schools and through the education of that still substantial proportion of their candidates that would continue to be admitted, that this change in Oxbridge's position was generally accepted as right. In so far, then, as these aims are successfully achieved, action which may once have been resented as partisan by the hitherto more powerful schools or social groups, will eventually be seen by them too as having been based on a vision of neutrality. But those individuals, groups or institutions, who, having first been neutralised, are thus led in due course to accept as proper the principles of their own neutralisation, will be ready to support or themselves to become the neutralisers in their turn, if the situation still calls for it. Indeed, if the lesson has been properly learned, they will see that the possibility must remain forever open that the situation will still call for it: either because the original imbalances have still not been removed or because new imbalances have arisen as the framework of potential conflict and neutrality has once again shifted around the university. It cannot be repeated too often that there is no position of final or absolute neutrality. As conflicts may continually arise, neutrality lies in the endlessly readjusted pursuit of an endlessly elusive goal; or, as Marin also puts it, in the unceasing readiness to bring once more into question whatever position at which one may temporarily have arrived.[23]

We may now return to my example of the father and his children. Marin characterises the father's intervention in this example as consisting 'in the paradox of "working" in favour of one of the conflicting parties to the detriment of the other in order to arrive at the state of neutralisation (*la situation neutre*) in which recourse to a judge is logically justified. This', he goes on to say, 'is the reason for his preliminary activity of practical intervention undertaken for the sake of a "neutre" that is to come and justifiable only by reference to it. In other words, "le neutre" is here defined as a power of neutralisation, whose aim is to neutralise the opposing parties, a "neutre" which receives its force from an "originary" position in a situation of dual conflict.'

As before, there is no question of attempting a faithful exegesis. But, all problems of textual exegesis aside, what sort of interpretation might this passage most plausibly suggest? It certainly presents a number of *prima facie* difficulties. Who or what, for instance, is the exact object of the neutralising power of the father? A few sentences before the passage quoted, Marin says that the father's aim in 'complementing the force of the weaker child' is to

[23] Already in the very different context of Part I, section 3, open-mindedness, there characterised as the readiness 'always to take into fresh consideration any new facts and any new interpretation of old facts', was seen to be so closely bound up with objectivity and impartiality as to form a constituent element of any sustained analysis of these latter. The point would be worth further exploration with its fresh suggestions of the links as well as the differences between the concepts of objectivity and impartiality and that of neutrality.

'create a real zero of opposition', that is, a dynamic equilibrium of opposing forces. On this view it must be the elder or stronger child who is at least temporarily neutralised. 'This is the reason for [the father's] preliminary activity of practical intervention. . .' But is it really no more than a simple restatement 'in other words' to go on to say that ' "le neutre" is here defined as a power of neutralisation whose aim is to neutralise the opposing parties'? The advent of the neutral judge, at any rate, actually awaits the establishment of the balance of opposing forces through their mutual neutralisation, perhaps to some extent helpfully contrived by third party inter-vention – though we must remember that there is in logic no neces-sity for any real equality of forces between them over and above their 'equal' acceptance of the rule of law or their 'equal' vulnerability to the power of the judge. (And in this latter case 'equal' need not mean that they must succumb equally easily to his power, but only that both are, in the event, 'equally' at its mercy.)

There seems already to have been a slide from one neutralising aim to another. It may be that to read the passage in this way would be wilfully superficial and that we should talk rather of a first aim subordinated to a second and deeper one. But now, we may ask, if the force of the father/judge is somehow derived from those of the opposing parties 'in a situation of dual conflict', in what sense is it then to be turned back upon them in order to neutralise them both? In La Fontaine's fable to which Marin had earlier referred in his analysis of the paradigm of the judge, Raminagrobis, the cat, resolves the conflict by the drastic means of gobbling up both the contending parties, the rabbit and the weasel. In general neither judges nor the law are expected actually to destroy the parties that appear to present a dispute before them, either through judgement or through the procedures involved in arriving at it. In principle, they aim rather to settle the conflict, that is to say, to neutralise it rather than the conflicting parties themselves. However, this may perhaps be seen as a neutralisation, an abolition of the parties *qua contestants*. Moreover, if they are thus neutralised or stripped of their role as contestants, it is only by virtue of the power that they have accorded the judge by their prior acceptance of him; or, to put it more generally, in virtue of the power that has been accorded to the whole legal system through its acceptance by the society in whose structure it occupies a key position. In as much as it is the father's aim to put himself in the neutral position of a judge in re-lation to his two children, he may be said to aim at neutralising – taking the sting out of – their opposition, rather than at neutralising either or both of them in themselves; if he is in a sense seeking to render them impotent, it is only that they should be impotent to carry on their contest. Though, we may add, in the banal practice of ordinary family life there may obviously be no need for him to go through any 'preliminary activity of practical intervention' to complement the force of the weaker child *before* stepping in to try and settle the conflict; in so far as the father has the overall power to impose his judgement, it is already in itself a force of equalisation.

It may at once be objected that this is to distort the whole point of Marin's discussion by transposing it into the superficial key of analysis by reference to everyday life. There is certainly something in this. Marin is far more concerned with symbolic structures than with empirical generalisations and, as he had started by pointing out, it is a '[principal supposition of the analysis] that the father's status as a referee in the children's games is given before this particular conflict breaks out'. The father is not a mere outsider who just happens to want to create for himself the position of a judge and so, out of this contingent desire, seeks to place the conflicting parties in such a position of equal and unresolvable tension in relation to each other that they have no other recourse but to ask him to adjudicate. He is already the neutralising father of a certain Freudian mythology who, as Marin goes on to argue, stands at the point of creation of rational conscience and of civil law. Within this perspective his is therefore the power to which his children must naturally turn for judgement – the power which it is their role to internalise as the voice of neutral and impartial law, whose first function it then is to neuterise and suppress their own 'illicit' desires.[24]

In these ways Marin effectively weaves together the themes of the neuter/neutral as it stands in relation to a conflict of equally matched and mutually inhibiting forces, those of one-sided interventions in conflicts as a form of, or for the sake of, a wider neutrality and those of a creative-type genesis of neutrality from neuterness. It may be that the passages between these themes have, so to speak, a 'natural' basis of their own; that is, that Marin is simply exposing to our view some of the ways in which the overlapping connections, both *de facto* and conceptual, that exist between these varied themes and sub-themes, constitute pathways along which the mind (both in its individual and its social, in its theoretical, attitudinal and behaviourial expressions) may pass backwards and forwards, continually reinforcing the links that facilitated its first passages by the mere fact of its repeated passing. So he expresses the instability of this neuterness/neutrality,

[24] To this it may be added, by way of a gloss on Marin's characterisation of the position of the father as that of 'a "third" (contentless) term in a more fundamental situation', that both this power and the law which is founded on it stand first and foremost and in general for the pure suppression or transcendence of conflict rather than for the imposition of any positive line of conduct.

its impossibility of any definitive or absolute foundation and its nevertheless parallel indispensability as a mark of open rationality, by locating it in the very movement or passage from one theme or embodiment to another. But whatever volatile truth may thus be expressed – or whatever the possibilities of expression that may thus be exploited – it is *also* important soberly and unimaginatively to point out that there is great heterogeneity not only among the themes so linked together, but also in the very modes of transition from one to the other; here by way of explicit conceptual relationships, there by way of possible psycho-sociological genesis, here by way of analogy or metaphor, there by way of a certain philosophical tradition.

So what does tend to happen to a discourse such as Marin's when translated into one which is governed by traditions of analysis and logical empiricism? Something is surely lost from this play of concepts and of the language within which they are continually built up and dissolved. But what is this philosophical play – the very 'concept' of which belongs to the tradition out of which his discourse is evolved rather than to that of its translation? It is among other things an exploration of the ways in which the mind can realise its own creative ideas – but a mind that is in part constituted by its proliferating explorations and by the language of their expression, a language of which it is both the creator and the creation. If it achieves full self-consciousness, such conceptual (or metaphysical?) seeking may also be understood as an exploration of the personal, social and institutional framework of life of the seeker or player and of the games out of which he emerges; and of the limits of what is possible within it, both as it is and as it may become. In relation to explorations conducted in terms such as these, the down-to-earth empiricist's reiterated insistence on distinguishing between one embodied individual and another will seem at once a crudeness and an ill-considered threat. Nevertheless, even if it is right, even if it is in some sense necessary in this day and age, to regard philosophy as a game, one of its rules (or so it seems to me) must still be that play be not the only dimension of philosophical activity. A certain kind of analysis is also needed to determine the sense of the game, even if such analysis can only maintain its own restricted claim to neutrality through the recognition that it too may be regarded as an extension of the game. One might put it another way: that neutrality here lies in the recognition that the analysis in which the very sense of the game demands that it be made explicit, is one by which part of the spirit of the game at least, and perhaps even of its sense itself, is at the same time dissipated and lost – except, may be, in so far as the analysis finds its own explicit meaning getting caught up and lost in a renewal of the game. It may be the peculiar nature of philosophy to be driven always to seek ways of having it both or all ways at once, at the risk always of ending up by having it no way at all. But then would not a form of philosophy that *both* had it both ways at once *and* had it neither way, be one in search of what Marin diagnoses as its own impossible but necessary basis of absolute, a utopian neutrality? Or should he have said, to be more analytically accurate, objectivity or impartiality?

If this sounds like a rhetorically satisfactory ending to this section, there is yet an important postscript to be added. It is one of Marin's principal themes that a crucial element in the would-be neutrality of philosophical discourse is its continual turning back upon itself to query its own context and status. But he has pointed out too, when speaking of Thrasymachus, that in a situation of force to transpose the dispute into the terms of open-minded, rational debate, to change the weapons and rules of combat from those of the sword to those of the undogmatic word, may be very unneutral in its bearing upon the outcome of the conflict. Indeed, while he sits theorising about the conflict and its stabilisation or neutralisation in highly abstract terms, the philosopher is at professional risk of mistaking intellectual justifications, solutions and formulations for the achievement of real social balance or change. And while it is easy to insist that we need in addition a discussion of the 'objective' forces themselves, it is also strangely easy in doing so to forget that this discussion too is in itself no more than a discussion and, as such, a possible non-neutral diversion of these very objective forces – (which means, of course, that in another sense it may be much more than a 'mere' discussion).

We have already noted the frequent radical objection that intellectual discussion, and especially intellectual discussion that is institutionalised within a university framework, may simply reflect some particular partisan position in a real social conflict and, in so reflecting, constitute an active reinforcement of it. The only honest reply to this objection is that it may sometimes in fact be correct. Rational discourse must indeed be continually alert to the hidden as well as to the overt meanings that it may contain, to its unavowed motivation and to its varying practical significance at different points of history. Notoriously it is not always rational to stop and reason; and even if it were, there would be those who would not necessarily choose to be rational. Nevertheless, the potential non-neutrality of a recourse to discourse should not be confused with that discourse's potential impartiality; and while it may be true that even self-understanding may at times be purchased only at the price of partisan intervention, and true too that there may be times when this price seems too high to be paid, this in itself is no reason to shrink from an openly partisan commitment of preference for such positions and causes as may demand silence and inarticulate action only at moments of very last resort – that is to say, moments at which all future possibilities for reflective speech and understanding seem definitively threatened.[25]

4   The concept of the political again

Section 5 of Part I was devoted to the concept of the political. Although there is little in the papers of Part II to call what was there said into direct question, I have been convinced by subsequent discussion[26] that some of its present inadequacies should at least be noted here.

The first and most pervasive of these lies in an over-simplification so serious as to amount to a straight mistake. In moving back from the notion of the political to that of the public, I in effect allowed the contrast between the public and the private, drawn by Sir George Cornewall Lewis and utilised by Bentham, to pass as providing for each of these terms its sole counterbalancing antithesis. But this is highly misleading. It is not merely that the contrast between the public and the private does not always have the same sense, that both terms possess a range of varying interpretations and applications (the differences, for example, between a public and a private company are not exactly the same as those between a politician's private and public life). It is, more importantly, that the notion of the public may draw its sense from different contrasts altogether. It may have a sense in societies where that of the private, as a sphere of especial rights and obligations, may appear to have very little; or, if it does, its relation to that of the public may be far from exhausting the sense or senses of this latter. It would be obviously unsatisfactory to find oneself having to claim that in societies where such a concept of the private was lacking, and hence that of any contrast between it and that of the public, so too would be lacking the concept and practice of politics. In fact, in societies where there appears to be little or no conception of privacy or of the private, the concepts of the public, the community and the body politic may still hold clo-

[25] It was only after having written this section that I discovered my ignorance of Maurice Blanchot's book *L'Entretien Infini* (Gallimard, Paris, 1969), in which he quite explicitly treats the theme of 'le neutre' in ways some of which bear comparison with some aspects of Louis Marin's treatment of the subject.

[26] In particular with Melvin Richter and Steven Lukes to whom, as well as to other members of seminars in which we all three took part at the Université de Montréal and at McGill during the spring of 1973, I owe grateful thanks.

sely together in joint contrast, for example, to all that is outside and foreign; or to that which is of a lower or purely ancillary order, as that which pertains to children, to women or to slaves; or, again, to all that belongs to the realms of morality or religion, where these may be conceived of as affecting men in their common humanity or in their common relationship to God and as having nothing to do with their assignability as particular individuals. In as much as any non-public domains of concern may serve to distract a man's attention from his public commitments within a given community, grounds no doubt exist for argument that the concept of the private must always be at least implicitly or potentially available, whatever the nature or structure of society. Nevertheless, the terms of my earlier analysis were undeniably inappropriately restrictive. The distinction between the realms of the private assignable individual and that of the public non-assignable citizen, if not invariably sharp, remains yet valid enough. But it does not provide the only antithesis into which the concept of the public, or indeed that of the private, can enter; nor is it one of universal application. The domains of public politics are wider and more varied than I implicitly allowed them to be.

None of this invalidates the contention that the boundaries between the public and the non-public, and with them those between the political and the non-political, are essentially and ineradicably contestable; but it does mean that it will need supporting by a wider range of arguments. Their full deployment, with proper historical backing, would necessarily constitute a considerable undertaking; their nature, however, will not be fundamentally different from those already sketched out in section 5 of Part I. What types or classes of persons may be acknowledged as belonging to the body politic? By what criteria or by whom are such questions to be decided? How freely and under what circumstances may this or that group declare itself to have adhered to or to have dissociated itself from the city or the republic? Or this or that individual? Where and of what nature are the boundaries between the laws of man and those of God alone? There may be long stable periods during which the answers to these questions will be, as it were, given in the assumptions and structures of society itself. But they are answers that may inevitably be called into question as the patterns of society change. None of the key concepts involved are hard at the edges; and the phenomena to which they apply are precisely those features of social life, practice and belief over whose nature men dispute both in theory and in practice with each other.

There is, however, an objection of almost classical pattern that has to be faced at this point. The remarks of section 5 make no pretence, it is true, of presenting 'a complete definition of the concept of "politics"'; nevertheless, the claim that the concept is by definition essentially contestable does constitute a contribution towards that end. But there are, of course, a number of other definitions of this concept in the field, some of them very well known and not all of them including essential contestability as one of their elements. So is my (partial) definition straightforwardly superior to all others in this respect? It seems that I have either to claim that it is – in which case I appear to present the essential contestability of the concept of 'politics' as itself incontestable; or, in allowing that its essential contestability must itself be contestable, I can no longer explain why my own account of the concept is to be preferred to anyone else's. The same difficulty reflects on the claim that disputes about the proper limits of the domain of the political are themselves of political significance. For whether this is so or not must likewise be essentially contestable. Of course, it may always be claimed that any resulting meta-conflict will be of political significance in its turn; but this is only to take a further step in the direction of an infinite regress.

To say that a concept is *essentially* contestable must be to say more than that it is open always to challenge in the ways in which the definition (lexical or stipulative) of any term whatsoever may be challenged as inadequate. Essentially contestable concepts are so in virtue of the nature of the material to which they apply and of their relation to it. The evident complication is that one cannot identify this material as that to which the concepts relate in direct and total independence of the meaning assigned to the concepts through whose application the identification is made. One has, therefore, to proceed indirectly, adjusting one's terms of discourse as one goes along.

In the present case we may start from a briefly crude distinction between an account of the functioning of terms like 'political' in contexts of practical discourse, of the meanings which it may there bear and of the forces with which it may be used; and, on the other hand, one of the elaboration of definitions within the frameworks of political theory or political science. In these latter contexts it may naturally appear that differing definitions of 'the political' may compete with each other under conditions of substantive political neutrality. This distinction goes deeper than one between the area of simple contemporary usage and that of theoretical study and debate. The body politic is, among other things, an arena of claims, privileges, rights and obligations. Rival attempts to demarcate this body in different ways and by reference to different criteria necessarily carry with them rival visions of who has what sorts of claims on whom else, of who should be entitled to what or have what obligations laid upon them. When trade unionists, church-men, industrialists and others argue about what forms of activity do or do not count as political, they are arguing about what can be expected of or imposed upon whom, of what efforts may properly be directed to what ends and under what circumstances. Thus, prac-tically orientated argument about what is to be counted as political may play a very direct part in active political contest and is in any case bound to have some potential relevance to it. Theoretical dis-course, on the contrary, may at first sight present itself as bearing no such necessary implications. The relative merits and demerits of characterising the political in terms of relationships between friend and foe, for example, rather than in terms of competition between rival pressure groups may be debated by reference to the power of the predications generated by the one as against the persuasiveness of the explanations furnished by the other. What people actually say and the ways in which they actually conceive of their actions form, of course, a crucial part of the material of which theoretical dis-course seeks to provide an account. But there is no reason why it should be limited in its construction to the concepts and concep-tions that are already to be found among its objects of study.

By now, however, we know all too well just how controversial are the possibilities or impossibilities of keeping this distinction sharp, particularly in the area of the human sciences. We may recall how all sorts of arguments, good, bad and indifferent, have been mar-shalled on one side or another of these controversies. For example: that the construction of theories about the nature of society itself takes place as a social act, which has in its turn to be studied as such in its social and historical context. But, of course, this further reflexive study may itself be considered both as a theoretical exercise and as a social act of additional complexity; it is clear that here too we may set ourselves upon a course if not of infinite regress, then at least of an endless series of shifts – and that Louis Marin's 'neutre' may be only just around this ever receding corner. Or again: that it is almost impossible seriously to envisage a society in which there is never any impact of theoretical upon practical dis-course, no *de facto* working interaction of the one with the other. More fundamentally, it will be argued that closer analysis reveals the very concepts of the theoretical and the practical to be over-lapping, so that the idea of a pure, wholly non-practical theoretical discourse turns out to be strictly meaningless. But – not surpris-ingly – the presentation of this apparently theoretical argument has itself to be assessed in the light of the practical implications which it may bear in the context in which it occurs. As Régis Debray com-ments on his student days as a pupil of Louis Althusser, 'All very fine: theory draws its effectiveness from its rigorousness, and its rigorousness is effective because it separates "development of reality" from "development in thought", "the operation of society" from the "operation of knowledge". In other words, all we had to do to become good theoreticians was to be lazy bastards.'[27] There is the difficult but important argument that there can be no full understanding of a contemporary political situation by someone who is not striving, through his understanding, to be at effective work within it. Finally, there are the problems, mentioned more than once in the course of this book, associated with the much contested and arguably essentially contestable doctrine of the Autonomy of Ethics; and with the further and equally contested contentions that beliefs as to values and even as to facts are in part actually constituted by the expressions that they may find in action.

Against this increasingly familiar background, it is clear that whether or not, and in whatever version, the distinction between theoretical and practical discourse may in the end be establishable, it cannot be taken as immediately obvious or straightforward. In the case here in question, my own account of the way in which the term 'political' functions in contemporary practical discourse is (necessarily) itself an interpretive theory, which has to take into account the language and views of those who at the ground level would explicitly or implicitly deny its claim that the concept was essentially contestable. If I point out that such views are natural in those who have a deep vested interest in the maintenance of a stable *status quo* or in the establishment of some future and thenceforth unchanging framework of politics; if I point out that their denial of the essential contestability of the political has a political function in the reinforcement of their own beliefs and in the effective imposition of them on those whose 'real' interests lie in maintaining a fundamentally open political situation; then, by doing so, I take sides against those whose views I characterise in this way. To what extent this taking of sides constitutes effective practical action will depend on the actual political context in which it takes place. A theoretician cannot without self-deception satisfy his conscience nor gratify a personal wish to see himself as a man of action simply by defining himself as such within his own theoretical frame of reference. But neither – as we have also seen – can he adopt a position of neutrality by any mere inverse theoretical fiat.

To sum up this not easily sum-uppable matter: In claiming that the concept of the political is essentially contestable I have to allow, as part of the point of my claim, that there may be other and incompatible views of its nature. I do not and cannot consistently claim

[27] *Prison Writings* (Allen Lane, London, 1973), p. 187.

that they need involve any internal logical incoherence or factual error, but rather that they would involve a certain narrowness, a certain blindness – something which is at once a theoretical and a practical limitation. But this thesis too must have a practical as well as a theoretical dimension; if I have on the one hand to claim to provide for a wider and better range of predictions or more persuasive explanations of the positions taken by those with whom I here differ than they can provide of mine, I have at the same time to recognise it as carrying potential political implications of its own. Though whether I personally enjoy them or am able or willing to do anything further about them is another, if not *quite* another, matter. Not *quite* another matter, since, as we know, there are all those points of view from which my failure to do anything further must be taken to reflect back on the very meaning of my claims, certainly on their status as acts of claiming and perhaps even in the last resort on their propositional contents.

There is one other possibly misleading limitation embedded in the terminology and presentation of my earlier discussion that calls for mention here. This lies in the particular association there established between the notions of 'policy' and 'politics'. That there is a very close association between them is obvious enough. But the notion of a policy also has close connections with that of an agent, be it individual, collective or institutional, whose policy it is; and this gives rise to certain problems. This is not an appropriate point at which to enter into the ramified controversies over who or what may be counted as a subject of action, as an initiator or pursuer of policies. But whatever the position that one may adopt in these complexities, we have to remember that anything that may affect the shaping and formulation or non-formulation of policy may fairly be counted as political, even though many such factors may in themselves relate to frameworks or structures rather than to policy conflicts as such. Thus it would be wrong to suppose that in fields where there is no actual policy and *a fortiori* no clash of policies that are incompatible, there is a complete absence of politics. It is enough that reference may be made to potential policies and to conflicts between them, policies whose possibility is implicit in the structure of the situation even if no one is able actually to envisage them at the period under study. A number of recent studies have indeed concentrated on this very point – that it has been a characteristic of much 'liberal' political practice and its accompanying theory to ignore the political importance of those features of its systems which function to prevent certain issues from arising as matters for policy formation at all. I do not think that there is anything in my earlier discussion to exclude taking account of these factors. But certainly no fully explicit account was there taken of them; and in a proper reworking of the discussion, it would have to be extended in order to make it clear how this should be done.

5   Weinstein, Graham and Ten

The papers of Part II are all written out of their authors' own varied experience; but this reference may be most explicit in the cases of Graham, Ten and Weinstein. Obviously this does not mean that these papers have no theoretical dimension. Nevertheless, it may appear that their main function in this volume is to provide illustrations of the practical relevance of the primarily theoretical discussions contained elsewhere within it. Indeed, this is one of their functions. But if there is a sense in which it is even their main function, it must immediately be added that this sense itself calls for theoretical illumination. The relation of illustrative examples to the theses which they are intended to illustrate is itself philosophically variable and problematic. One of the principal purposes of this section will be, then, to see how far it may be possible to make theoretically explicit the contribution which such more or less 'practical' discussions may make to the whole through their role of providing not merely illustrations but also 'grounding' examples.

We may start, however, with a point arising from one of Weinstein's discussions. The last of his examples – not of world importance in itself – concerns a series of controversies over the content of the Oxford course in philosophy, politics and economics. 'It was intensively criticised', as he says, 'as excessively narrow in its coverage of rival doctrines in all three subjects (and therefore not impartial in so far as not all relevant views on contemporary issues were included) . . .' And in fact he himself agreed with his students' contention, if not with all their supporting arguments, 'that Marxism and other important radical theories were not given sufficient scope, and that this represented a defeat of *academic* balance, operating as a discouragement to open-mindedness and impartiality in teachers and students'. Finally, to quote a longer passage: '. . . part of my conscious response to the criticism of the syllabus as politically non-neutral because of its imbalanced coverage of controversial ideas was to react in liberal academic style – that is, by striving to restore the impartial treatment that would lend credibility to the separation of academic and political considerations. I now see more clearly . . . that on this account it may not be absurd to suggest that I was acting politically in defence of academic values. For the partiality or bias that some students thought to be sinister was a ground for *political* criticism of the university's overall position in society; though . . . I was mainly conscious of the need to meet well-founded criticism based on *academic* standards, the criticisms of the syllabus were sometimes connected with wider issues about the position of the university.'

The two major criticisms to which Weinstein here refers are directed to the syllabus's alleged narrowness and imbalance. In fact, these do not necessarily come to the same thing. Balance can presumably be secured on a wider or a narrower front; and a broad coverage of all rival doctrines in the field may be exceedingly unbalanced in the manner of its presentation. But Weinstein is here, I think, assuming a reasonably impartial exposition of whatever views may actually be expounded; and assuming too that the particular kind of narrowness that was being attacked in fact involved an important kind of imbalance. There is, also, the very obvious assumption that an imbalance is undesirable as such. So the important questions to be asked seem first to be in what exactly does academic balance consist, and what is it that makes it so desirable?

Weinstein is writing about the teaching of politics, philosophy and economics. But a course in, say, mathematics may also be open to criticism as either narrow or unbalanced. That is, it is easy to suppose a course so constructed and a department so staffed as to give great weight to certain aspects of the subject and correspondingly little to others. The judgement as to whether this involves an imbalance or not calls no doubt for some sort of evaluative commitment. But to speak of an imbalance as being non-neutral or biased is already implicitly to refer to some sort of conflict, in this sort of case presumably a conflict of views as to the proper nature of the subject and how best it may be studied and taught. It would be difficult not to agree that 'a proper balance' within the teaching of the subject is *ceteris paribus* desirable in as much as this is almost an analytic proposition. But is it obviously desirable that the department or the curriculum should be so organised as to produce a neutral balance of all conflicting views as to what the proper balance of emphasis within the subject should actually be? This is a very different matter; and if one *does* think it desirable to aim at such a balancing out of the conflict, it cannot be on the basis of one's view of the nature and teaching of mathematics alone. There is further and crucial reference to some Millsian-type view of the value, both instrumental and intrinsic, of the free play of contrasting ideas of which Taylor writes in his article; and beyond that, most probably, to the value of balance and neutrality itself.

Thus there could well be a conflict between one's essentially liberal wish that the department and course should reflect a balance of opposing views about the overall nature of mathematics and one's own view of how it should be studied and taught. The outcome might be a resolution on *general academic* grounds that one's own *academic mathematical* views and interests should be represented only as one set among others that should also find equal representation in the department. Any claim that such a view of what constitutes a strong *general academic* case has no wider *political* implications would, as we have seen often enough, be either too simple or itself essentially political or both; this is after all just one more instance of the way in which the political case for restricting the domain of politics needs to be made out with constant and self-conscious vigilance. Weinstein, however, is a teacher not of mathematics but of politics itself; and the objects of study in departments of politics may naturally be expected to include what are the teachers' own real political views. But while some real life political views would demand as free and balanced an expression and study as possible of all remotely relevant political views to be found actively 'on the market', others of course would not. Moreover, on the view of politics propounded in Part I of this book – which is *not* that of every teacher of the subject – political views are by definition views on what policies to adopt in situations of policy conflict. On this view, therefore, a proper understanding of the nature of politics, such as the teacher of the subject must aim to bring about in his students, must include an awareness of the nature of such conflicts, a consideration that does not apply in a domain such as that of mathematics. So here we may find not just two or three, but even four abstractly distinguishable sorts of consideration running substantively together: one's *general pedagogical* views on the instrumental teaching value of exposing the student to a conflicting variety of views on whatever may be the subject matter concerned – pedagogical views which a mathematician might equally well hold in the context of the teaching of mathematics; one's *special academic* views on the nature of politics as a field of academic study: one's *general academic* views as to whether the department or the university should seek a representative balance of special academic views at all appropriate levels of the university: and one's *general political* views as to whether, on other than purely academic grounds, universities should be encouraged, compelled or allowed to seek such all round representation or not.[28] When one further

---

[28] No one could sensibly suggest that room must always be found for the expression and study of all views whatsoever no matter what their degree of combined lunacy and unimportance. Clearly, the distinctions here are, as ever, essentially contestable; there are no indisputably given criteria of lunacy or unimportance. Moreover, the weight to be given to the one factor or the other may properly vary between disciplines; even very absurd views need to be studied in departments of politics if they carry enough weight in social and political practice,

reflects that it will be a matter both of dispute and possible study whether these distinctions can be properly made out or not, or whether their acceptance or refusal must of itself be of direct or indirect political significance, one realises yet again the extraordinarily regressive nature of any sustained attempt to maintain the distinction that Weinstein is struggling to maintain between the political and the academic. For the liberal – I am here tempted to say the 'true' liberal – the battle has always to be fought; but it has to be fought in the clear understanding that to seek a final and absolute victory is to lose the essential before one has begun. That is, there is no proper victory without full self-awareness, including the reflexive awareness of the political implications of the refusal to admit any political implications of one's own position. We are back to one of the central themes of Marin's analysis of 'le neutre' – who may, as indeed he must, be prepared to stand up and be counted, but who cannot merely remain standing where he is to be counted a simple second, third and fourth time. If he is prepared to be counted again, as again indeed he must, it can be only when he has *come back* to his position of neutrality, the enabling context of which has constantly to be checked – and, often enough, re-established.

But why after all is it so important to achieve a balance? Here we may recognise another central Marin theme. To quote from one of the most abstractly speculative passages of his paper: 'Once "le neutre" is made into an object of thought it can be seen as making manifest the "neutralisation" of opposites or, to put it another way, their opposition as the reciprocal annulment of their forces. "Le neutre" is that which presents to thought this movement of mutual annulment as such; it makes it appear as a theme in itself before returning to the conflict from which it, "le neutre", arose and over which it will henceforth assume its authority as judge and arbiter.' Neutrality, as a position to be filled by a possible neutral if such a one actually appears, only comes into existence as effect and reflection of a conflict in which the diverse opposing forces balance each other out into an equilibrium in which there may be intense activity but no change actually takes place. The neutral university allows everyone to speak but in doing so puts everyone in his place; it pretends to claim no particular voice for itself, but, speaking through the counter-balancing voices of all, to present them in their joint diversity to themselves, each as the complement of the others and their several inter-negations as the truth of them all. Within the total equilibrium, each view stands as a question mark to each other.

---

while this is markedly not the case in such areas as mathematics. Nevertheless, contestable though the drawing of such lines may be, they have necessarily always to be drawn and – if necessary – revised and redrawn again.

Neutrality, one might say, is to lie in the overall dominance of the question mark as the basic condition of self-awareness; or rather, perhaps, in the constant endeavour to catch up with one's awareness of one's own ever shifting (if yet unchanging) position as one among others rather than as the unique and unquestionable framework of truth itself.

The reciprocal dependence of self-awareness and knowledge of objective truth is an old theme; and the liberal university is aware of itself as defined by the pursuit of knowledge. It is at any level dangerous, however, to take it too lightly for granted that self-awareness and self-realisation must necessarily come at once to the same thing. If there is a kind of self-awareness and truth to be found in the interconnected open-mindedness, impartiality and neutrality – Weinstein uses all of these terms – of the 'liberal' academic balance, what if this self-awareness comes, as it does with Weinstein, to a perception of itself as both supporting and defending, in its neutrality, certain partisan political interests? At this stage of the argument the possibility of finding any satisfactory answer may depend on the recognition of another danger, the danger (that will be more than apparent to philosophers of the analytic tradition) that may lie in the exhilaration of free-floating speculative discourse. After all, it is also a presupposition of the possibility of the concept of truth that '*not* both A and not-A'; and the voice of neutrality is itself but one voice competing among others. In working fact, it is often impossible both to create or to preserve a neutral balance of all competing tendencies and to work for what one may regard as necessary change and progress. The practical inability to have it both ways at once cannot be mended and should not be masked by the 'speculative' consideration that to fall between two stools may be thought of as a special form of neutrality – a way of having it *neither* way at once. Neutrality is not always desirable; and even from a liberal point of view a temporary abandonment of neutrality of the word may be justified by the effort to create a position for a future neutrality of greater and more equal substance.

There are other aspects to this need to keep abstract speculation and detailed practical consideration in their own appropriate balance, for it has always to be remembered that academic balance and neutrality have necessarily to find their expression within the context of actual institutions. We have been speaking so far of a possible balance of topics or views within the framework of particular courses or departments. But why *should* all points of view be represented within the courses and departments of each different university – why should there not be a measure of specialisation between one university and another with the balance sought only in the university system as a whole with one major tendency or interest being represented only in one university and others in others? There can be no general *a priori* answer to this question, for it must always depend on a whole range of features of the university system actually in question. Is entry equally accessible to students, and perhaps staff, across the system as a whole? Is its financing equal and equally with or without strings throughout? Are back-up facilities of roughly comparable strength? How effective are channels of communication between the different universities? And so on. In fact, what one needs in detail to know is whether there is sufficient interlocking balance within the system as a whole for it to be regarded really as one whole.

These questions about the relations of different universities with each other within the framework of any one system connect, inevitably, with others. What of the relations between teaching and research within any one institution? What of their relations at the level of distinctive, specialised institutions? Does the liberal ideal of academic neutrality require also a balance between these two functions – and if so, would the argument apply to university graduate schools and to research institutes alike? Does academic neutrality within a university also require some sort of balance of effective influence on the determination of its syllabuses and of its programmes of research? And if so, *whose* influence is to be secured and balanced out with that of the academic staff itself – that of the students, of university administrators, of outside supporters, of the government and of who else? And once this is decided, how – through what subsidiary institutions – is such a balance to be achieved? Once again, there is emphatically no general *a priori* answer to be sought to any of these questions; and it would be quite outside the scope or intention of the present discussion to make any attempt to pursue them through the intricate detail of such actual and possible academic and political circumstances as may or might obtain. What can be said, however, is that any search for a balance of academic neutrality must in general depend on a sufficiently sensitive estimate of the sorts of conflict that are or should be most likely to arise in the relevant social, political and university contexts. Will it matter, for instance, whether one's whole department is going to consist of Jews, Catholics, Marxists, blacks or women? This depends. It is, for example, probably more or less true to say that a philosophy department staffed exclusively by Catholics would be felt to be not just politically but also academically unbalanced (and therefore implicitly unneutral) in any country in which the position of the Catholic Church and its teaching had recently been or was still a source of public conflict and dispute. In exclusively and take-it-for-granted Catholic countries, on the other hand, the point would not arise; nor, most probably, would it in societies in which a clear distinction existed between the public and the strictly personal or private and in which matters of religion were universally regarded as belonging to the latter sphere alone – though whether that is a possible position for the Catholic or any other church is, perhaps, a matter that is properly contestable. But this is just one further exemplification of the general point that where there is no question of a conflict, there by the same token no question of neutrality will arise.

Of course, as must by now be clear enough, even where the question does arise, the 'liberal' answer to it must by no means be taken for granted. It would, certainly, be a principle of any 'liberal' appointments policy in, say, a philosophy department, that one should choose on each particular occasion the best man for the particular post to be filled, where 'best' is to be determined on the basis of 'academic' criteria alone and not, for example, on that of the candidate's personal religious allegiance. Let us assume that no problems arise for anyone concerned in the making of this crucial distinction. It may still happen, perhaps for extraneous but intelligible reasons of social or cultural structure or perhaps by sheer coincidence, that over a series of years the best candidate for each separate post that arises is each time a Catholic so that after a time Catholics come in this unintended way to form the overwhelming majority of the department. If now the surrounding social context is one in which Catholic outlook and* commitment or noncommitment is a source of widespread conflict, the department – and with it perhaps the whole university – may find itself knitted in to the fabric of conflict itself in this subjectively inadvert way; and if the conflict exists on the same level as that on which material support for the university is determined and provided (if, for example, the university obtains a substantial proportion of its funds from either pro- or anti-Catholic sources), then it is clear that there can be no persisting option of neutrality once the balance is lost in this way; that is, the department and university will no longer be able even to pretend to be standing aside from the wider conflicts in their choice of their own members. In such circumstances the 'liberal' demands of, on the one hand, neutrality, (independence and impartiality) in the appointment of individual candidates and, on the other hand, of general academic/political neutrality in the overall balance of department, university or system of education as a whole may come to run in opposite directions to each other; so that the neutrality of relevant balance may only be purchasable at the price of loading the dice of appointment against the candidates who are 'academically the best'. In which case one perfectly good 'liberal' response would be to reject any attempt at present neutrality of balance as being if not actually impossible then at least quite unjustifiable; on the contrary the proper task of the university might rather be to contribute towards changing the surrounding context so as to transform it into one where an acceptable neutrality of academic and political balance would no longer have to be bought at this sort of price. This would be another example of deliberately partisan action aimed at establishing future positions of possible neutrality. In practice, of course, one may expect to find different parties, equally convinced of their own 'liberalism', opting for quite different solutions of this sort of contradiction.

The whole of this question is clearly bound up with that of earlier discussions of the conditions under which it may be possible to mark off the academic from other domains, most notably the political. In return, the possibility of preserving the clarity of any such line as one may have been able to draw is going to depend on that of preserving some balance of academic and political neutrality. And while both possibilities must together depend on the working out of detailed practical situations, to speak of them in such terms as they have been spoken of throughout this book must carry its potentially practical as well as its perhaps more apparent theoretical implications. This constitutes a quite general double reason for including within the total discourse of the book discussions of certain more specific and practical problems concerning issues of academic or political impartiality, objectivity, independence or neutrality; for they serve here not merely as illustrations of what, in its own terms, might otherwise be taken as an essentially autonomous theoretical body of discourse, but more urgently as constituting that element within its overall body which it needs if it is to remain in full appropriate contact with the non-discursive world to which it also belongs – that is, the world in which men do other things with language than play, however seriously, intricate conceptual games. Moreover, in constituting that element of limit or of anchorage, they serve not merely as logically dispensable illustrations or as contingently necessary reminders. Given the nature of the (necessarily connected) social, academic and political contexts in which intellectuals are bound by *their* nature to work, what they say, write or teach on social, academic or political matters has always also to be assessed as potential, if not already actual, social, academic or political action or inaction. This is not to say that it has always some direct, practical relevance or impact. Indeed, we have seen how one typical function of 'le neutre' is to inhibit such impact in regard to whatever conflict may be in directly relevant question. On the other hand, and as we have also seen often enough, there may always be some other conflict in relation to which neutrality in relation to the first conflict may constitute directly intervening action; and, in such cases as we have been considering here, the first may sometimes undergo disconcerting transformation into the second. In practice the degree to which theoretical discourse may also constitute effective practical intervention is bound to depend on the terms in which it is carried on. Ten's paper is here perhaps the most direct and obvious instance of potential practical engagement. But it is not just an example. It finds its place within the total body of theoretical-cum-practical discourse from which it draws in part its strength not only as the taking of a practical stand, but also as contributing its own share of theoretical illumination of how even the most theoretical arguments of moral or political philosophy depend for their ultimate viability on the fact that the *same* discourse may also be carried on (or refused) in quite *other* and primarily practical terms.

It is important, of course, that this claim should not be exaggerated. Not only was the book not in fact planned in such cunning advance dialectical detail; in principle it could not honestly have been so. The precise actual relations between the different elements of the whole could not be given in advance. And it may be that in the outcome the interplay between theoretical elaboration, description of practical dilemma and acts of practical intervention or commitment (as presented, for example, by Graham) has been made insufficiently explicit or left incompletely and imperfectly developed in other parts of the book. Nevertheless, not all such interplay *can* be made fully explicit and any attempt to do so must not only always find itself going one step beyond itself, but, more importantly, must involve some degree of distorting self-misunderstanding of what the enterprise must be. There must, evidently, be some limits beyond which proffered contributions would have to be irrelevant or impossible to integrate within the theoretical structure of the whole; one cannot simply play the trick of deeming every theoretically recalcitrant discussion to be a theoretically indispensable element of the reverse side of theory itself. But these limits too are necessarily indeterminate; and the trick is not always a mere trick. What is here most important about the apparently primarily 'exemplary' discussions is not so much the incidental use they may make of one member or another of the set of *words* under principal examination in Part I as their tracing out of certain institutional conditions under which struggles of neutrality or partisanship, impartiality, independence, objectivity or open-mindedness may actually develop and take place. One does not have to use the theoretically more or less self-conscious words to be faced with such issues; and one's use of the words will remain free-floating if one is insufficiently aware of any actual issues. The interrelation of pure theory, of theoretical description of practice and of practice itself needs practical exemplification as well as theoretical statement – in so far as this is possible within the bounds of discourse and within the covers of a book.

These remarks must be understood not so much as *ex post facto* justification of the overall contents and ordering of the book as an attempted '*prise de conscience après coup*'. But the more 'concrete' discussions of 'examples' constitutes (in retrospect) an essential moment of the movement towards this '*prise de conscience*'; merely to have referred to their possibility would not have been the same thing. The fact of their variety is also important – though it has here, of practical necessity, to stand for a variety far more diverse, a diversity through which, as Marin might say, the theoretical unity of 'le neutre' is indicated, though it can never be 'given', in the figures of its endlessly different practical appearances. The differences and similarities, exhibited by Graham, between the roles of economic adviser to politicians and of teacher of economics to university students, the nature and reasons for the pressures, presented by Ten, which a government may be led to bring on a university and its individual members to adopt positions of political commitment together with the reasons which they may have for attempting to avoid such commitments, the ways in which the sometimes almost trivial internal problems of a university, which Weinstein discusses, may involve inescapable entanglement with issues of broad political principle – it is only in the discussion of particular instances of these and related sorts that the interwoven texture of the themes presented and debated in this book may be exhibited in their proper complexity. Even the shifting idiomatic interplay of one key term with another throughout the varied 'practical' discussions provides a proper counterpoint to the more explicit theoretical discussion of the conceptual interrelationships. Indeed, such 'neutrality' as the book may itself exemplify and precariously achieve between the conflicting demands of theoretical understanding and practical commitment may depend on such balance as may be found within it of philosophical statement and analysis with practical performance and exhibition of what can never be exhaustively statable but whose statement must be constantly attempted. But if this discussion indeed provides in itself an instance of that neutrality which has, by its own nature, constantly to put itself into question, let it not end in the illusion, whose condemnation is contained throughout, of some kind of derivatively absolute neutrality to be secured at some ever higher level of discourse. He who looks to establish a position of academic neutrality with respect to all political conflicts in full awareness of what he is attempting must understand that from the battle for his own academic soul he can find no ultimately neutral political refuge.

It is appropriate that I should here return to stop (not, of course, to conclude) at a point of possible mutual convergence and interference of certain 'continental' and 'analytic' modes of discourse. My own growing but uncertainly intermittent use of some of Marin's themes and devices was (at least subjectively) an unexpected development in the writing of my own contribution. Is it largely some sort of affectation, a merely temporarily intoxicating and slightly pretentious intellectual game? Or does it achieve a serious and in part non-discursive purpose that might not be achieved in any other way? It is certainly faithful to Marin's conception of 'le neutre' to end on a? that claims to defy any attempt at complete and definitive spelling out – but which, in doing so, suggests the problematic possibility of a new philosophical balance that may be, as Marin says, 'to come'.

Appendix   The concept of evaluation

Throughout the discussions of this book comparatively little use has been made of the vocabulary of evaluation – of terms such as 'value-judgement', 'value word', 'evaluative meaning' and so on – and there has been no direct, systematic examination of it at all. Many of the questions that have been discussed, however, clearly relate to familiar debates over the essential *Wertfreiheit* of philosophy and the human sciences or over what is sometimes alleged, conversely, to be their inextricable entanglement with values. A full examination of the uses and misuses to which this network of concepts has been put, of its internal articulations and of its relations with surrounding and overlapping networks would call for a substantial book in itself, a book in which, as already indicated in passing reference to the doctrine of the Autonomy of Ethics, we should once again find ourselves dealing with issues that are essentially contestable. In this appendix I cannot pretend even to supply notes towards the writing of such a book. Nevertheless, there are three or four points which may be made in brief indication of why it has here seemed best to avoid getting caught up in arguments overly dependent on or concerned with this particular set of terms.

There is first the simple fact that the terminology of values has been grossly overworked. It has been used in too many different ways by too many different kinds of theorists with too many varying degrees of precision and imprecision. On the one hand, economists, sociologists, psychologists, men of literature, philosophers and even more or less ordinary people may use it with a familiarity that suggests that everyone knows well enough what it means without having to worry whether the next man's use and understanding may not depend on a partly different set of assumptions. On the other hand, when as self-conscious professionals they become only too aware of the underlying confusions of the situation, they tend to feel each a need to work out for themselves some more precisely stipulated way of systematising the terminology; the result is that we now have embarrasingly many professional variations on the theme. Any set of terms, no doubt, that comes to play a key role for a while, will naturally collect so much work and reworking around it that it may end up by being worked out until it has been sent for a period of recuperation into the terminological wilderness. On these grounds alone it is unsurprising that the vocabulary of evaluation should have become temporarily unhandy as a tool for reasonably concise and exact analysis and debate.

This first consideration is of a very general order. One of its more specific consequences is that wherever the network of concepts of

evaluation overlaps those with which we have been directly concerned in this book, whatever potential complexities or confusions
lie hidden in the one may enter only too easily into union with those
that lie hidden in the others. A good example of this may be found in
the different and much disputed ways in which the language of evaluation has beeen related to those of preference, wish, desire and
choice. These notions already give rise, of course, to enough problems of their own – on their own and in their further ramified connections, in particular with the concepts of interest and indifference.
We have indeed looked at one or two of these problems in the main
text of this book; and for immediate purposes there is greater risk of
further confusion than of illumination in the prospect of trying to
sort out, for example, the pros and cons of treating every expression
of preference as already carrying evaluative implications; or of
trying to mark off as evaluative certain types of preference or choice
as opposed to others. The history of the concepts of value and evaluation seem to have generated powerful conflicting pressures in
this area, so that one can find differently convincing reasons for
moving in a number of incompatible directions at once. A man's ultimate preferences may be held to determine or even to constitute
his values; but then, on the other hand, may not a man prefer to surrender or to abandon all that he holds most valuable? If these and
many similarly intricately woven conflicts are not explicitly sorted
out, the main result of trying to cope with the issues of this book in
terms of values, value-judgements and evaluation would almost
inevitably be to further entangle distinctions and relations whose
criss-crossing and overlapping are already entangled enough.

But what *is* the substance of this debate about the *Wertfreiheit* of
philosophy and the human sciences? At the heart of it, so it has so
often been said, lies the question of whether value-judgements can
be derived from statements of fact. But what, then, is to be counted
as valid or proper derivation? Can the purely technical or factual
elements in causal or theoretical analysis be clearly separated out
from its evaluative assumptions? What are the relations between
these (and similar) questions? One thing that is noteworthy about
the developing history of these arguments, within the framework of
analytical philosophy at any rate, is the way in which the issues have
been more and more closely defined as belonging to the realm of
logic alone; until, quite recently, the advent of speech act theory has
seen the start, on analytic grounds, of a move in the reverse direction and we now have to face a whole new range of questions. Are
value-judgements after all to be treated as the sort of items which
can enter into logical relations – as a class of sentences, for example,
as Hare once put it in *The Language of Morals?* Or are they rather to

be analysed as acts, acts which paradigmatically may be performed by the enunciation in certain recognised circumstances of certain standard forms of sentence, but acts, or events, all the same? What, indeed, of statements of fact? Are we to think of them too as constituting a particular kind of speech act? Or as that which is produced as the correlative result of such an act? But what then marks the act as being one of fact-stating as opposed to one of evaluation? Is there any reason why both acts should not be performed at once through the enunciation in appropriately complex circumstances of one and the same sentence? How in any case are we to conceive of the relations between the *meaning* of the sentences through the utterance of which such acts are typically performed and the *force* of their utterance? How, above all, are we to adapt our discussion of the logical relationships that may or may not obtain between one kind of logical or linguistic item and another to one of the relationships that may hold between different kinds of (speech) act?

All these are important and puzzling questions of present debate. Failure to notice them as questions, let alone to propose answers to them, has no doubt vitiated many of the innumerable discussions of the relations between factual and evaluative discourse that have taken place in the past. It may have been cowardly to avoid entering into the problems of concepts of evaluation here; but such discretion has at least the advantage of enabling us to keep partially and temporarily clear of one great range of complications. And it is worth noting, perhaps, that in virtually all our discussions of neutrality, objectivity, impartiality, disinterestedness and the rest we have been concerned directly or indirectly with certain kinds of attitudes and actions. If impartiality may not always be neutral and neutrality not always disinterested, it remains for the moment unclear whether our understanding of these notions is likely to be obscured or helped forward by worrying over whether partiality, bias and interest should or should not be treated as so many forms of evaluative commitment.

DATE DUE

5.13 87	
FEB 16 1999	

BRODART, INC.

Cat. No. 23-221